995

Holmes and Watson searching for clues in 'The Adventure of the Second Stain', illustrated by Sidney Paget, *Strand*, December 1904

A **Sherlock Holmes** COMPENDIUM

By the same author

THE SHERLOCK HOLMES SCRAPBOOK
GHOSTS: THE ILLUSTRATED HISTORY
SUPERSTITIONS
THE MAN WHO WAS FRANKENSTEIN
MOVABLE BOOKS
SWEENEY TODD

A Sherlock Holmes COMPENDIUM

Edited by
Peter Haining

CASTLE
BOOKS

For Ken and Joan Chapman with gratitude
'You are a fixed point in a changing age.'
His Last Bow

Arrangement has been made to publish this edition by Castle Books,
a division of Book Sales Inc. of Secaucus, New Jersey

Manufactured in the United States of America

JANUARY-1981

ISBN No.: 0-89009-406-3

Contents

Introduction

A SHORT while ago in America I picked up a copy of *The Chicago Tribune* and under a picture of the familiar hawk-like features, curved pipe and deerstalker hat, I read, 'It might take Sherlock Holmes himself to crack this one. The mystery: Why are Holmes and his creator, Sir Arthur Conan Doyle (1859–1930), suddenly the hottest fad since exorcism?'

The answer, of course, is elementary, my dear Watson—as Holmes might have said, but in actual fact never did. For in our disorderly, troubled world, a hero who solves problems through logical deduction is surely just the kind of person everybody needs.

It is a fact, however, that Holmes has been the centre of a cult for generations and there is probably no other character who so suddenly sprang to life from the pages of a book and thereafter assumed such a universal immortality. Conan Doyle's brother-in-law, E. W. Hornung (who himself created a revered character in the master cracksman, Raffles), put it most aptly when he remarked, 'Though he might be more humble, there's no police like Holmes!'

It is, I believe, most appropriate to be issuing this latest addition to the library of Sherlockiana in the year which marks the fiftieth anniversary of the death of the Great Detective's creator. Other milestones in the history of Holmes have been suitably marked, but in this year all Sir Arthur's works come out of copyright and fall into the Public Domain, and a veritable flood of reprints can be confidently expected in many of the dozens of languages in which the 56 Sherlock short stories and four novel-length adventures have already appeared. My purpose in this compendium has been to make generally available some of the best essays and articles written about the legend by Sherlockians of all shades of opinions and convictions. To them I have added a generous helping of unusual pictures and photographs associated with the canon and—with a bow to Holmes himself—a group of quizzes and crossword puzzles to test the reader's knowledge of his adventures.

A number of the items reflect what most enthusiasts consider the best part of the Sherlockian game—detecting the detective. This is the study of the various cases and the deduction from them of such esoteric matters as the dates of Holmes's birth, which university he attended and what his attitude was to women. Watson has also come in for similar treatment, and apart from the persistent debate about the number and dates of his marriages, one American detective story writer, Rex Stout, not so long ago set the world of Sherlockiana on its ear by advancing the outrageous theory that the good doctor was actually a woman in disguise—Holmes's mistress, no less! But though humour does intrude into such discussions from time to time (whether intentional or not), there is a widely shared belief that these exercises must be played according to specific rules. The late Dorothy L. Sayers explained it best when she wrote in her *Unpopular Opinions* (1946), 'The [games] must be played as solemnly as a county cricket match at Lord's: the slightest touch of extravagence or burlesque ruins the atmosphere.'

It's generally agreed that the man to have started these 'games' was Father Ronald Knox, the essayist and theologian, who delivered a paper entitled 'Studies in the Literature of Sherlock Holmes' to the Gryphon Club at Trinity College in 1911. This fascinating item is reprinted here by way of an opening, along with an assessment of the Holmes cult by Sir Sydney Roberts, the Master of Pembroke College, Cambridge, who was also an expert on the life of Holmes and for many years the President of the Sherlock Holmes Society of London. Among the other renowned Sherlockians to be found herein are Gavin Brend, who guides us around the Great Detective's English haunts, and Michael Kaser who takes us abroad to Europe, both of them augmented with some splendid maps by Dr Julian Wolff. Steam historian J. Alan Rannie is our conductor on the fascinating subject of the railway journeys of Sherlock Holmes, J. P. W. Mallalieu has some strong views on the less-publicised side of Sherlock's character, and William Leonard sees evidence of the Un-dead (vampires, to you) in the Holmes legend. For the

VIOLIN CONCERTS

PURE HONEY

Mr. Sherlock Holmes

CONSULTING DETECTIVE

LONDON: 01-486-5555
WASHINGTON: (202) 338-180
NEW MEXICO: (505) 832-44

221-B BAKER ST.
LONDON. W.C. 1

sake of balance, I have also included an argument on behalf of the Funda-mentalists'—Sherlockians who wish the Adventures to be taken at face value and no more—written by one of the leaders of their number, Bernard Darwin. Alongside these are to be found other intriguing items such as the London *Times* leader on the use (or non use) of the phrase 'Elementary, my dear Watson' in the canon, a search for the actual location of 221b Baker Street, and a description by Winifred Paget of how her father, Sidney, came to create the most famous of all portraits of Holmes. Conan Doyle himself is also present, introducing a competition which has not been reprinted since it first appeared in 1927 (here complete with the results), and he even answers some questions from beyond the grave put to him by a group of Sherlockians at a seance!

To set the whole legend in perspective I have included an essay about the Great Detective's forerunners taken from the magazine in which he first appeared, *The Strand*, and an article by a former editor of the periodical, Macdonald Hastings, who offers a revealing insight into how Conan Doyle came to hate the character who made him world-famous. I have also found space for a fresh look at Mycroft Holmes, Sherlock's older brother and allegedly a detective, too, as well as the Master's arch-enemy, Professor Moriarty, who very nearly brought a premature end to the saga and whose fame is still inextricably entwined with it.

Among the famous authors who crowd these pages are such as J. M. Barrie (a friend and collaborator of Conan Doyle), P. G. Wodehouse and John Gardner, not to mention such unexpected names as President Roosevelt (who purported to believe Holmes was an American!), actor Basil Rathbone (perhaps the screen's most famous Sherlock Holmes who reports a quite extraordinary encounter in New York) and Police Commissioner Sir Robert Mark, with Scotland Yard's view on Holmes. By way of some final icing on such a feast of Sherlockiana, I have included a number of parodies of the Adventures by such as 'Cunnin Toil' (actually humourist R. C. Lehmann), Peter Todd (also known as Frank Richards of Billy Bunter fame) and Maurice Baring (who puts us into Holmes's shoes rather than Watson's so to speak).

Such, and more, are to be found in the Compendium. I wish there had been room for more, for there is such a richness of Sherlockian writings that there was much I had regretfully to omit. Yet, whether you are an expert on the Adventures or simply a lover of the stories, I think you will find a great deal to enjoy, to ponder over and to help increase your knowledge of some of the most famous and widely loved tales in all literature. And by way of conclusion I can only echo the words of Sherlock Holmes himself in 'The Red Circle': 'Education never ends, Watson. It's a series of lessons, with the greatest for the last.'

PETER HAINING

THE BIBLIOGRAPHY OF
SHERLOCK HOLMES

Before March 1881	*On the Distinction between the Ashes of Various Tobaccos.* A monograph enumerating 140 varieties of cigar, cigarette, and pipe tobacco, with coloured plates illustrating the difference in the ash. This was probably Holmes's first and favourite child. He continually refers to it. (*A Study in Scarlet, The Sign of Four, The Boscombe Valley Mystery.*)
March 1881	*The Book of Life.* An article in a magazine on the science of observation and deduction. (*A Study in Scalet.*)
March 1886	*On Variations in the Human Ear.* Two short monographs in the *Anthropological Journal.* (*The Cardboard Box.*)
Before July 1887	*On the Tracing of Footsteps.* A monograph containing, *inter alia*, some remarks on the use of plaster of Paris as a preserver of impresses. (*The Sign of Four.*)
Before July 1887	*The influence of a Trade upon the Form of the Hand.* Containing lithotypes of hands of slaters, sailors, cork-cutters, compositors, weavers, and diamond polishers. (*The Sign of Four.*)
Before October 1890	*On Tattoo Marks.* It is probable that this is one of Holmes's earliest works and that his interest in this subject dates back to his undergraduate days when he made his first successful deduction from the tattoo marks on the elder Trevor's arm. (*The Red-Headed League.*)
Probably 1896	*The Polyphonic Motets of Lassus.* A monograph printed for private circulation and said by the experts to be the last word on the subject. (*The Bruce-Partington Plans.*)
Before July 1897	*On Secret Writings.* A monograph which analyses one hundred and sixty separate ciphers. (*The Dancing Men.*)
Before October 1899	*On the Dating of Documents.* A brief monograph. (*The Hound of the Baskervilles.*)
Between 1904 and 1912	*The Practical Handbook of Bee Culture with some Observations upon the Segregation of the Queen.* The *magnum opus* of Holmes's later years. "The fruit of pensive nights and laborious days." (*His Last Bow.*)

The Cult of Sherlock

S. C. Roberts

To begin this collection here is a perceptive examination of the appeal of the Great Detective by a leading Sherlockian and former President of the Sherlock Holmes Society of London. S. C. Roberts was for a time Vice Chancellor of Cambridge University and the author of several works on both Holmes and Watson. This article appeared in JOHN O'LONDON'S WEEKLY *of 19 February 1954, to mark the centenary of Sherlock Holmes.*

S IR,' said Dr. Johnson to Boswell, 'you have but two topicks, yourself and me. I am sick of both.'

So today, perhaps, there are some who are sick both of Holmes and Watson. Writing of my own recent book on the subject, a reviewer concluded that while it would be delicious to the enthusiast it was for the outsider intolerable.

Evidently the reviewer belonged to the second category and I have no quarrel with him. Nor do I complain of the indignant correspondent who wrote to me at an earlier date: 'I see that you are President of the Sherlock Holmes Society!! I could hardly believe the evidence of my eyes when I read about it. Sherlock Holmes and Watson were fictitious characters invented by Conan Doyle. All there is about these two invented people is what Conan Doyle wrote. There is nothing more to it and very little at that!'

My correspondent's factual statement is indeed incontrovertible. What he has failed to appreciate is, to use a notable expression of an old Cambridge don, that Holmes and Watson have earned their title to be 'emancipated from the bonds of fact'. They have been canonized not by a literary pope or a college of scholastic cardinals but by that 'common sense of readers incorrupted with literary prejudices' which Johnson proclaimed to be the ultimate criterion of literary fame.

If the cult of Sherlock Holmes were confined to a few devotees, would this publication devote even a page to him at this time? Would *The Times* have thought it worth while to make the centenary of his birth the subject of a fourth leader?

Of course, the refinements of critical scholarship may well provoke irritation even amongst those who are genuine lovers of the Adventures. If every date and every relationship were entirely consistent throughout the long series of stories, the critics would have been deprived of a lot of their fun, but the common reader would still have maintained his love of the saga for its own sake.

Of the many thousands who visited the Baker Street exhibition of 1951, the great majority were not interested in the dating of Watson's first marriage or in the identification of Holmes's university; what they came to see was the reconstruction of the sitting-room at 221b, with all the dear, familiar features—the scrap-books and the pipe-racks; the newspapers and the test-tubes; Dr. Watson's stethoscope hanging behind the door and Holmes's shag reposing in the toe of the Persian slipper.

These are the images which come to the mind of the common reader when he is reminded of the centenary of the birth of Sherlock Holmes. To the professed student, of course, the event suggests problems of deeper import. When, in fact, was Holmes born? The vagaries and the pitfalls of the Higher Criticism are well illustrated in this context.

The late H. W. Bell (perhaps the most laborious and methodical of all investigators of Holmesian chronology) wrote: 'Since eighteen is the average age of students entering Oxford and Cambridge, he was probably born in 1855 or late in 1854'; while Mr. Gavin Brend in his book *My Dear Holmes* writes: 'Since most undergraduates start at the age of eighteen, it would seem that the most likely year for his birth would be 1853.'

Behind these contradictory inferences from an identical premise lies much conjecture about the length of Holmes's residence at the University and the correct interpretation of Watson's remark that Holmes was 'in active practice for twenty-three years.'

On the other hand, there is the categorical statement in *His Last Bow* that on August 2nd, 1914 ('the most terrible August in the history of the world') Holmes, disguised as an Irish-American with a goatee-beard, was 'a man of sixty.' It is clear, therefore, that he was born either in the later months of 1853 or between January 1st and August 1st, 1854, with a fairly strong presumption in favour of 1854.

So, whatever the precise date of birth may have been, we may picture Holmes growing to manhood in the 1860s and 1870s, that mid-Victorian period of which the stability and security are now so frequently, though not always justifiably, contrasted with the baffling insecurity of our own epoch. In boyhood, he would hear stories of the Crimean War and the Indian Mutiny. He came of 'a long line of country squires' and it is difficult to imagine that his elder kinsmen were not represented in the regiments of the British and Indian Armies.

Later, he doubtless heard much discussion of the American Civil War. It will be remembered that a portrait of Henry Ward Beecher stood upon the top of a bookshelf in 221b Baker Street and that Watson's contemplation of it provoked one of the most brilliant of Holmes's deductions. Undoubtedly the

Three Sherlockian societies: Hugo's Companions of Chicago, The Trained Cormorants of Los Angeles and the Danish Baker Street Irregulars

THE HOUND

HUGO'S COMPANIONS
CHICAGO

A Scion Society of the

Baker Street Irregulars

THE TRAINED CORMORANTS
of Los Angeles County

SCION SOCIETY OF

THE BAKER STREET IRREGULARS

"We Can But Try"

Sherlockiana
Meddelelser fra
SHERLOCK HOLMES KLUBBEN I DANMARK
THE DANISH BAKER STREET IRREGULARS
Rønnekrogen 1, Bagsværd
Telefon 98 10 15

This is the last Will and Testament

of me _Sherlock Holmes_

of _221B, Baker Street in the parish of St. Marylebone_

in the County of _London_ _____ made this _Sixteenth_

day of _April, 1891_ _____ in the year of our Lord

I hereby revoke all former testamentary dispositions made by me and declare this to be my last Will.
I appoint _my brother_

Mycroft Holmes

_____

to be my Executor   and direct that all my just Debts and Funeral and Testamentary Expenses shall
be paid as soon as conveniently may be after my decease.

I give and bequeath unto _____

_my devoted friend and associate, Dr. John H. Watson,
often tried, sometimes trying, but never found wanting
in loyalty; my well-intentioned though unavailing
mentor against the blandishments of vice; my indispensable
foil and whetstone; the perfect sop to my wounded
vanity and too tactful to whisper "Norbury" in my ear
when necessary; the ideal listener and the audience
par excellence for those little tricks which others more
discerning might well have deemed meretricious; the
faithful Boswell to whose literary efforts – despite my
occasional unkindly gibes – I owe whatever little fame
I have enjoyed: in short, to the one true friend I
have ever had, the sum of £5,000; also the choice
of any books in my personal library (with such
reservations as are mentioned below), including my
commonplace books and the complete file of my
cases, published and unpublished, with the sole
exception of the papers in pigeonhole "M," contained
in a blue envelope and marked "Moriarty" which
the proper authorities will take over in the event
my demise should make it impossible for me to
hand them over in person._

A hotly-debated document: Sherlock Holmes's Last Will, as 'discovered' by New York Sherlockian Nathan L. Bengis in 1955

— To George Lestrade, of Scotland Yard, my gilt-edged German dictionary, in the hope he will find it useful should he again see the handwriting of Miss Rachel on the wall.

— To Tobias Gregson, ditto, my leatherbound Hafiz, the study of whose poetry may supply a dash of that imagination so necessary to the ideal reasoner.

— To the authorities of Scotland Yard, one copy of each of my trifling monographs on crime detection, unless happily they shall feel they have outgrown the need for the elementary suggestions of an amateur detective.

— To my good brother, Mycroft Holmes, the remainder and residue of my estate, which he will be agreeably surprised to find, even after the foregoing bequests, to be not inconsiderable, and which will enable him, I hope, to take a much needed holiday from governmental cares to surroundings more congenial than those of the Diogenes Club; in the expectation that he will remain celibate for the rest of his natural life — and unnatural too, for that matter.

Sherlock Holmes

Signed by the Testator in the presence of us, present at the same time, who at his request, in his presence, and in the presence of each other, have subscribed our names as Witnesses .. .. ..

1st WITNESS—Name *Thomas P. Stockton*
Address *Staple Inn, Holborn*
Occupation *Solicitor*

2nd WITNESS—Name *Philip H Mason*
Address *Staple Inn, Holborn*
Occupation *Solicitor*

N.B.—The person making the will should sign it at the end of the Will itself, that is, immediately at the end of the writing.

trend of American history exercised a powerful influence on Holmes and on one famous occasion he rose to a rhapsodical height in reflecting upon the ultimate potentialities of Anglo-American unity; he even visualized a world-wide country whose flag would be 'a quartering of the Union Jack with the Stars and Stripes'.

Still more powerful an influence on the young Holmes was the spirit of France. His grandmother was a Vernet and it was from that distinguished family of painters that both Mycroft and Sherlock inherited their artistic tendencies. There can be little doubt, then, about the direction of Holmes's sympathies during the Franco-Prussian War and his lonely undergraduate life must have been further saddened by the débâcle of the early 1870s.

Later, when he had begun his professional career, Holmes displayed a marked preference for French cases. His reputation stood high amongst French investigators and the story of the energy he displayed in defeating the machinations of Baron Maupertuis and in securing the conviction of the boulevard assassin Huret is well known to all readers of the Adventures. The French government, as well as private clients, liked to retain his services in important cases and it is noteworthy that he accepted the Order of the Legion of Honour, though in later years he refused the offer of knighthood.

Such are a few of the reflections provoked by the contemplation of the youthful Holmes. Lack of detailed records of his early years destroys any hope of biographical certainty. Undoubtedly, however, the union of the country squires with the Vernets produced in Sherlock Holmes certain warring elements of heredity. On the whole, the Vernet strain was dominant; and yet, when his artistic passion was spent, it was to the 'soothing life of Nature', that immemorial refuge of country squires, that he retired.

WORD SHIFT

By changing only one letter at a time (making sure that you form a proper word with every go), can you go from **SPOT** *to* **CLUE**? *Now try going from* **SEEK** *to* **FIND**.

```
S  P  O  T        C  L  U  E
S  E  E  K        F  I  N  D
```

Sherlock Holmes disguised as an Irish-American in 'His Last
Bow , as referred to by S. C. Roberts

Conan Doyle Hated Sherlock Holmes!

Macdonald Hastings

Macdonald Hastings, a former Editor of the STRAND MAGAZINE, *describes the development of the Sherlock Holmes legend in the pages of that publication. Although Mr Hastings did not occupy the editorial chair until the final years of the* STRAND *(1944–50), he had access to the magazine's files and records, enabling him to produce this fascinating insight which first appeared in* JOHN O'LONDON'S *in the issue of 4 February 1949.*

C ONAN DOYLE and the *Strand Magazine* are associated with each other as inseparably as Diogenes with his tub or D'Artagnan with his sword. Together, the author and the magazine came to London; together, they adventured for fame and fortune; and together, in an unbroken alliance of forty years, they each of them achieved reputations which made publishing and literary history.

The *Strand* was first published at Christmas time, 1890, in the same month and in the same year that Dr. Conan Doyle, then a not very successful medical man in Portsmouth, decided to give up general practice and chance his luck as a consultant, and perhaps as a writer too, in London. The last proofs of the first issue of the *Strand Magazine* were being passed for press when the President of the Portsmouth Literary and Scientific Society—a certain Dr. Watson—rose to his feet to propose the health of his popular fellow member and professional colleague, Dr Conan Doyle, at a farewell banquet at Southsea on the occasion of the latter's departure 'for a few months' study and rest in Vienna prior to settling down in the West End of London.' And although the fact is not recorded in his biography, it may be regarded as certain that, in that Christmas of 1890 when Dr. Conan Doyle and his wife left London for Austria, the travellers took along with them to read in the train a copy of the newly-published magazine which everybody was talking about.

For the success of the *Strand*, from the very first issue, was unprecedented in publishing annals. A young magazine proprietor, named George Newnes, who had amassed a fortune out of a periodical called *Tit-Bits*, had conceived the then novel notion of producing a magazine 'with a picture on every page'. And, although George Newnes can hardly have guessed the

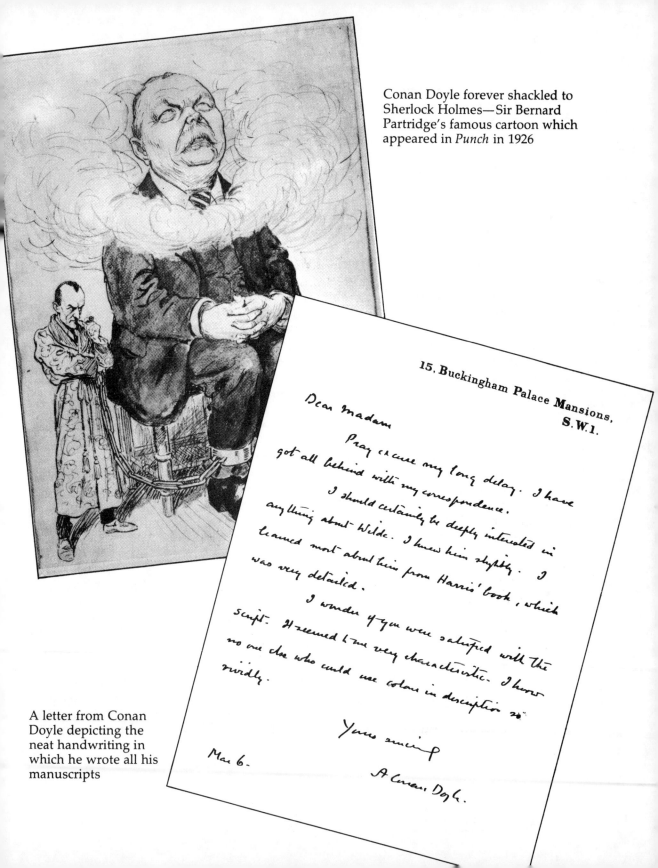

Conan Doyle forever shackled to Sherlock Holmes—Sir Bernard Partridge's famous cartoon which appeared in *Punch* in 1926

A letter from Conan Doyle depicting the neat handwriting in which he wrote all his manuscripts

15, Buckingham Palace Mansions,
S.W.1.

Dear Madam

Pray excuse my long delay. I have got all behind with my correspondence.

I should certainly be deeply interested in anything about Wilde. I knew him slightly. I learned most about him from Harris' book, which was very detailed.

I wonder if you were satisfied with the script. It seemed to me very characteristic. I know no one else who could use colour in description so vividly.

Yours sincerely

A Conan Doyle.

Mar 6.

ultimate implications of that formula, the coming of the *Strand* marked the beginning of the modern periodical industry. In a single issue, the new magazine established a new style—a style which was subsequently copied throughout the world—in the presentation of popular reading. And we may be sure that Dr Conan Doyle, for whom it was still an anxious business getting his literary work into print, studied this potential new market with immediate and careful attention.

At that time Doyle had published several books, *Girdlestone* and *Micah Clarke* among them. He had completed *The White Company* which, throughout his life, he believed was his best and most important book (it was serialized in the *Cornhill Magazine* by the great editor, James Payn, who also had the distinction of publishing Doyle's first story: July 15, 1883). And the first of the Sherlock Holmes stories had been written. *A Study in Scarlet*—sold with the complete copyright for £25—had appeared in 1887 in *Beeton's Annual* (owned, incidentally, by the husband of Mrs Beeton, the cookery-book writer). Messrs. Spencer Blackett had published the adventure called *The Sign of Four* in book form. But *A Study in Scarlet* had aroused no particular interest and the first edition of *The Sign of Four* attracted nothing but the dust in the publisher's warehouse. In that Christmas of 1890 Conan Doyle had a little money in the bank, but solid literary success evaded him.

Only one year later Doyle himself was a celebrity and his characters, Sherlock Holmes and Dr. Watson, were national figures. Early in 1891, presumably after reading the first issues of the new magazine, Conan Doyle tentatively submitted a story to the *Strand*. Unbeknown to his future biographer, for Dickson Carr makes no reference to it, the story, called 'The Voice of Science', was published anonymously in the third issue of the new periodical. Presumably, Mr. Greenhough Smith, then acting editor, afterwards editor for so many glorious years, wrote to Dr. Conan Doyle a letter of mild encouragement, even perhaps suggesting further contributions. Anyhow, sometime in 1891, Doyle completed the first of the Holmes short stories and sent it off, not very optimistically, to the *Strand*.

He had no reason for feeling particularly hopeful. The longer stories on Holmes and Watson had apparently failed. James Payn, of the *Cornhill*, had turned down *A Study in Scarlet* with the shattering phrase 'Shilling dreadful.' But George Newnes and Greenhough Smith thought differently. The *Strand* took the first story—that great story 'A Scandal in Bohemia' which begins with the memorable sentence, 'To my friend Sherlock Holmes, she was always THE WOMAN'—and the *Strand* asked for more. The price, generous for those days, was to be £35, less agent's fee, for each of six stories. By the end of Doyle's life the *Strand* was paying £800 and more a story for the British rights only and Conan Doyle was averaging, with world rights included, a

BEETON'S · CHRISTMAS · ANNUAL

A STUDY IN SCARLET

By A. CONAN DOYLE

Containing also
Two Original
DRAWING ROOM PLAYS.
1
FOOD FOR POWDER.
By R. ANDRE
2
THE FOUR LEAVED SHAMROCK
By C. J. HAMILTON

With ENGRAVINGS
By D. H. FRISTON
Matt STRETCH,
AND
R. ANDRÉ

This Number Contains a Complete Story,

THE SIGN OF THE FOUR

BY A. CONAN DOYLE.

FEBRUARY, 1890.

LIPPINCOTT'S

MONTHLY MAGAZINE.

CONTENTS.

RICE ONE SHILLING.

D CO., Salisbury Square, E.C.
PINCOTT Co.

on's Christmas
ual of 1887, in
ch the first Holmes
enture was
lished. The figure
he front cover is
eved to be the first
orial representation
e Great Detective

The second Holmes
adventure, 'The Sign of
the Four', made its first
appearance in the
American magazine
Lippincott's, in
February 1890

es Payn, the Editor of
hill Magazine who rejected
irst Holmes story, 'A Study
carlet' as a 'shilling dreadful'.
s been suggested that Payn
equently became the model for
essor Moriarty!

total of ten shillings a word. The original six stories increased to over fifty. The last of them, 'The Mystery of Shoscombe Old Place', was published in the *Strand* in 1927, three years before its creator's death.

Apart from the first six, all the Sherlock Holmes stories were dragged out of Conan Doyle by the pertinacity of editors, Greenhough Smith in particular, and the fatness of the publisher's cheques in general. The most remarkable fact about Conan Doyle—and his biographer brings it out brilliantly—is that Doyle himself was never able to share his readers' affection for Holmes and Watson.

Even in the first rapture of literary success, after only the fifth Holmes story had appeared in the *Strand*, he was writing to his mother about a thought to slay Holmes in the twelfth adventure 'and winding him up for good and all.' 'He takes my mind from better things,' he said. His mother expressed a proper horror at the suggestion. And, with people fighting at the bookstalls for the new Holmes story on the first of every month, we can imagine what Greenhough Smith was saying in his letters to the author.

Doyle roared with exasperation. After only the first six stories had been delivered, he tried to back out. When the *Strand* got frantic, he asked a price for future stories which he thought was so steep that it would settle the matter once and for all. The price was to be £50 each for the next half a dozen. Then, in February, 1892, he wrote to his mother: 'They've been bothering me for more Sherlock Holmes tales. Under pressure, I offered to do a dozen for a thousand pounds, but I sincerely hope they won't accept it now.' But they did accept it, immediately. And Holmes's life was saved from his unloving creator for another twelve stories. But, in the twenty-fourth tale, at the Reichenbach Falls, he struck. 'I am in the middle of the last Holmes story,' he told his mother, 'after which the gentleman vanishes, never to return. I am weary of him.'

The deed was done in the December issue of the *Strand* for 1893. There was a public clamour. The editor of the *Strand* was in disgrace. Letters of anger and abuse poured on Conan Doyle himself. Sporting young City men, Dickson Carr records, went to their offices with crêpe bands tied round their hats for the death of 'S. H.'

But Doyle didn't care. He wanted to do 'better work.' He was cheered that *The White Company*, now selling edition after edition, showed that the public shared his own judgment of its merits: merits, in Doyle's opinion, so much greater than any Holmes. It never occurred to him—or, if it did, he never referred to it—that the fame of Sherlock Holmes was selling his other books, fine story books though they were in their own métier.

He went on to write *Brigadier Gerard*, *Rodney Stone*, and more short stories, all of which Greenhough Smith published in the *Strand*. But all the time they nagged him for more Sherlock Holmes stories. At last, in 1901, Doyle produced *The Hound of the Baskervilles*. When Sir George Newnes—he had now become a baronet—heard the news, he felt it was so important that he even announced it to the annual meeting of his shareholders. But he also made it clear that the detective had not been recalled to life. This new adventure, he explained, occurred before Holmes's 'unhappy and dreadful' death.

'Can't you bring him back to life?' moaned millions of readers. 'He's at the foot of the Reichenbach Falls,' retorted Conan Doyle, 'and there he stays.' He didn't give a hoot. He allowed William Gillette, the American actor, to present a play about Holmes which murdered the facts as Doyle had written them. Doyle himself was much more interested in a long pamphlet he was writing defending the conduct of British soldiers in the Boer War. But, in 1903, an American publishing house called the highest price yet for the reprieve of Holmes's death warrant. 'If Conan Doyle would bring Holmes to life,' they said, 'explain away that wretched matter of the Reichenbach Falls, they were prepared to pay at the rate of five thousand dollars a story for as many stories as they could get.' And that was only the American rights. Sir George Newnes, too, was ready to pay plenty. On a postcard to his agent Conan Doyle wrote briefly, 'Very well A. C. D.' And the new adventures started.

After all, Doyle consoled himself, he would soon write other books, create new characters—perhaps in another mediæval romance like *The White Company*—when he would show the world the error of its ways. But, meanwhile, if it was Holmes they wanted, they should have it. It was Holmes that they wanted. 'The scenes at the railway bookstalls,' says Mr. Dickson Carr, quoting a woman who vividly remembers the return of Holmes to the *Strand*, 'were worse than anything I ever saw at a bargain sale.'

Thenceforward, Sir Arthur Conan Doyle—as he now was—wrote occasional Holmes stories for the rest of his working life. But every story was always the last. Even his titles, like *His Last Bow*, were meant to indicate it. Greenhough Smith delicately changed the latter title, when it appeared in the *Strand*, to *The War Service of Sherlock Holmes*.

What Holmes lovers owe to the editor of the *Strand*, Greenhough Smith, for the way he wheedled the stories out of a reluctant Conan Doyle, year by year, can never be calculated. In character, the two men were poles apart. Conan Doyle, magnificent in physique, was emotional, exuberant, obstinate, proud and brilliant. Greenhough Smith, physically slight, was shy and eccentric, with a passion for puzzles, a detestation of meeting authors, and such a dislike of any demonstration of emotion that his fellow clubmen nicknamed him 'Calamity'. Reginald Pound, who was responsible for the fortunes of the *Strand* during the war years, tells in his new book, *A Maypole in the Strand*, the story of how a well-known actor invited Greenhough Smith, with a hearty slap on the back, to join him in a game of billiards. Seeing that Greenhough Smith hesitated, the actor said: 'What, you refuse?' 'I don't refuse to play billiards' said Greenhough Smith dryly, and without removing his long, thin cigarette holder, 'I refuse to be genial.' In the light of that story, consider the alarm of the great editor when his great author Conan Doyle wrote *The Lost World* and seriously suggested that it should be illustrated with photographs of Doyle himself disguised as Professor Challenger in an immense black beard, with adhesive eyebrows and a wig.

Greenhough Smith stopped that one. But there must have been days of acute anxiety for the dry little editor in his Southampton Street office. Yet, in all the years when Greenhough Smith and Conan Doyle rubbed together in the friction of editor and author, there is no evidence—not in the *Strand* archives and not in the fascinating Doyle papers which are now revealed for the first time in Mr. Dickson Carr's official biography—there is no hint of a real difference of opinion; except, of course, in that little controversy involving Sherlock Holmes and Dr. Watson.

In addition to the Sherlock Holmes stories, Greenhough Smith published every important work that Conan Doyle wrote during their long association; and he published him loyally if a little reluctantly, even in the latter years, when Sir Arthur was interested in little else except the proselytizing of Spiritualism. The great author predeceased his old editor by five years.

From the present editor, beyond raising his hat to the memory of his great predecessor and murmuring a heartfelt prayer that the day may come when another story-teller as great as Conan Doyle drops a manuscript into the post to us, there is nothing to add except to record one more fact about Sir Arthur Conan Doyle as a writer which his biographer has somehow missed mentioning. Alone of all the great and popular authors in that astonishing flowering of letters which marked the beginning of this century, and the beginning of the popular illustrated magazine, Conan Doyle, writing Sherlock Holmes, was the only one—Kipling and Wells not excepted—whose name on the cover as a contributor was sufficient to justify the publisher in increasing by many thousands the print run for that particular issue.

THE GAME OF THE NAME

Taking the letters of Sir Arthur Conan Doyle's two family names—CONAN DOYLE—how many three-letter words can you make? Each letter may be used only once in each word: we've made thirty and are still counting!

A Sherlock Holmes Competition

A. Conan Doyle

At intervals throughout this book there are a number of Holmesian diversions—and it is perhaps only fitting that the first of these should be a competition set by Conan Doyle himself for the readers of the STRAND magazine in March 1927. It simply asked them to list what they considered to be the twelve best stories in the canon. I think it's still of particular interest today, for apart from giving the modern reader a chance to pick his favourites it also provides an intriguing insight into Doyle's own opinion of his work—his selections are printed at the end of the book. (Regretably, the original prizes for the competition—a cheque for £100 and a hundred autographed copies of Conan Doyle's autobiography, MEMORIES AND ADVENTURES—cannot be offered by the present Editor or his publishers!)

I FEAR that Mr. Sherlock Holmes may become like one of those popular tenors who, having outlived their time, are still tempted to make repeated farewell bows to their indulgent audiences. This must cease and he must go the way of all flesh, material or imaginary. One likes to think that there is some fantastic limbo for the children of imagination, some strange, impossible place where the beaux of Fielding may still make love to the belles of Richardson, where Scott's heroes still may strut, Dickens's delightful Cockneys still raise a laugh, and Thackeray's worldlings continue to carry on their reprehensible careers. Perhaps in some humble corner of such a Valhalla, Sherlock and his Watson may for a time find a place, while some more astute sleuth with some even less astute comrade may fill the stage which they have vacated.

His career has been a long one—though it is possible to exaggerate it. Decrepit gentlemen who approach me and declare that his adventures formed the reading of their boyhood do not meet the response from me which they seem to expect. One is not anxious to have one's personal dates handled so unkindly. As a matter of cold fact, Holmes made his *début* in *A Study in Scarlet* and in *The Sign of Four*, two small booklets which appeared between 1887 and 1889. It was in 1891 that A Scandal in Bohemia', the first of the long series of short stories, appeared in THE STRAND MAGAZINE. The public seemed appreciative and desirous of more, so that from that date, thirty-six years ago, they have been produced in a broken series which now contains no fewer than fifty-six stories. These have been re-published in *The Adventures, The Memoirs, The Return,* and *His Last Bow,* and there remain twelve published during the last few years which Sir John Murray is about to produce under the title of *The Case-Book of Sherlock Holmes.*

Holmes puzzling over a piece of evidence in 'The Adventure of the Golden Pince-Nez' *Strand*, July 1904.

He began his adventures in the very heart of the later Victorian Era, carried it through the all-too-short reign of Edward, and has managed to hold his own little niche even in these feverish days. Thus it would be true to say that those who first read of him as young men have lived to see their own grown-up children following the same adventures in the same magazine. It is a striking example of the patience and loyalty of the British public.

I had fully determined at the conclusion of *The Memoirs* to bring Holmes to an end, as I felt that my literary energies should not be directed too much into one channel. That pale, clear-cut face and loose-limbed figure were taking up an undue share of my imagination. I did the deed, but, fortunately, no coroner had pronounced upon the remains, and so; after a long interval, it was not difficult for me to respond to the flattering demand and to explain my rash act away. I have never regretted it, for I have not in actual practice found that these lighter sketches have prevented me from exploring and finding my limitations in such varied branches of literature as history, poetry, historical novels, psychic research, and the drama. Had Holmes never existed I could not have done more, though he may perhaps have stood a little in the way of the recognition of my more serious literary work.

There has been some debate as to whether the Adventures of Holmes, or the narrative powers of Watson, declined with the passage of the years. When the same string is still harped upon, however cunningly one may vary the melody, there is still the danger of monotony. The mind of the reader is less fresh and responsive, which may unjustly prejudice him against the writer. To compare great things to small, Scott in his autobiographical notes has remarked that each of Voltaire's later pamphlets was declared to be a declension from the last one, and yet when the collected works were assembled they were found to be among the most brilliant. Scott also was depreciated by critics for some of his most solid work. Therefore, with such illustrious examples before one, let me preserve the hope that he who in days to come may read my series backwards will not find that his impressions are very different from those of his neighbour who reads them forwards.

It is as a little test of the opinion of the public that I inaugurate this small competition. I have drawn up a list of the twelve short stories contained in the four published volumes which I consider to be the best, and I should like to know to what extent my choice agrees with that of STRAND readers. I have left my list in a sealed envelope with the Editor of THE STRAND MAGAZINE.

And so, reader, farewell to Sherlock Holmes! I thank you for your constancy, and can but hope that some return has been made in the shape of that distraction from the worries of life and stimulating change of thought which can only be found in the fairy kingdom of romance.

Forerunners of Sherlock Holmes

Anonymous

Like all great literary creations, Sherlock Holmes was modelled to a degree on both factual and fictional characters. Conan Doyle admitted that the Great Detective was based in part on Dr Joseph Bell, the Edinburgh professor who taught him while he was a medical student, and also on the fictional sleuths created by two Frenchman, Voltaire and Emile Gaboriau, and the American, Edgar Allan Poe. Appropriately this 'paternity' was fully discussed in an interesting but anonymous article in the STRAND MAGAZINE of July 1906, reprinted here for the first time. I believe the author may well have been the Editor, Greenhough Smith, who played such an important role in the development of Sherlock Holmes.

SHERLOCK HOLMES has achieved that rarest of all reputations in literature, for he has become the symbol of a vital force in the language, and has taken his place among the small band of men who are types of their calling. For anyone to be described as a Sherlock Holmes is for all the world to understand that he is an individual gifted with an extraordinary sense of logical deduction, the ability to reason clearly from cause to effect, or from effect back again to cause, and to arrange a series of given facts in their ordered sequence for the elucidation of a mystery.

Brilliant creation as he was, however, Sherlock Holmes stands forth as another example of the famous dictum, 'There is nothing new under the sun.' All his admirers know that the author of his being derived the idea of his character from a famous professor of Edinburgh, under whom Sir Arthur Conan Doyle, as a medical student, studied long before he had any intention of devoting himself to the service of letters.

Professor Bell, however, took to his lecture-room and to the out-patient department of the hospital no new idea, for the process of drawing deductions from established facts was as old as the sun, and the application of the principle to literature had fascinated writers from the earliest ages. Like much of our knowledge, it came from the East. One of its oldest forms is the Eastern fable which may be familiar to many readers, since it has been seized upon for translation in all European languages.

A dervish was journeying alone in the desert, when he met two merchants. 'You have lost a camel,' said he to the merchants.

'It is true, we have,' they replied.

'Was he not blind in his right eye and lame in his left leg?' inquired the dervish

'He was,' replied the merchants.

'And had he not lost a tooth?'

'He had,' said the merchants.

'And was he not loaded with honey on one side and wheat on the other?'

'Most certainly he was,' they replied; 'and, as you have evidently just seen him, we pray you to tell us where to find him.'

'My friends,' said the dervish, 'I have never seen your camel, nor ever heard of him except from you.'

'A pretty story, truly,' said the merchants. 'But where are the jewels which formed part of his cargo?'

'I have neither seen your camel nor your jewels,' repeated the dervish.

On this they seized his person and forthwith hurried him before a justice, where, on the strictest search, no proof could be found against him, either of falsehood or of theft.

They were about to proceed against him as a sorcerer when the dervish, with great calmness, thus addressed the Court: 'I have been much pleased with your surprise, and own that there has been some ground for your suspicions; but I have lived long and alone, and I can find ample scope for observation even in a desert. I knew that I had crossed the track of a camel that had strayed from its owner because I saw no mark of any human footstep on the same route. I knew that the animal was blind in one eye because it had cropped the herbage only on one side of its path; and I perceived that it was lame in one leg from the faint impression which that particular foot had produced upon the sand. I concluded that the animal had lost one tooth because wherever it had grazed a small tuft of herbage was left un-injured in the centre of its bite. As to that which formed the burden of the beast, the busy ants informed me that it was corn which had dropped on the one side, and the clustering flies that it was honey on the other.'

This idea of deduction may be traced in a Persian book called *Nigaristan*, which may be translated as *The Picture Gallery*. It is a miscellany of stories and poetry on moral subjects, written by Muin-al-din Juvaini in 1335. Later on an Italian found it, and translated it. The Italian work was used by Gueulette as the basis of his *Soirées Bretonnes*—a work on which, it is believed, Voltaire founded 'Zadig,' the hero of a series of incidents in exactly the same way as Sherlock became the hero of a series of problems, so that the most famous character of The Strand Magazine can trace back his ancestry to a period which might make most of our bluest-blooded aristocracy turn green with envy.

Zadig sought his happiness in the study of Nature. 'No one is happier,' he said, 'than the philosopher who reads this great book which God has placed under his eyes. The truths which he discovers are his own; he nourishes and elevates his soul; he lives a tranquil life; he fears nothing from man.' 'Full of these ideas,' we are told, 'he withdrew to his house in the country on the borders of the Euphrates. There he occupied himself solely in calculating

An early illustration of Poe's pionee[r]
detective, C. Auguste Dupin (*right*[)]
in 'The Murders in the Rue Morgue'[.]
Dupin's companion here bears [a]
striking resemblance to Poe himsel[f]

Edgar Allan Poe—'The Father o[f]
the Detective Story'

how many inches of water ran under the arches of a bridge in a second, or if there fell a cubic inch of rain in the Month of Mice more than in the Month of Sheep. It did not enter his imagination to make silk of spiders' webs or porcelain with broken bottles; but he made a special study of the properties of animals and plants, and he soon acquired a sagacity by means of which he discovered a thousand differences where other men saw nothing but uniformity.'

It was this capacity which distinguished him, as it was similar capacity which distinguished Sherlock, though the latter used his deductive powers only in the elucidation of crime.

One day when Zadig was walking near a little wood he saw the Queen's chief attendants and several officers running towards him. He noticed that they were in great anxiety, for they ran about as if they were quite bewildered, looking for something of great value which they had lost. When they came up to him the chief Eunuch said: 'Have you seen the Queen's pet dog?'

Zadig replied, 'It is a little female dog.'

'You are right,' said the Eunuch.

'It is a very small spaniel,' added Zadig; 'she has recently had puppies, she has a limp of the left forefoot, and she has very long ears.'

'You have seen her, then?' exclaimed the Eunuch, joyfully.

'No,' replied Zadig, 'I have never seen her, I did not know that the Queen had such a dog.'

Precisely at the same time, by an extra-ordinary coincidence, the most beautiful horse in the King's stable had escaped from the hands of the stable attendants and galloped out on the plains of Babylon. The Grand Vizier and all the other officers ran after it with as much anxiety as the first Eunuch after the spaniel. The Grand Vizier addressed himself to Zadig, and asked him if he had seen the King's horse pass. Zadig replied, 'It is a horse which gallops to perfection; it is five feet high, with very small hoofs. It has a tail three and a half feet long; the bit of its bridle is of twenty-three-carat gold; its shoes are of silver.'

'What road has it taken? Where is it?' demanded the Vizier.

'I have never seen it,' replied Zadig, 'and I have never heard it spoken of.'

The Grand Vizier and the first Eunuch had no doubt that Zadig had stolen the King's horse and the Queen's dog. They had him conveyed before the Great Desterhan, who condemned him to the knout and to pass the rest of his days in Siberia. The judgment had scarcely been pronounced when the horse and the dog were found. The judges were under the sad necessity of reversing their judgment, but they condemned Zadig to pay four hundred ounces of gold for having said that he had never seen what he had seen. He was first obliged to pay this fine; after which he was permitted to plead his cause before the council of the Great Desterhan. He spoke in these terms:—

'Stars of Justice, Abysses of Science, Mirrors of Truth which have the weight of lead, the hardness of iron and the brilliance of the diamond, and much affinity with gold: Since I am permitted to speak before this august assembly I swear to you by Orosmede that I have never seen the respected dog of the Queen nor the sacred horse of the King of Kings. This is what happened to me. I was walking towards the little wood, where I lately encountered the venerable Eunuch and the most illustrious Grand Vizier. I had seen on the sand the traces of an animal, and I had easily judged that they were those of a little dog. The light and long furrows imprinted on the little eminences of sand between the traces of the feet showed me that it was a female that had lately given birth to pups. Other traces which appeared to have continually raised the surface of the sand by the side of the front feet told me that she had long ears. As I remarked that the sand was always less crushed by one foot than by the three others, I understood that the dog of our august Queen was, if I may dare say so, a little lame.

Illustration from the first book publication of 'The Purloined Letter' by Clarke Beeton, London, 1851

'With regard to the King's horse, you must know that while I was walking in the roads of this wood I perceived the marks of the hoofs of a horse. They were all at equal distances. 'Here,' said I, 'is a horse which gallops perfectly.' The dust of the trees in a narrow route only seven feet broad was brushed off here and there, to right and left, at three and a half feet from the middle of the road. 'This horse,' I added, 'has a tail of three and a half feet long, which, by its movement right and left, has scattered the dust.' I had seen under the trees, which formed a canopy five feet high, newly fallen leaves from the branches, and I knew that this horse had touched them, and therefore it was five feet high. As to the bridle, it must be of twenty-three-carat gold, for it had rubbed its bit against a stone, and I had made the assay of it. I judged, finally, by the marks which its shoes had left on the pebbles of another kind, that it was shod with silver of a fineness of twelve deniers,'

All the judges admired the profound and subtle discernment of Zadig. The news of it reached the King and Queen. Nothing else was spoken of in the ante-chambers, the chambers, and the Cabinet; and though the Magis were of opinion that he ought to be burnt for sorcery, the King ordered that they should give him back the fine of four hundred ounces of gold to which he had been condemned. The officers came to him in their grand robes bearing the four hundred ounces; they only retained three hundred and ninety-eight for the expenses of justice, while their valets demanded a 'tip.'

The first application of the idea embodied in these stories to the detective belongs to Edgar Allan Poe, who, in the estimation of many competent judges, still holds pride of place, supreme and unassailable, among the short-story writers of the world. In C. Auguste Dupin he introduced a detective whose paternity Sherlock Holmes might be proud to claim. Like Sherlock Holmes, he was interested in the detection of crime, not as a professional, but as an amateur, to whom the placing of each insignificant fact in its proper place was as fascinating as to the worker in mosaic is the placing of each tiny tessera in the design.

While thrown prominently into view in 'The Murders in the Rue Morgue' —the story which reaches the high-water mark of its class as an acknowledged masterpiece among short stories, unless Poe's own 'Gold Bug' may be regarded as taking its place—the methods Dupin adopted in 'The Purloined Letter' may be taken as most typical of his method. In that case, as in so many of Sherlock Holmes's investigations, the police were entirely baffled. The Prefect of the Parisian police went to consult him on the mystery, to which the only objection from Dupin's point of view was that there was no mystery.

Those who have read the story will remember that a document of supreme importance had been stolen from the Royal apartments. The thief was known, for he was seen to take the letter, which was in his possession. He was an exalted personage—a Minister of State. While the lady to whom the letter was addressed was reading it she was interrupted by the unexpected arrival of someone from whom she wished to conceal it. She tried to put it into a drawer, but failed, and she had to leave it on the table, relying on the fact that things which are not hidden at all are often most free from observation. This fact, it may be remarked, was made use of by Sardou in his famous comedy, known in its English dress as 'The Scrap of Paper',

As soon as the Minister entered he saw the paper, recognised the handwriting, and, having a letter somewhat similar in his possession, substituted the one for the other. The lady to whom the letter belonged saw what he did, but did not dare prevent him, in consequence of the presence of the third person. The situation thus developed became interesting, for, while the

Minister was using the information obtained to his great advantage, the lady robbed was unable to demand her letter from him. She therefore put the case into the hands of the police.

The police searched the Minister's house while he was away, but found nothing. That was the position of affairs when the police called on Dupin, who obtained from them an exact description of the letter. After a few weeks the Prefect returned to the amateur and acknowledged that he had again searched the Minister's house without any result. In despair he offered fifty thousand francs for the letter. With exquisite simplicity Dupin replied, 'You may as well fill in a cheque for the amount mentioned; when you have signed it I will hand you the letter.'

To the amazement of the head of the profession of police Dupin explained his method, which may be said to be summed up in the familiar axiom, 'Put yourself in his place,' a method which Sherlock Holmes himself adopted with conspicuous success on more than one occasion. The imagination, indeed, which Sherlock so frequently insisted upon in his conversations with Dr. Watson, Dupin applied to the case, and began by putting himself in the place of the Minister, who, being a courtier and a bold intriguer, could not fail to anticipate that the police would do exactly what they did—waylay him and search his house. Indeed, he frequently absented himself from his house in order to enable them to search for the letter, and arrive at the conclusion that it was not on the premises.

Dupin, however, concluded that, as most self-evident things pass unnoticed, the Minister had not attempted to hide the letter at all. Accordingly, he went to his house, where he found the Minister. In order to obtain the excuse of wearing spectacles of smoked glasses Dupin complained of weak eyes, and so minutely examined the room without appearing to do so. While he was talking he noticed a little card rack of pasteboard dangling by a little dirty blue ribbon from a brass knob beneath the middle of the mantelpiece.

It had three or four compartments, containing five or six visiting cards and a single letter, which was soiled, crumpled, and torn nearly in two, and had a large black seal bearing the Minister's cipher very conspicuously. It was addressed in a female hand to the Minister himself, and looked as if it had been carelessly thrown into one of the upper divisions of the rack.

Dupin concluded that it was the letter he was in search of, for he noticed that the edges of the paper seemed to be more chafed than was necessary. He concluded that it had been turned inside out, redirected, and re-sealed: for it must be remembered that those were the days in which envelopes were not commonly used. Dupin bade the Minister good day and went away, having taken the precaution to leave his gold snuff-box on the table.

Next morning he called for it. In the middle of a conversation with the Minister there was a sudden report of a pistol beneath the window, followed by fearful screams and loud shouting, all previously arranged for the

The French pioneer of the detective story, Emile Gaboriau

Cover for 'Monsieur Lecoq', one of the influences on the concept of Sherlock Holmes

amateur detective. The Minister rushed to the window, threw it open, and looked out; where upon Dupin, to use his own words, 'stepped to the card-rack, took the letter, and replaced it by a facsimile carefully prepared at my lodgings.' Having secured the letter, Dupin bade the Minister farewell and left.

The firing of the revolver to distract the attention of the Minister is closely akin to the alarm of fire which Sherlock caused his accomplice to raise at the house of the Larrabees when he was investigating the mystery of the purloined documents, which formed the subject of the famous play bearing his name.

Closely allied to Dupin is M. Lecoq, who, thanks to the invention of Emile Gaboriau, has become the beau-ideal of the detective in France. Unlike Dupin, however, and therefore unlike Sherlock Holmes, he was not an amateur, but a professional member of the police force, which he entered to make a career for himself. The orginality of his methods caused his colleagues to be antagonistic to him, and in this way the author introduced that hostility to the deductive philosophy which has always been characteristic of detective stories.

If one turns to Gaboriau's story, 'File No. 113, the closeness of the methods of Lecoq, Dupin, and Holmes is seen at a glance.

A safe had been robbed, and it is of the utmost importance to discover who robbed it. In discussing the matter with one of his subordinates, Lecoq says: 'Do you remember the scratch you discovered on the green paint of the safe-door? You were so struck by it that you broke into an exclamation directly you saw it. You carefully examined it, and were convinced that it was a fresh scratch only a few hours old. Now, with what was it made? Evidently with a key. That being the case, you should have asked for the keys both of the banker and the cashier; one of them would have had some of the hard green paint sticking to it,'

Might not that little speech, so lucid in its statement, have been made by Sherlock himself?

Lecoq had a photograph made of the safe, which showed the scratch with great exactness. It ran from top to bottom, starting from the hole of the lock, and went from left to right. Although very deep at the keyhole, it ended off in a scarcely perceptible mark.

'Naturally you thought,' said Lecoq to his subordinate, 'the scratch was made by the person who took the money. Let us see if you are right. I have a little iron box painted with green varnish like the safe. Here it is. Take the key and try to scratch it.' The assistant tried and failed. 'It is very hard, my friend,'' said Lecoq, 'and yet that on the safe is still harder and thicker, so you see the scratch you discovered could not have been made by the trembling hand of a thief letting the key slip.'

'It certainly required great force to make that scratch.'

'Yes; but how was that force employed? I have been racking my brains for the last three days, and only yesterday did I come to a conclusion.' Lecoq went to the door of the room, took the key from the lock, and called the subordinate over to him. 'Now, suppose,' he said, 'I want to open this door and you don't want it opened; when you saw me about to insert the key what would be your first impulse?'

'To put my hand on your arm and draw it towards me so as to prevent you introducing the key.'

'Precisely so. Now let us try it.'

The assistant obeyed, and the key, held by M. Lecoq, pulled aside from the lock, slipped along the door and traced upon it a diagonal scratch from top to bottom, the exact reproduction of the one in the photograph.

'What a man you are!' said the subordinate. 'Two persons were present at the robbery; one wished to take the money and the other wished to prevent its being taken.'

If one substitutes the names of Sherlock and of Watson for those of Lecoq and his subordinate, might not the little dialogue have been written by the accomplished hand of Sir Arthur Conan Doyle?

By the way, Lecoq, like Sherlock, always worked alone. He took a pride in his solutions, and refused assistance because he wished to share neither the pleasure of success nor the pain of defeat.

In the course of one of his cases he had occasion to examine a letter composed of printed words cut out and pasted on a sheet of paper—a similar course, it will be remembered, to that which Sherlock Holmes had to adopt in elucidating the mystery of *The Hound of the Baskervilles*. From certain words it contained, which men never use, Lecoq quickly came to the conclusion that the letter was composed by a woman. He approached the window and began to study the pasted words with the scrupulous attention which an antiquarian would devote to an old, half-effaced manuscript.

'Small type, very slender and clear; the paper is thin and glossy—consequently these words have not been cut from a newspaper, magazine, or even a novel. I have seen type like this. I recognise it at once.'

He stopped, his mouth open and his eyes fixed, appealing laboriously to his memory. Suddenly he struck his forehead exultingly. 'Now I have it. Why did I not see it at once? These words have been cut from a prayer-book.'

He moistened with his tongue one of the words pasted on the paper, and, when it was sufficiently softened, detached it with a pin. On the other side of this word was printed the Latin word *'Deus'*. 'What became of the mutilated prayer-book? Could it have been burnt?' 'No,' he replied to himself, 'because a heavily-bound book is not usually burnt! It is thrown into some corner.' And in a corner it was eventually found.

Surely that was Sherlock all over, even to the fact that the man whose very fate depended upon the success of his investigations almost forgot the circumstance in his admiration of Lecoq's method; for his energy, his bantering coolness when he wished to discover anything, the surety of his deductions, the fertility of his expedients, and the rapidity of his movements were astonishing.

In *The Moonstone* Wilkie Collins, the king of constructive novelists, gave us a detective to whom in some respects Sherlock bears a by no means slight resemblance. This is his description:—

'Sergeant Cuff was a grizzled, elderly man, so miserably thin that he looked as if he had not got an ounce of flesh on his bones in any part of him. His face was as sharp as a hatchet, and the skin of it was as yellow and dry and withered as an autumn leaf. His eyes, of a steely light grey, had a disconcerting trick whenever they encountered your eyes of looking as if they expected something more from you than you were aware of yourself. His walk was soft, his voice was melancholy, his long, lanky fingers were hooked like claws. He might have been a parson or an undertaker, or anything else you like, except what he really was.'

Sergeant Cuff formulated into words the theory which Sherlock put into action. He was investigating a smear on a newly-painted door when he was called in to unravel the mystery of the disappearance of the moonstone. He was told by the superintendent who had the case in hand that it was made by the petticoats of the women-servants as they crowded into the room for the inquiry.

'Did you ascertain which petticoat?' he asked.

'I cannot charge myself with such trifles,' said the superintendent. Cuff's rejoinder might have been made by Sherlock.

'I made a private inquiry last week; at one end of the inquiry there was a murder, and at the other end there was a spot of ink which could not be accounted for. In all my experience along the dirtiest ways of this dirty little world I have never met such a thing as a trifle yet. We must see the petticoat that made the smear, and we must know for certain that the paint was wet.'

Not very long ago a writer in one of the weekly papers declared that the detective in literature is passing to decay. It may be doubted, however, whether, so long as deduction exercises its fascination, he will ever disappear from the pages of fiction. The processes on which he works are, as we have seen, of the most remote antiquity, and they have not lost their fascination yet.

The Artist Who Made Holmes Real

Winifred Paget

Sherlock Holmes has, of course, been pictured by countless artists over the years, but despite this the most popular and enduring idea of him remains that of the lean, aquiline figure who was created for the STRAND *by one of its artists, Sidney Paget. In the following article from* JOHN O'LONDON's *of 19 February 1954, Paget's daughter, Winifred, describes how her father helped make Holmes 'the most universally familiar imaginary figure in two hemispheres'.*

LITTLE did I realize how much the name of Sherlock Holmes would mean to me in the years to come when as a child I watched my father, Sidney Paget, drawing the now famous features. In those far-off days Sherlock Holmes was just a name associated with happy times, for when the great detective was hot on the trail it meant that we spent a month at the sea instead of the usual fortnight.

My father was the eldest of three brothers, all of whom became artists. His first recorded drawings of Sherlock Holmes appeared in the *Strand Magazine* in 1891 and it was his brother Walter, with his lean aquiline features, who became the model for the great detective.

Strangely enough, it appears that Walter should have been the artist and not the model. The Editor of the *Strand* was seeking an illustrator and remembered an artist named Paget, who had been the representative of the *Illustrated London News* with the Gordon Relief Expedition. He had forgotten his christian name, however, and wrote to my father instead; so Sidney got the commission and Walter, who should have had it, became the model.

Walter was an artist who took great pains to get every detail accurate. It is thus possible that he would have given the world a less handsome Holmes, portraying him perhaps more as the author saw him 'with a great hawks-bill of a nose and two small eyes set close together.'

That the detective and the model looked alike is proved by the following story—and it seems that they also shared the same tastes.

My uncle was attending a Musical Recital at the Bechstein Hall and as he walked to his seat near the front a woman in the audience was heard to say 'Look, there's Sherlock Holmes.'

On another occasion he was dining with friends in St. John's Wood and

Sidney Paget, the first man to draw Sherlock Holmes

One of Paget's drawings of Holmes, utilising the artist's own furniture. From 'The Adventure of the Greek Interpreter', 1893

when he appeared on the doorstep their young son, who had been watching the guests arrive from the window, called out: 'Mummy, Mr. Sherlock Holmes has come!'

One hopes he did the thing properly and arrived in a hansom.

As a model for Watson I think it is true to say that my father took an architect friend of student days, though there have been other claims to this honour. For the other characters in the ever-changing scene he relied entirely on the written word and his imagination, though I have been told by his sister, who is still living, that she and others sometimes acted as models. Glancing at the illustrations in the *Strand*, one can spot an odd chair or other piece of furniture which is still in the possession of some member of the family.

In 1951 I lent to the Sherlock Holmes Exhibition an old cane chair that we had kept all these years out of sentiment, and it can be seen well to the fore in any photograph taken of the living room at 221b, Baker Street at that time. This chair appears at least twice in the *Memoirs*—once in 'The Greek Interpreter' and again in 'The Stockbroker's Clerk,' where for some unknown reason it appears to have acquired rockers.

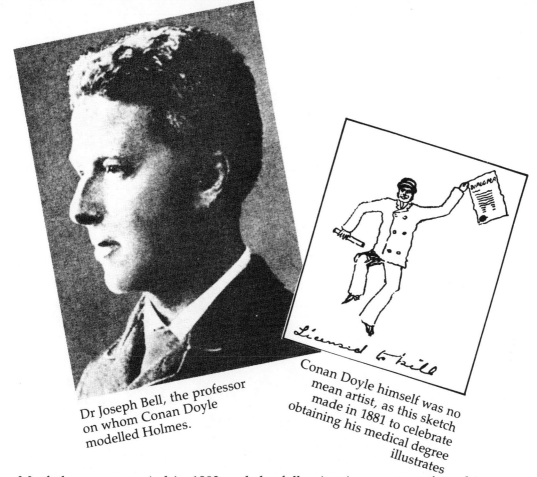

Dr Joseph Bell, the professor on whom Conan Doyle modelled Holmes.

Conan Doyle himself was no mean artist, as this sketch made in 1881 to celebrate obtaining his medical degree illustrates

My father was married in 1893 and the following is an extract from his diary:

June 1st, 1893. Our Wedding Day . . . Was most delighted at breakfast time to find a beautiful silver cigarette case from 'Sherlock Holmes' had come as a present. [The cigarette case was, of course, from the late Sir Arthur Conan Doyle.] Pipe also from Dr. Parker. . . .

One feels there is something wrong with the last name!

Even on his honeymoon the man from Baker Street kept him company. Only six days after the wedding appear these words in the diary: 'Wrote letters and read Sherlock Holmes,' then again on the 12th: 'After breakfast began drawing (S. H.) worked till 1 o'clock.' On this morning he apparently missed his bride and found her under a tree in the meadow.

My parents set up their home in a village in Hertfordshire and here my father built a studio in one corner of the orchard that surrounded the house. During the summer I fear he sometimes spent more time in that orchard than he did in the studio with the result that when the time came for the next batch of drawings to go to the publishers he would have to sit up half the night working hard to get them finished. It was worth it, I suppose, for those

A portrait of Sherlock Holmes by Sidney Paget which the artist had thrown into the wastepaper basket, where it was rescued by his wife. It was later reproduced by his daughter, Winifred Paget

sunny days spent hay-making in the orchard.

Even creative work can become monotonous through repetition and when eventually my father was commissioned to portray the death of Holmes at the Reichenbach Falls, he did so with few regrets; indeed the author and artist must have been the only persons then living who appeared to be quite indifferent to his fate!

It was during the time that my father lived in the country that he wore that surely now most famous of all hats—the deerstalker; and the fact that he liked it and found it comfortable inspired him to depict Holmes wearing it on so many occasions.

My father had been a regular exhibitor in the Academy since 1879 and I recently found the ticket for that first Exhibition between the pages of his diary. He liked to be known as a portrait painter, but he is remembered for his drawings of Sherlock Holmes. (One of his portraits was of a former head of Mill Hill School; two others were bought by local authorities in London.)

As a 'black and white' artist for the *Illustrated London News*, the *Graphic* and the *Sphere*, he had to attend many functions of one sort or another to make rough sketches for the final picture and on very rare occasions we were allowed to go with him. I still remember the thrill of a visit to the Military Tournament with the noise and the flying tan as the Indians engaged in tent pegging thundered past on their horses and, last but not least, the biggest thrill of all—a ride in a hansom cab on the way home when one kept one's eyes fixed on the little trap-door in the roof hoping every moment it would open once more to expose the face of the driver who seemed like a veritable Jack-in-the-Box so quickly did he come and go! Surely these vehicles with their jingling bells and the 'man up there in the roof' were specially designed for the delight of small children!

After my father's death at the early age of forty-seven, the figures of Holmes and Watson faded into the background of my life, to reappear now and again in some newspaper or magazine which my mother would carefully preserve, so much did these names and all the old associations connected with them still mean to her. I well remember her joy one day when the milkman standing at the door suddenly craned his neck and, gazing at a sketch of Holmes hanging in the hall exclaimed, 'Well, if it ain't Sherlock Holmes!' Could this rather stout little Cockney have been a descendant of Wiggins, I wonder. Whoever he was he knew the Master well and from that day became a friend instead of 'just the milkman'.

The mysterious gas-lit London of the eighties and nineties has vanished for ever, but Sherlock Holmes lives on!

'I Play the Game for the Game's Own Sake'

Here are thirty questions on the titles of cases in the Holmesian canon set by American Sherlockian John Bennett Shaw of the scion society, The Brothers Three of Moriarty. Note that only the key words of each title are needed, and that in most cases a pun is used or implied. The answers are provided at the back of the book.

1. If the first Pope had been a Negro. _____
2. A sewing group in Leningrad. _____
3. After a train wreck the operator hitches to town. _____
4. An uncomplaining tenant. _____
5. An employer carefully searching a mountain area for someone or something. _____
6. Fags at play. _____
7. Three Raquel Welchs. _____
8. What the dying dog uttered. _____
9. Hurting teeth. _____
10. Private swimming area for police. _____
11. An unmarried male who tells the truth. _____
12. More than two socially prominent young ladies in a filthy Indiana town. _____
13. An agreement to allow belly dances. _____
14. For rent. _____
15. A marching musical group with measles. _____
16. Day of Judgement. _____
17. Comment of a gentleman who does not want yellow trousers. _____
18. Posted warning of safety measure at golf tee. _____
19. Possibly Sir Walter's daughter. _____
20. Several happy young cattle looking at cows. _____
21. Case history of character in GONE WITH THE WIND. _____
22. Impoverished private eye working in a cleaning shop. _____
23. A pasture owned by a noted lady newspaper columnist. _____
24. Bridge player, dead of ennui, in a casket. _____
25. If Schoendinst rather than Cronin had lead the junior circuit. _____
26. Spit it out, spit it out, spit it out, spit it out, spit it out. _____
27. When he worked, he summoned hogs. _____
28. A deformity of the face named after a mammal of the genus *Lepus*. _____
29. If baseball was played in southern England, the man who would 'call 'em' would be. _____
30. If I went in for phone tapping, bribery, destroying evidence, and so on I would be? _____

[46]

Studies in the Literature of Sherlock Holmes

Ronald Knox

This is widely considered the most important of all the many hundreds of essays that have been written about Sherlock Holmes. For as a result of Ronald Knox delivering the paper in the form of an address to members of The Gryphon Club at Trinity College, Oxford, in 1911, and later having it published in THE BLUE BOOK *magazine, he initiated what has subsequently become an obsession with a world-wide band of enthusiasts who use the sixty* Adventures *of the Master Detective as the source material for endless discussion and argument about the finer points of the cases. Father Knox's trenchant and satirical essay is undoubtedly required reading for all newcomers to the realms of Sherlockiana.*

IF THERE is anything pleasant in life, it is doing what we aren't meant to do. If there is anything pleasant in criticism, it is finding out what we aren't meant to find out. It is the method by which we treat as significant what the author did not mean to be significant, by which we single out as essential what the author regarded as incidental. Thus, if one brings out a book on turnips, the modern scholar tries to discover from it whether the author was on good terms with his wife; if a poet writes on buttercups, every word he says may be used as evidence against him at an inquest of his views on a future existence. On this fascinating principle, we delight to extort economic evidence from Aristophanes, because Aristophanes knew nothing of economics: we try to extract cryptograms from Shakespeare, because we are inwardly certain that Shakespeare never put them there: we sift and winnow the Gospel of St. Luke, in order to produce a Synoptic problem, because St. Luke, poor man, never knew the Synoptic problem to exist.

There is, however, a special fascination in applying this method to Sherlock Holmes, because it is, in a sense, Holmes's own method. 'It has long been an axiom of mine,' he says, 'that the little things are infinitely the most important.' It might be the motto of his life's work. And it is, is it not, as we clergymen say, by the little things, the apparently unimportant things, that we judge of a man's character.

If anyone objects, that the study of Holmes literature is unworthy of sholarly attention, I might content myself with replying that to the scholarly mind anything is worthy of study, if that study be thorough and systematic. But I will go further, and say that at the present time we need a far closer familiarity with Sherlock's methods. The evil that he did lived after him, the good is interred with him in the Reichenbach. It is a known fact, that is, that several people contracted the dirty and deleterious habit of taking cocaine as a result of reading the books. It is equally obvious that Scotland Yard has benefited not a whit either by his satire or by his example. When Holmes, in the 'Mystery of the Red-Headed League,' discovered that certain criminals were burrowing their way into the cellars of a bank, he sat with a dark lantern in the cellar, and nabbed them quietly as they came through. But when the Houndsditch gang were found to be meditating an exactly similar design, what did the police authorities do? They sent a small detachment of constables, who battered on the door of the scene of operations at the bank, shouting, 'We think there is a burglary going on in here.' They were of course shot down, and the Home Office had to call out a whole regiment with guns and a fire brigade, in order to hunt down the suvivors.

Any studies in Sherlock Holmes must be, first and foremost, studies in Dr. Watson. Let us treat at once of the literary and bibliographical aspect of the question. First, as to authenticity. There are several grave inconsistencies in the Holmes cycle. For example the *Study in Scarlet* and the *Reminiscences* are from the hand of John H. Watson, M.D., but in the story of the 'Man with the Twisted Lip', Mrs. Watson addresses her husband as James. The present writer, together with three brothers, wrote to ask Sir Arthur Conan Doyle for an explanation, appending their names in the proper style with crosses after them, and an indication that this was the sign of the Four. The answer was that it was an error, an error, in fact, of editing. 'Nihil aliud hic latet,' says the great Sauwosch, 'nisi redactor ignorantissimus.' Yet this error gave the original impetus to Backnecke's theory of the Deutero-Watson, to whom he assigns the *Study in Scarlet*, the 'Gloria Scott', and the 'Return of Sherlock Holmes'. He leaves to the proto-Watson the rest of the *Memoirs*, the Adventures, the *Sign of Four* and the *Hound of the Baskervilles*. He disputed the *Study in Scarlet* on other grounds, the statement in it, for example, that Holmes's knowledge of literature and philosophy was nil, whereas it is clear and the true Holmes was a man of wide reading and deep thought. We shall deal with this in its proper place.

The 'Gloria Scott' is condemned by Backnecke partly on the ground of the statement that Holmes was only up for two years at College, while he speaks in the 'Musgrave Ritual' of 'my last years' at the University; which Backnecke supposes to prove that the two stories do not come from the same hand. The 'Gloria Scott' further represents Percy Trevor's bull-dog as having bitten Holmes on his way down to Chapel, which is clearly untrue, since dogs are not allowed within the gates at either university. 'The bull-dog is more at home' he adds 'on the Chapel steps, that this fraudulent imitation among the divine products of the Watsons-genius.' A further objection to the 'Gloria Scott' is that it exhibits only four divisions out of the eleven-fold division (to be mentioned later) of the complete Holmes-episode, a lower percentage than is found in any other genuine story. For myself, however, I am content to believe that this irregularity is due merely to the exceptional character of the investigation, while the two inaccuracies are too slight (*me judice*) to form the basis for so elaborate a theory. I would include both the 'Gloria' Scott and the *Study in Scarlet* as genuine incidents of Holmes-biography.

When we come to the 'Final Problem', the alleged death of Holmes, and his subsequent return in an unimpaired and even vigorous condition, the problem grows darker. Some critics, accepting the Return stories as genuine, regard the 'Final Problem' as an incident faked by Watson for his own purposes; thus M. Piff-Pouff represents it as an old dodge of the thaumaturgist, and quotes the example of Salmoxis or Gebeleizis among the Getae, who hid underground for two years, and then returned to preach the doctrine of immortality. In fact, M. Piff-Pouff's verdict is thus expressed: 'Sherlockholmes has not at all fallen from the Reichenbach, it is Vatson who has fallen from the pinnacle of his mendacity.' In a similar vein, Bilgemann asserts that the episode is a weak imitation of Empedocles on Etna, the alpenstock being left behind to represent the famous slipper which was revomited by the volcano. 'The episode of the "Final Problem" ', in his own immortal language, 'has the Watsons-applecart completely overturned.'

Others, Backnecke of course among them, regard the 'Final Problem' as genuine, and the Return stories as a fabrication. The evidence against these stories may be divided into (a) those suggested by changes in the character and methods of Holmes, (b) those resting on impossibilities in the narrative itself, (c) inconsistencies found by comparison with the previous narrative.

(a) The true Holmes is never discourteous to a client: the Holmes of the 'Adventure of the Three Students' 'shrugged his shoulders in ungracious acquiescence while our visitor . . . poured forth his story.' On the other hand, the true Holmes has no morbid craving for serious crime; but when John Hector Macfarlane talks of the probability of being arrested, the detective is represented as saying 'Arrest you! this is most grati—— most interesting.' Twice in the Return he gibes at his prisoner, a habit from which the true Holmes, whether from professional etiquette or for other reasons, invariably abstains. Again, the false Holmes actually calls a client by her Christian name, an impossible thing to an author whose views had not been distorted by the erroneous presentation of him in the play. He deliberately abstains from food while at work: the real Holmes only does so through absent-mindedness, as in the 'Case of the Five Orange Pips'. He quotes Shakespeare in these stories alone, and that three times, without acknowledgement. He gives way to ludicrously bad logic in the 'Dancing Men'. He sends Watson as his emissary in the 'Solitary Cyclist,' and this is elsewhere unparalleled, for in the *Hound of the Baskervilles* he himself goes down to Dartmoor as well, to watch the case incognito. The true Holmes never splits an infinitive; the Holmes of the Return-stories splits at least three.

(b) It is likely that a University scholarship paper—nay, an Oxford scholarship paper, for the Quadrangle is mentioned in connexion with it—should be printed only one day before the examination? That it should consist of only half a chapter of Thucydides? That this half-chapter should take the examiner an hour and a half to correct for the press? That the proofs of the half-chapter should be in three consecutive slips? Moreover, if a pencil was marked with the name JOHANN FABER, how could the two letters NN, and these two only, be left on the stump? Prof. J. A. Smith has further pointed out that it would be impossible to find out from the superimposition of the tracks of front and back bicycle tyres, whether the cyclist was going or coming.

(c) As to actual inconsistencies. In the mystery of the 'Solitary Cyclist' a marriage is performed with no one present except the happy couple and the officiating clergyman. In the 'Scandal in Bohemia' Holmes, disguised as a loafer, is deliberately called in to give away an unknown bride on the ground that the marriage will not be valid without a witness. In the 'Final Problem', the police secure 'the whole gang with the exception of Moriarty.' In the 'Story of the Empty House' we hear that they failed to incriminate Colonel Moran. Professor Moriarty, in the Return, is called Professor James Moriarty, whereas we know from the 'Final Problem' that James was really the name of his military brother, who survived him. And, worst of all, the dummy in the Baker Street window is draped in *the old mouse-coloured dressing-gown*'! As if we had forgotten that it was in a *blue* dressing-gown that Holmes smoked an ounce of shag tobacco at a sitting, while he unravelled the dark complication of 'The Man with the Twisted Lip'! 'The detective,' says M. Papier Maché, 'has become a chameleon.' 'This is not the first time', says the more ponderous Sauwosch, 'that a coat of many colours has been as a deception used! But in truth Sherlock, our modern Joseph, has altogether disappeared, and the evil beast Watson has him devoured.'

To this criticism I assent: I cannot assent, however, to the theory of the deutero-Watson. I believe that all the stories were written by Watson, but whereas the genuine cycle actually happened, the spurious adventures are the lucubrations of his own unaided invention. Surely we may reconstruct the facts thus. Watson has been a bit of a gad-about. He is a spendthrift: so much we know from the beginning of the *Study in Scarlet*. His brother, as Holmes finds out by examining the scratches on the keyhole of his watch, was a confirmed drunkard. He himself, as a bachelor, haunts the Criterion Bar: in the *Sign of Four* he admits having had too much Beaune for lunch, behaves strangely at lunch, speakes of firing off a double-barrelled tiger-cub at a musket, and cautions his future wife against taking more than two drops of castor-oil, while recommending strychnine in large doses as a sedative. What happens? His Elijah is taken away from him: his wife, as we know, dies: he slips back into the grip of his old enemy; his practice, already diminished by continued neglect, vanishes away; he is forced to earn a livelihood by patching together clumsy travesties of the wonderful incidents of which he was once the faithful recorder.

Sauwosch has even worked out an elaborate table of his debts to other authors, and to the earlier stories. Holmes's stay in Thibet with the Grand Lama is due to Dr. Nikola; the cipher of the 'Dancing Men' is read in the same manner as that in the 'Gold Bug', by Edgar Allan Poe; the 'Adventure of Charles Augustus Milverton' shows the influence of Raffles; the 'Norwood Builder' owes much to the 'Scandal in Bohemia'; the 'Solitary Cyclist' has the plot of the 'Greek Interpreter'; the 'Six Napoleons' of the 'Blue Carbuncle'; the 'Adventure of the Second Stain' is a doublet of the 'Naval Treaty', and so on.

We now pass on to the dating of the various pieces, so far as it can be determined by internal evidence, implicit or explicit. The results may be tabulated thus:

The Criterion Long Bar, Piccadilly, in 1881, where Dr Watson met Dr Stamford—a meeting which was to result in Watson being introduced to Sherlock Holmes

The plaque erected at the Criterion Bar to commemorate the meeting

THE CRITERION BAR.

THIS PLAQUE COMMEMORATES THE HISTORIC MEETING AT THE ORIGINAL LONG BAR AT THIS HOTEL ON JANUARY 1st 1881 OF Dr STAMFORD AND Dr JOHN H. WATSON WHICH LED TO THE INTRODUCTION OF Dr WATSON TO Mr SHERLOCK HOLMES.

(1) The 'Gloria Scott'—Holmes's first case.
(2) The 'Musgrave Ritual'—his second.
(3) The *Study in Scarlet*—Watson first appears, i.e. the first of the We-Stories. Date 1879.
(4) 1883, the 'Speckled Band'.
(5) 1887, April, the 'Reigate Squires'.
(6) Same year, the 'Five Orange Pips'.
(7) 1888, the *Sign of Four*—Watson becomes engaged.
(8) The 'Noble Bachelor'. Then comes Watson's marriage, followed closely by
(9) The 'Crooked Man'.
(10) The 'Scandal in Bohemia', and
(11) The 'Naval Treaty', apparently in that order.

To some period in the year '88 we must assign 12, 13, and 14, that is, the 'Stockbroker's Clerk', the Case of Identity, and the 'Red-Headed League'. In the June of '89 we have (15) the 'Man with the Twisted Lip', (16) the 'Engineer's Thumb' (Summer), and (17) the 'Blue Carbuncle' (somewhere in the octave of Christmas). The 'Final Problem' is dated '91. Of the remainder, 'Silver Blaze', the 'Yellow Face', the 'Resident Patient', the 'Greek Interpreter', the 'Beryl Coronet', and the 'Copper Beeches' are apparently before Watson's marriage, the 'Boscombe Valley Mystery' after it: otherwise they are undated.

There remains only the *Hound of the Baskervilles*. This is explicitly dated 1889, that is, it does not pretend to be after the Return. Sauwosch, who believes it to be spurious, points out that the *Times* would never have had a leader on Free Trade till after 1903. But this argument from internal evidence defeats itself: we can show by a method somewhat akin to that of Blunt's *Undesigned Coincidences in Holy Scriptures* that it was meant to be before 1901. The old crank who wants to have a law-suit against the police says it will be known as the case of Frankland versus REGINA—King Edward, as we all know, succeeded in 1901.

I must not waste time over other evidences (very unsatisfactory) which have been adduced to show the spuriousness of the *Hound of the Baskervilles*. Holmes's 'cat-like love of personal cleanliness' is not really inconsistent with the statement in the *Study in Scarlet* that he had pinpricks all over his hand covered with plaster—though this is also used by Backnecke to tell against the genuineness of the earlier production. A more serious question is that of Watson's breakfast-hour. Both in the *Study in Scarlet* and in the Adventures we hear that Watson breakfasted after Holmes: in the *Hound* we are told that Holmes breakfasted late. But then, the true inference from this is that Watson breakfasted very late indeed.

Taking, then, as the basis of our study, the three long stories, *The Sign of Four, A Study in Scarlet,* and *The Hound of the Baskervilles,* together with the twenty-three short stories, twelve in the *Adventures,* and eleven in the

Dr Stamford introduces his friend Dr Watson to Sherlock Holmes
at St Bartholomew's Hospital, London

Memoirs, we may proceed to examine the construction and the literary antecedents of this form of art. The actual scheme of each should consist, according to the German scholar, Ratzegger, followed by most of his successors, of eleven distinct parts; the order of them may in some cases be changed about, and more or less of them may appear as the story is closer to or further from the ideal type. Only *A Study in Scarlet* exhibits all the eleven; *The Sign of Four* and 'Silver Blaze' have ten, the 'Boscombe Valley Mystery' and the 'Beryl Coronet' nine, *The Hound of the Baskervilles*, the 'Speckled Band', the 'Reigate Squires', and the 'Naval Treaty' eight, and so on till we reach 'The Five Orange Pips', the 'Crooked Man', and the 'Final Problem' with five, and the 'Gloria Scott' with only four.

The first part is the Proöimion, a homely Baker Street scene, with invaluable personal touches, and sometimes a demonstration by the detective. Then follows the first explanation, or Exegesis kata ton diokonta, that is, the client's statement of the case, followed by the Ichneusis, or personal investigation, often including the famous floor-walk on hands and knees. No. 1 is invariable, Nos. 2 and 3 almost always present. Nos. 4, 5 and 6 are less necessary: they include the Anaskeue, or refutation on its own merits of the official theory of Scotland Yard, the first Promenusis (exoterike) which gives a few stray hints to the police, which they never adopt, and the second Promenusis (esoterike), which adumbrates the true course of the investigation to Watson alone. This is sometimes wrong, as in the 'Yellow Face'. No. 7 is the Exetasis, or further following up of the trial, including the cross-questioning of relatives, dependants, etc., of the corpse (if there is one), visits to the Record Office, and various investigations in an assumed character. No. 8 is the Anagnorisis, in which the criminal is caught or exposed, No. 9 the second Exegesis (kata ton pheugonta), that is to say the criminal's confession, No. 10 the Metamenusis, in which Holmes describes what his clues were and how he followed them, and No. 11 the Epilogos, sometimes comprised in a single sentence. This conclusion is, like the Proöimion, invariable, and often contains a gnome or quotation from some standard author.

Although the *Study in Scarlet* is in a certain sense the type and ideal of a Holmes story, it is also to some extent a primitive type, of which elements were later discarded. The Exegesis kata ton pheugonta is told for the most part, not in the words of the criminal, but as a separate story in the mouth of the narrator: it also occupies a disproportionate amount of the total space. This shows directly the influence of Gaboriau: his *Detective's Dilemma* is one volume, containing an account of the tracing of the crime back to its author, who is of course a duke: the second volume, the *Detective's Triumph*, is almost entirely a retailing of the duke's family history, dating back to the Revolution, and we only rejoin Lecoq, the detective, in the last chapter. Of course, this method of telling the story was found long and cumbrous, but the French school has not yet seen through it, since the 'Mystery of the Yellow

Room' leaves a whole unexplained problem to provide copy for 'The Perfume of the Lady in Black'.

But the literary affinities of Dr. Watson's masterly style are to be looked for further afield than Gaboriau, or Poe, or Wilkie Collins. M. Piff-Pouff especially, in his *Psychologie de Vatson*, has instituted some very remarkable parallels with the *Dialogues of Plato*, and with the Greek drama. He reminds us of the blustering manner of Thrasymachus when he first breaks into the argument of the Republic, and compares the entry of Athelney Jones: 'Oh, come, now, come! Never be ashamed to own up! But what's all this? Bad business, bad business! Stern facts here, no room for theories,' and so on. And when the detective comes back crestfallen after a few days, wiping his brow with a red handkerchief, we remember how Socrates describes the first time in his life when he ever saw Thrasymachus blushing. The rival theories of Gregson and Lestrade only serve to illustrate the multiformity of error.

But the most important point is the nature of the Scotland Yard criticism. Lecoq has his rival, but the rival is his own superior in the detective force, thwarts his schemes out of pique, and actually connives at the prisoner's receiving notes through the window of his cell. The jealousy of a Lestrade has none of this paltry spirit about it, it is a combination of intellectual pride and professional pique. It is the opposition of the regular force to the amateur. Socrates was hated by the sophists because they took money, and he did not. The cases in which Holmes takes money, explicitly at any rate, are few. In the 'Scandal in Bohemia' he is given £1,000, but this would seem to be only for current expenses, and may well have been refunded. At the end, he refuses the gift of an emerald ring. He will not allow the City and Suburban Bank to do more than pay his expenses in connection with the Red-headed League. He says the same elsewhere: 'As for my reward, my profession is my reward.' On the other hand, he takes £4,000 from Mr. Holder when he has recovered the missing beryls for £3,000. In *A Study in Scarlet*, when setting out in business, he says: 'I listen to their story, they listen to my comments, and then I pocket my fee.' In the 'Greek Interpreter' he affirms that detection is a means of livelihood with him. And in the 'Final Problem' we hear that he has been so well paid for his services in several instances to crowned heads that he is thinking of retiring from business and taking to chemistry. We must suppose, therefore, that he did sometimes take payment, but perhaps only where his clients could well afford it. None the less, as compared with the officials, he is a free lance: he has no axe to grind, no promotion to seek. And further, there is an antithesis of method. Holmes is determined not to be led away by side issues and apparent pressure of facts: this it is that raises him above the level of the sophists.

If the sophists have been borrowed from the Platonic dialogue, one element at least had been borrowed from the Greek drama. Gaboriau has no Watson. The confidant of Lecoq is an old soldier, preternaturally stupid, inconceivably inefficient. Watson provides what the Holmes drama needs—a Chorus. He represents the solid, orthodox, respectable view of the world in general; his drabness is accentuated by contrast with the limelight which beats upon the central figure. He remains stable amid the eddy and flux of circumstance.

> *Ille bonis faveatque, et consilietur amicis,*
> *Et regat iratos, et amet peccare timentes:*
> *Ille dapes laudet mensae brevis, ille salubrem*
> *Justitiam, legesque, et apertis otia portis.*
> *Ille tegat commissa, deosque precetur et oret*
> *wut redeat miseris, abeat fortuna superbis.*

It is to Professor Sabaglione that we owe the profoundest study of Watson in this his choric character. He compares such passages as that in the *'Speckled Band'*:

Holmes: 'The lady could not move her bed. It must always be in the same relative position to the ventilator and the rope—for such we may call it, since it was clearly never meant for a bell-pull.'

Watson: 'Holmes, I seem to see what you are hinting at. We are only just in time to prevent some subtle and horrible crime.'

with the well-known passage in the Agamemnon:

Cassandra: 'Ah, ah, keep away the bull from the cow! She takes him, the black-horned one, in a net by her device, and smites him; he falls in a watery vessel—I speak to thee of the Mystery of the Treacherous Cauldron.'

Chorus: 'Far be it from me to boast of any particular skill in oracles, but I deduce from these words some impending evil.'

Watson, like the Chorus, is ever in touch with the main action, and seems to share the full privileges of the audience; yet, like the Chorus, he is always about three stages behind the audience in the unravelling of the plot.

And the seal, and symbol, and secret of Watson is, of course, his bowler. It is not like other bowlers: it is a priestly vestment, an *insigne* of office. Holmes may wear a squash hat, but Watson cleaves to his bowler, even at midnight in the silence of Dartmoor, or on the solitary slopes of the Reichenbach. He wears it constantly, even as the archimandrite or the rabbi wears his hat: to remove it would be akin to the shearing of Samson's locks by Delilah. 'Watson and his bowler' says M. Piff-Pouff, 'they are separable only in thought.' It is his apex of wool, his petasus of invisibility, his *mitra pretiosa*, his triple tiara, his halo. The bowler stands for all that is immutable and irrefragable, for law and justice, for the established order of things, for the rights of humanity, for the triumph of the man over the brute. It towers colossal over sordidness and misery and crime: it shames and heals and hallows. The curve of its brim is the curve of perfect symmetry, the rotundity of its crown is the rotundity of the world. 'From the hats of Holmes's clients,' writes Professor Sabaglione, 'deduce themselves the traits, the habits, the idiosyncrasies: from the hat of Guatson deduces itself his character.' Watson

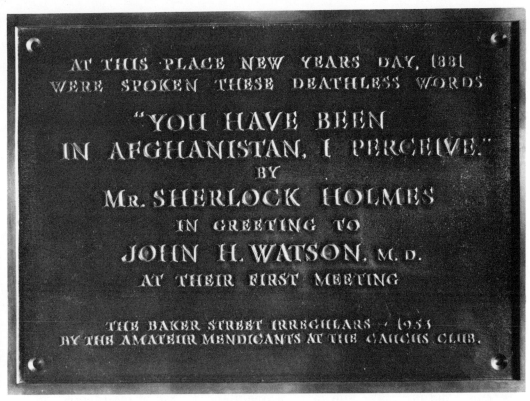

The wall plaque at St Bartholomew's Hospital commemorating
an historic event

is everything to Holmes—his medical adviser, his foil, his philosopher, his
confidant, his sympathizer, his biographer, his domestic chaplain, but above
all things else he stands exalted in history as the wearer of the unconquerable
bowler hat.

And if the rival detectives are the sophists, and Watson is the Chorus,
what of the clients, and what of the criminals? It is most important to
remember that these are only secondary figures. 'The murderers of the
Holmes cycle,' M. Papier Maché assures us, 'are of no more importance than
the murderers are not in Macbeth.' Holmes himself often deprecates Watson's habit of making the stories too sensational, but he does him an injus-
tice. The authors of crime are not, in Watson, of personal interest, like the
Duke in Gaboriau; they have no relation to the detective other than that
which subsists between the sleuth-hound and its quarry—the author of the
'Mystery of the Yellow Room' was a bungler when he made Jacques
Rouletabille the criminal's natural son—they are not animated by lofty or
religious motives like the high-flown villains in Mr. Chesterton's *Innocence of
Father Brown*. All clients are model clients: they state their case in flawless
journalese; all criminals are model criminals: they do the cleverest thing a
criminal could possibly do in the given circumstances. By a sort of Socratic

paradox, we might say that the best detective can only catch the best thief. A single blunder on the part of the guilty man would have thrown all Holmes's deductions out of joint. Love and money are their only incentives: brutality and cunning their indefeasible qualities.

And thus we arrive at the central figure himself, and must try to gather together a few threads in the complex and many-sided character. There is an irony in the process, for Holmes liked to look upon himself as a machine, an inhuman and undifferentiated sleuth-hound. 'L'homme, c'est rien; l'œuvre, c'est tout,' was one of his favourite quotations.

Sherlock Holmes was descended from a long line of country squires: his grandmother was the sister of a French artist: his elder brother Mycroft was, as we all know, more gifted than himself, but found an occupation, if the Reminiscences are to be trusted, in a confidential audit of Government accounts. Of Sherlock's school career we know nothing; Watson was at school, and one of his schoolmates was the nephew of a peer, but this seems to have been exceptional there, since it was considered good fun to 'chevy him about the playground and hit him over the shins with a wicket.' This seems to dispose of the idea that Watson was an Etonian. On the other hand, we have no evidence as to his University career, except the testimony (always doubtful) of one of the Return stories that he was unacquainted with the scenery of Cambridgeshire. Of Holmes's student days our knowledge is much fuller: he was reserved by nature, and his recreations—boxing and fencing—did not make him many acquaintances. One of his friends was Percy Trevor, son of an ex-convict, who had made his money in the Australian goldfields; another Reginald Musgrave, whose ancestors went back to the Conquest—quite the last word in aristocracy. He lived in a College, but what College? And at which University? The argument that his scientific bent would have naturally taken him to Cambridge defeats itself: for why should he have been only up two years if he wanted a proper scientific training? More and more as I consider the wealth of his two friends, the exclusive aristocracy of the one, and the doggy tendencies of the other, together with the isolation which put even so brilliant a light as Holmes's under a bushel—more and more I incline to the opinion that he was up at the House. But we have no sure evidence.

If he was an Oxford man, he was not a Greats' man. Yet when Watson describes his first impressions of the man at the beginning of the *Study in Scarlet*—the *locus classicus* for Holmes's characteristics—he wrongs him in saying that his knowledge of philosophy is nil, and his knowledge of literature nil. The fact is, clearly, that Holmes did not let his talents appear till he had been living with Watson for some time, and had come to recognize his sterling qualities. In fact, he compares Hafiz with Horace, quotes Tacitus, Jean Paul, Flaubert, Goethe, and Thoreau, and reads Petrarch in a G.W.R. carriage. He has no definite interest in philosophy as such, yet he holds certain definite views on scientific method. A philosopher could not have said, 'when you have eliminated the impossible, whatever remains, however improbable, must be the truth.' He could not have confused observation with inference, as Holmes does when he says: 'Observation shows me you have been to the Post Office' judging by the mud on Watson's boots. There must be inference here, though it may be called implicit inference, however rapid be the transition of thought. Yet Holmes was no Sensationalist. What sublimer confession of faith could any realist make that the remark in the *Study in Scarlet:* 'I ought to know by this time that when a fact appears to be opposed to a long train of deductions, it invariably proves to be capable of bearing some other interpretation'?

And here I must say a word on the so-called 'method of deduction'. M. Papier Maché has boldly asserted that it was stolen from Gaboriau. M. Piff-Pouff in his well-known article, 'Qu'est-ce que c'est que la déduction?' declares roundly that Holmes's methods were inductive. The two fallacies rest on a common ground. Lecoq has observation: he notices footsteps on the snow. He has powers of inference, for he can infer from such footsteps the behaviour of those who have left them. He has not the method of deduction—he never sits down and reasons out what it is probable the man would have done next. Lecoq has his lens and his forceps: he has not the dressing-gown and the pipe. That is why he has to depend on mere chance, again and again, for picking up lost threads. Holmes no more depended on a chance than he prayed for a miracle. That is why Lecoq, baffled after a long investigation, has to have recourse to a sort of arm-chair detective, who, without leaving the arm-chair, tells him exactly what must have happened. It is wrong to call this latter character, as M. Papier Maché does, the original of Mycroft: he is the original, if you will, of Sherlock. Lecoq is but the Stanley Hopkins, almost the Lestrade, of his period. Holmes himself has explained for us the difference between observation (or inference) and deduction. It is by observation *a posteriori* that he recognizes Watson's visit to the Post Office from the mud on his trousers; it is by deduction *a priori* that he knows he has been sending a telegram, since he has seen plenty of stamps and postcards in Watson's desk.

Let us now take two pictures of Sherlock Holmes, the one at leisure, the other at work. Leisure was, of course, abhorrent to him—more so than to Watson. Watson says he was reckoned fleet of foot, but we have only his own word for it, and Holmes always beat him; beyond this alleged prowess we have no evidence of Watson's athleticism, except that he could throw a rocket through a first-floor window. But Holmes had been a boxer and a fencer; during periods of enforced inactivity he fired a revolver at the opposite wall till he had 'marked it with the patriotic device V.R.' Violin playing occupied leisure moments when Watson first knew him, but later it seems to be nothing more than a relaxation after hard work. And—this is very important—in this music was the exact antithesis of cocaine. We never hear of the drug being used in order to stimulate the mental faculties for hard work. All the stimulus needed he derived from tobacco. We all know, of course, that he smoked shag; few people could say off-hand what his pipe was made of. As a matter of fact, his tastes were various. The long vigil in Neville St. Clair's house was solaced by a briar—this is when he is hard at work; when he sees his way through a problem by inspection, as in the 'Case of Identity,' he takes down 'the old and oily clay pipe, which was to him as a counsellor.' In the 'Copper Beeches' he takes down 'The long cherrywood pipe with which he was wont to replace his clay when he was in a disputatious rather than a meditative mood.' On one occasion he offers Watson snuff. Watson, by the way, smoked Ship's tobacco when he went into lodgings with Holmes, but must have replaced it soon after with a sterner stuff, thinly veiled under the *nom de plume* of Arcadia Mixture. This expensive product he did not abandon even under the exigencies of married life; though his circumstances were not those of affluence, since he had linoleum laid down in the front hall. But the pipe is not to Watson what it is to Holmes: to Holmes belongs the immortal phrase: 'This will be a three-pipe problem.' He is one of the world's great smokers.

Now let us see Holmes at work. We all know how brisk he becomes at the appearance of a client; how, according to the inimitable phrase in the Reminiscences: 'Holmes sat up in his chair and took his pipe out of his mouth like a hound that has heard the View Halloo.' We have seen him in the mind's eye prowling round the room with his nose an inch from the ground, on the look-out for cigarette-ends, orange-peel, false teeth, domes of silence, and what not, that may have been left behind by the criminal. 'It is not a man,' says M. Binsk, the great Polish critic, 'it is either a beast or a god.'

It is this charge of inhumanity brought against Holmes that I wish specially to rebut. True, he is reported to have been found beating the dead subjects in the laboratory, to see whether or no bruises could be produced after death. True, he was a scientist. True, we get passages like that in the *Sign of Four:*

'Miss Morstan: From that day to this no word has been heard of my unfortunate father. He came home with his heart full of hope, to find some peace, some comfort, and instead——

She put her hand to her throat, and a choking sob cut short her utterance. 'The date?' asked Holmes, opening his notebook.'

But is it true to say that Holmes's anxiety to catch the criminal was not, like Watson's, due to a passion for justice, but to a purely scientific interest in deduction? Such truths are never more than half-truths: it would be hard to say that the footballer plays only for the goal, or that he plays only for the sake of exercise. Humanity and science in Holmes are strangely blended. At one moment we find him saying 'Women are never to be trusted, not even the best of them' (the coward!) or asserting that he cannot agree with those who rank modesty among the virtues, since the logician must see all things exactly as they are. Even his little sermon on the rose in the *Naval Treaty* is delivered in order to cover the fact that he is examining the window-frame for scratches. At another moment he is purchasing 'something a little choice in white wines,' and discoursing on miracle plays, on Stradivarius violins, on the Buddhism of Ceylon, and on the warships of the future.

But there are two specially human characteristics which come out at the very moment of action. One is a taste for theatrical arrangement, as when he sends back five orange pips to the murderers of John Openshaw, or takes a sponge into prison with which to unmask the man with the Twisted Lip, or serves up the Naval Treaty under a cover as a breakfast dish. The other is a taste for epigram. When he gets a letter from a duke, he says: 'It looks like one of those social summonses which call upon a man either to be bored or to lie.' There is a special kind of epigram, known as the Sherlockismus, of which the indefatigable Ratzegger has collected no less than one hundred and seventy-three instances. The following may serve as examples:

'Let me call your attention to the curious incident of the dog in the night-time.'

'The dog did nothing at all in the night-time.'

'That was the curious incident,' said Sherlock Holmes.

And again:

'I was following you, of course.'

'Following me? I saw nobody.'

'That is what you must expect to see when I am following you,' said Sherlock Holmes.

To write fully on this subject would need two terms' lectures at least. Some time, when leisure and enterprise allow, I hope to deliver them. Meanwhile, I have thrown out these hints, drawn these outlines of a possible mode of treatment. You know my methods, Watson: apply them.

A selection of sixteen of the characters from the Sherlock Holmes stories featured in a set of twenty-five cigarette cards issued in the 1920s by Turf Cigarettes under the title 'Conan Doyle Characters'

1. **SHERLOCK HOLMES**   The nature of a detective's work makes it essential that he should avoid publicity. Perhaps that is why no 'real life' detective has won the notoriety of Sherlock Homes, the hero of so many of Sir Arthur Conan Doyle's tales. One cannot help wondering, however, if there exists, outside the pages of history, anyone *quite* so clever at unravelling mysteries as this remarkable man, with his ingenious methods of work and extraordinary powers of observation.

2. **SHERLOCK HOLMES IN DISGUISE**   Besides hoodwinking criminals whom he wished to track, Sherlock Holmes used to get fun out of the way in which his disguises deceived even his intimate friends. In *The Sign Of Four* he appeared as 'an aged man, clad in seafaring garb, with an old peajacket buttoned up to his throat,' and until he resumed his natural voice, Dr Watson had no suspicion that he was anything but 'a respectable master mariner who had fallen into years and poverty.'

3. **DR WATSON**   Dr Watson, Sherlock Holmes's friend, often appears unobservant, and even a little stupid, in contrast with the famous detective. Those who are inclined to despise him, however, should try their own hand at playing the part of Sherlock Holmes and learn humility! Holmes was lucky in having a friend who was willing to play second fiddle, yet always ready with his help when required, even if he knew it meant risking his life.

4. **INSPECTOR LESTRADE**   It is hardly surprising that Sherlock Holmes' success in clearing up mysteries which they had failed to elucidate sometimes aroused the jealousy of professional detectives. And he had an irritating way of talking as if everybody ought to be capable of acquiring his almost uncanny powers of observation. Lestrade, the Scotland Yard detective, was often reluctantly compelled to seek the help of Sherlock Holmes, though the latter accused him of readiness to 'pocket all the credit.'

5. MISS MARY MORSTAN   Dr Watson owed his happy marriage to the fact that Mary Morstan called to consult the great detective in *The Sign of Four*. Sherlock Holmes refused to congratulate his friend on his engagement, remarking characteristically that 'love is an emotional thing, and whatever is emotional is opposed to that true cold reason which I place above all things.' He admitted, however, that Miss Morstan was 'one of the most charming young ladies' he had ever met.

6. TONGA (*The Sign of Four*)   The murder of Bartholomew Sholto presented many mysterious features, but Sherlock Holmes discovered that it had been accomplished by means of a poisoned dart. The murderer was Tonga, a little black man, the imprint of whose tiny feet had led Dr Watson to the horrified conclusion that the criminal was a child. Tonga was one of the aborigines of the Andaman Islands, who are described as 'naturally hideuos, having large mis-shapen heads, small fierce eyes and distorted features.'

7. PROFESSOR MORIARTY   Professor Moriarty was Sherlock Holmes's arch enemy, whom the latter once described as 'The Napoleon of Crime' and recognised as his intellectual equal. A life-and-death struggle between the two men took place on the edge of a precipice, and in order to mislead the members of Dr Moriarty's gang who were seeking his life, Sherlock Holmes let people go on for several years thinking that he, as well as his enemy, had been killed.

8. LUCY FERRIER (*A Study in Scarlet*)   John Ferrier and little Lucy, the five-year-old child whom he afterwards adopted, were on the point of perishing from thirst and hunger in the desert when they were rescued by a party of Mormons. Poor Lucy, however, met with a still more tragic fate in after years. After the murder of her adopted father, separation from her lover and her forced marriage with one of the Mormons, the unfortunate girl died of a broken heart.

9. **JEFFERSON HOPE** (*A Study in Scarlet*)   Jefferson Hope devoted his life to avenging the death of Lucy Ferrier, the girl he loved, but more than twenty years passed before his revenge was accomplished. Whatever one may think of the way in which Hope took the law into his own hands, few readers of his story would deny that his two victims deserved their fate, or regret that Jefferson Hope did not live to be tried as a murderer.

10. **MISS HELEN STONER** ('The Speckled Band')   When Helen Stoner went to ask the advice of Sherlock Holmes, Dr Watson noticed that she was 'in a pitiable state of agitation, her face was all drawn and grey, with restless, frightened eyes, like those of some hunted animal.' But her condition of terror can hardly have surprised those who listened to the story of her sister's tragic fate and the danger which she herself had reason to fear.

11. **DR GRIMESBY ROYLOTT** ('The Speckled Band')   If 'truth is strange than fiction' one feels, after reading 'The Adventures of Sherlock Holmes,' that it must be very strange indeed! Who, for instance, ever thought out such a plan as Dr Grimesby Roylott evolved to prevent the marriage of his step-daughter, Helen Stoner? This tale of a bed clamped to the floor, a poisonous snake and a wandering cheetah and baboon can safely be recommended to all who love a 'creepy' yarn.

12. **THE HOUND OF THE BASKERVILLES**   When Sherlock Holmes succeeded in 'laying the family ghost,' it was discovered that the terrifying appearance of the Hound of the Baskervilles was due to the use of phosphorus. Although Holmes's assistants were not superstitious men, their nerves were severely tried as the gigantic beast sprang into view from the fog, fire bursting from its open mouth, its eyes glowing with a smouldering glare, its muzzle and hackles and dewlap outlined in flickering flame!

13. **THE MAN WITH THE TWISTED LIP**   Relentless as Sherlock Holmes was in tracking down the murderer, the blackmailer, and the criminals who preyed upon the weak and helpless, there were occasions when he would 'hush up' a breach of the law. The case of 'the man with the twisted lip' is an example. But Sherlock Holmes exacted from Mr Neville St Clair a solemn oath that his double life—every morning a squalid beggar, every evening a well-dressed man-about-town—should cease.

14. **KING OF BOHEMIA** ('A Scandal in Bohemia')   Wilhelm Gottreich Sigismund von Ormstein, Grand Duke of Cassel-Felstein and hereditary King of Bohemia, wore a mask and adopted an assumed name when visiting Sherlock Holmes, and was therefore startled when the latter addressed him as 'Your Majesty.' This was one of the very few cases in which Homes was outwitted. Fortunately, however, Irene Adler, for reasons of her own, decided not to make use of the incriminating photograph which was the cause of the trouble.

15. **MR JABEZ WILSON** ('The Red-Headed League')   Mr Jabez Wilson seems to have been of the type of those men who are victims of 'the confidence trick.' One feels that he ought to have guessed there was something rather 'fishy' about the advertisment which he answered. But perhaps there are others among us who would not ask too many questions if they were offered £4 a week for merely copying matter from the *Encyclopedia Britannica* during four hours a day!

16. **IRENE ADLER** ('A Scandal in Bohemia')   To Sherlock Holmes, Irene Adler was always *'the* woman'—not because he had fallen in love with her—that emotion being 'abhorrent to his cold, precise, but admirably balanced mind'—but because she had seen through his plan of campaign and frustrated it. After meeting this woman whose brains were a match for his own, we are told that Sherlock Holmes ceased to make merry over the cleverness of women.

A Sherlock Holmes Crossword Puzzle

(See pages 79–80 for key)

Devised by Dorothy Rowe Shaw

Across

1. Initials of the Peerless Detective.
2. Selden's beard was dripping from a _____ of blood. (HOUN)
7. Name of the gang arrested by Birdy Edwards. (VALL)
11. H was a fine single-stick player and in the Middle Ages he would do this in tournaments.
12. H asked Mary Maberley if she would like to go there. (3GAB)
14. Initials of the scene of The Adventure of the Dancing Men.
15. A succulent item in the story without slush. (BLUE) (two words)
17. The condition of W's trousers after H examined his wound. (3GAR)
18. The 'best of the professionals'. (HOUN)
21. The day of the month of March when McCauley was cleared. (FIVE)
22. The sixth note on the musical scale, often played by H on violin.
23. Initials of the place to which Openshaw was lured and killed. (FIVE)
24. H says his _____ figures in no newspaper. (SIGN)
25. H's statue was in the bow window (MAZA) perhaps there was this kind of a window also.
26. How some of the loafers in Briony Lane would refer to Godfrey Norton. (SCAN)
27. The initials on the note which said 'For God's sake come at once'. (RESI)
29. H listened while Irene Adler said 'I _____'. (SCAN)
30. Initials of One of the Four. (SIGN)
31. The part where some think W was shot—if so why not call him Jack not John?
32. The name of the story about the nicest time of year and a rock. (two words)
36. First two letters of the name of the stockbroker of Throgmorton Street. (BLAN)
37. Four of H's published Cases had this word in the title.
40. W drank wine pronounced like this. (SIGN)
41. The Literary Agent is reputed to have invented this as a sport.

43. Sounds like first name of Phelps's fiancée (NAVA) and first name of mathematics coach (LION)
44. Abbr. of first name of notorious husband of Mary Holder. (BERY)
45. Like the goose this too hangs high, and some of those caught by H ended up in it.
46. A seed which caused fear. (FIVE)
47. A product with which H was most concerned in later life.
48. H wrote on this subject in *Anthropological Journal*. (CARD)
49. The first name of a Chicago criminal. (DANC)
50. First word in name on the inn near The Priory School.
53. H's use of cocaine did _____ but only when boredom set in.
55. First syllable of the name of The Separation Case. (IDEN)
57. Initials of last name of bibliographer of Holmes who will soon be famous.
58. First word engraved on Mortimer's stick. (HOUN)
59. Initials of female in Coram's household. (GOLD)
60. The great poineer who influenced Watson-Doyle.
61. What Lord Mount-James was. (MISS)
63. Of all the villains in The Canon this one with the unlikely name of Angel is surely one. (IDEN)
65. Abbr. of place where Hattie and Flora walked. (NOBL)
66. First name of Old Jacob's daughter who was married in 1875. (VALL)
67. Part of the Devil, and we shouldn't root for him. (DEVI)
68. After the fake message W had to go back _____ the mountain. (FINA)
69. A clue in BLUE.
70. The initials of the Literary Agent.
73. The initials of the world's first consulting detective.
74. Initials for the correct way to file the forger's name in H's index. (SUSS)
75. Initials of a girl who married a sergeant. (CROO)
76. 'Tobacco, said Coram, and my work, that is all that is left to _____'. (GOLD)
77. Abbr. of the Inn where H and W stayed. (BOSC)
81. Initials of the Ship of The Adelaide-Southampton Line. (ABBE)
82. W stated that H's knowledge of Literature was this. (STUD)
84. A title used a number of times in The Canon.
85. A college where an ex Mormon stole some poison. (STUD)
88. The surname of both a great eye and a great brian, one private and one public.
91. Initials of the name of the British ship lost at sea. (FIVE)
92. What H and W owed to Mrs. Hudson.
93. H's advertisement for this said it was lost in the roadway. (STUD)
95. A city once referred to as 'that cesspool'. (STUD)
99. When Mrs. Hudson was 'knocked up', (SPEC)
100. An appropriate adjective already applied to H in this Crossword.

102. The substance sold at The Bar of Gold. (TWIS)
103. 'She flew to what an agitated woman will'. (CROO)
105. The magic number for N. Garrideb. (3GAR)
106. The substance to which W objected.
107. An exclamation used when H said 'a trusty comrade is always of use'. (TWIS)
108. The antiquarian was real, the other _____ were not. (3GAR)
110. Initials of the soft-voiced lover. (IDEN)
111. The abused vicar of Little Purlington. (RETI)
113. The direction from London of Riding Thorpe Manor in Norfolk. (DANC)
114. First syllable of what Norton did to get Irene's yes. (SCAN)
115. A dictionary abbr. for the probable nationality of Moriarty's parents.
116. W had a pair of shoes of a type named after this word. (CHAS)
117. Initials of the call name of the butler to Col. Emsworth. (BLAN)
118. Initials for a part of London where Wilson the Canary-Trainer plagued society. (BLAC)
119. He was, sometimes, the government. (BRUC)

Down
1. Nickname for Scotland Yard Inspector—Holmes had high hopes for him. (BLAC)
2. A description of a window sill in Caulfield Gardens. (BRUC)
3. 'There is, of course, the other woman, the drink, the _____, the blow. . .' (IDEN)
4. The bird would have been of no _____ to anyone had it not been eaten. (BLUE)
5. Abbr. part of Trelawney Hope's title. (SECO)
6. H and W had some with cold partridge. (VEIL)
7. What never set on the Queen's Empire.
8. The chronicler.
9. Add an 's' and you have the alias of a bad Chicago native. (3GAR)
10. As to his practice H says 'it _____ to be degenerating'. (COPP)
11. First name of a bad builder and bachelor. (NORW)
12. Initials of the captain of the Varsity Rugger Team. (MISS)
13. About this W said H had the crudest of ideas. (HOUN)
16. Former senator or western US state. (THOR)
17. H tapped his finger on its edge. (BLUE)
19. Initials of the tragic lady who worried about the childish figure writing. (DANC)
20. A slang word which Sam Merton would probably apply to a group of ladies. (MAZA)
22. Part of that which was in the parcel received by Miss Cushing. (CARD)

27. Recently some so-called scholars indicate H might have been this.
28. Two of these helped H solve the riddle. (MUSG)
29. A letter from Openshaw was postmarked here. (FIVE)
31. Moran murdered him. (EMPT)
33. A word which means the same as the first word of the hotel in THE COPPER BEECHES.
34. An unusual call used by the McCarthys. (BOSC)
35. Of this H said 'I never needed it more'. (DYIN)
37. Initials of the story about some spectacles. (GOLD)
38. Sir Henry was this to the estate of Sir Charles. (HOUN)
39. What W saw but could not determine its purpose. (SPEC)

42. The real 'Queen' in H's life.
45. In the upper parts of which Brother Bartholomew lived. (SIGN)
47. The 'Drone' in H's life.
49. Name of the inn near the British Museum. (BLUE)
51. First name of Trevor Bennett's fiancée. (CREE)
52. One of the items on Baker's hat. (BLUE)
54. First word of the name of Rucastle's house. (COPP)
56. The former senator's first name. (THOR)
58. He lost a 50-guinea fee and one of these. (ENGR)
61. In summary what W thought of H's habits as a roommate.
62. Abbr. of J. C. Rlman's title. (RETI)
64. Initials of the beloved of him who was followed. (DEVI)
69. A conveyance often used in the Canon.
71. It was here on the banks of the Amoy River that the gem was found. (BLUE)
72. Where Small opined he'd live out his life. (SIGN)
78. A pipe mentioned in only one story. (SIGN)
79. Last name of the wife of the Secretary of European Affairs. (SECO)
80. Initials of Lady Beatrice's maid. (SHOS)
83. First name of fellow who hated a dog, loved a lady and taught figures. (LION)
84. The direction from London of an island from whence the 'Lone Star' sailed. (FIVE)
86. Violet Hunter was one. (COPP)
87. What H looked at when he visited J. Wilson's hock shop. (REDH)
89. Head trainer of Shoscombe stables. (SHOS)
90. N. Garrideb strove to be the one for his age. (3AGR)
94. Nationality of the interpreter. (GREE)
96. What H did when a three-pile problem arose. (REDH)
97. What old Shafter probably said to McMurdo when he asked first for Ettie's hand. (VALL)
98. Forbes said of Tangey 'His pension was _____', (NAVA)
101. This mendicant designed a good one. (TWIS)
103. Name of a stone span over a pool. (THOR)
104. Initials of the girl in love with J. McCarthy. (BOSC)
105. Could be abbr. for ship that rescued Armitage and Evans. (GLOR)
107. Abbr. for three words that were probably used to refer to the retired Amberley. (RETI)
109. Boone was at the end of this for lack of money. (TWIS)
112. Possibly a nickname used by the stockbroker's clerk's friends. (STOC)
112. H suggested to Villard that he study a case that occured in this US state (abbr). (SIGN)

A Times leader

The catch-phrase 'Elementary, my dear Watson' is surely one of the most famous to be found anywhere in the world. Yet the truth of the matter is that although Holmes uttered both 'elementary' and 'my dear Watson' on several occasions, not once did he do so together. Indeed, so widespread has the acceptance of the phrase become that even a leading article in that most authentic of newspapers, THE TIMES, *has failed to dispel the belief. It is reprinted here from the issue of 12 May 1953, in the hope that a further airing might settle the matter—though I cannot help feeling that it will not, so deeply ingrained is the phrase in the public vocabulary.*

SOME of the most famous and familiar sayings when run to earth in books of reference are found to bear the stigma of being 'attributed.' The DUKE OF WELLINGTON'S remark about the playing fields of Eton is, to say the least of it, suspect and there seems little doubt that he never said 'Up, Guards, and at 'em' although in his own words he 'must have said and probably did say "Stand up, Guards."' Regarding a more peaceful battlefield another and a bitter blow has lately fallen; GEORGE HIRST has broken all our hearts by declaring that he did not say 'Wilfred, we'll get them by singles.' He has pointed out that no batsman would thus deliberately deny himself the chance of a boundary, though we certainly have heard of Yorkshire doing so before lunch on the first day of the Lancashire match. Yet with all our cherished quotations being 'debunked' one by one we had held fast to 'Elementary, my dear Watson.' And now there comes along an iconoclastic and disenchanting gentleman (writing in *The Spectator* from the scene of 'The Adventure of the Stockbroker's Clerk') who roundly asserts that Sherlock Holmes never used those words. What is worse, a hurried and imperfect search seems to show that he is right. 'My dear Watson' is easy; as the two men grew better acquainted it gradually superseded 'My dear Doctor.' The component parts of the desiderated phrase can nearly but, alas, not quite be found together in 'The Crooked Man.' 'I have the advantage of knowing your habits, my dear Watson,' said Holmes and deduced that the practice justified a hansom. 'Excellent!' I cried. 'Elementary,' said he.

This exclamation of 'Excellent!' produced a particular reaction so nearly identical, that students capable of a decent second class might well fall into error. In 'The Reigate Squires' after a demonstration as to handwriting 'Excellent!' cried Mr. Acton 'But very superficial,' said Holmes. Again, in *A*

'It was quite a simple case after all.'
Holmes elucidating in 'The Adventure of
the Crooked Man', *Strand*, 1893

Study in Scarlet, the earliest of all the writings, is the passage 'Wonderful!' I
ejaculated. 'Commonplace,' said Holmes. That is the best that can be made
of a bad job on the spur of the moment. Heaven forbid that we should
absolutely deny that those now almost sacred words can be discovered but
they do not seem to be there. Holmes often used far more unkind expres-
sions towards his friend as when (in 'The Sussex Vampire') he tartly
observed in response to a suggestion 'We must not let him think this Agency
is a home for the weakminded.' So too 'Good old Watson' implied a certain
derision not to be found in 'My dear Watson.' But that peculiarly galling
epithet 'elementary' appears to occur but once. It is a little sad; it would have
been better, if the expression be permissible, to let sleeping attributions lie.
And yet all but the most scholarly of us will soon get over the blow and will
go on happily misquoting to the end of time.

The Problem of
Baker Street

Another perennial source of discussion among Sherlockians has been the precise location of 221b Baker Street, the home of Sherlock Holmes. THE TIMES looked into the matter in some detail in the spring of 1951 and subsequently ran the following report in the issue of Saturday, 21 April.

AFTER prolonged study of the letters, published and unpublished, which *The Times* has received, it seems improbable that any generally acceptable answer will ever be given to what may be termed 'The Problem of the Vanished 221B, Baker Street'.

Mrs. Bruce Stevenson's letter has given her reasons for placing Sherlock Holmes's lodgings between the Paddington Street-Crawford Street crossing of Baker Street and Portman Square. Mr. G. F. Higginson has supported her to the extent of contending that they must have been farther from Baker Street station than is the present Abbey House, just over the road. But in a later communication Mr. P. S. Clarence, of Beaconsfield, on psychological grounds finds Mr. Higginson's argument from *The Beryl Coronet* unconvincing. He considers that '221B must have been a long way from Oxford Street,'

Some authorities maintain that Holmes lived at 111, Baker Street, disguised as 221B by Dr. Watson for no doubt sufficient reasons. Number 111 was so badly damaged by bombing in the war that only the front wall survives. But Dr. Douglas Guthrie, of Edinburgh, thinks there can be little question that it is the right house. He writes: 'True, there is no bow window; on the other hand it faces Camden House, now a shop, but once the "Empty House" which the notorious Colonel Moran entered from behind, by way of a lane now labelled David Mews, to fire his air-gun at the wax model of Holmes across the street, so skilfully manipulated by Mrs. Hudson. Moreover, until a few years ago one was able to count the 17 steps of the staircase which still remained.'

Mr. H. W. Mansfield, of Orpington, quotes from the same adventure Watson's account of the devious ways from Blandford Street by which he and Holmes made their way into Camden House from the back. He concludes that Holmes's lodgings were 20 doors or so nearer Oxford Street than 111—which is in fact only about 100 yards south of Marylebone Road. If 111 was indeed the 221B of the stories, Camden House was the building opposite, now numbered 120, on the wall of which is a circular plaque, recording that in it lived William Pitt the Younger in 1803–4. Had the L.C.C. put up the tablet in time it would have made an admirable target for Holmes's revolver practice.

Mr. John Shand, assistant editor of the *London Mystery Magazine*, plumps uncompromisingly for Abbey House. His letter is written on the stationery of his magazine, which is headed '221B, Baker Street'—a small mystery in itself. It is Mr. Shand's argument that when Watson, in *The Beryl Coronet*, saw Mr. Holder approaching from the station he himself was 'looking down the street.' The client was therefore coming 'up' Baker Street, and could not have done so had 221B been to the south. And Watson during his night walk with Holmes in 'The Empty House', was too confused by excitement to identify their route from Blandford Street, which led them through back streets to the top of Baker Street.

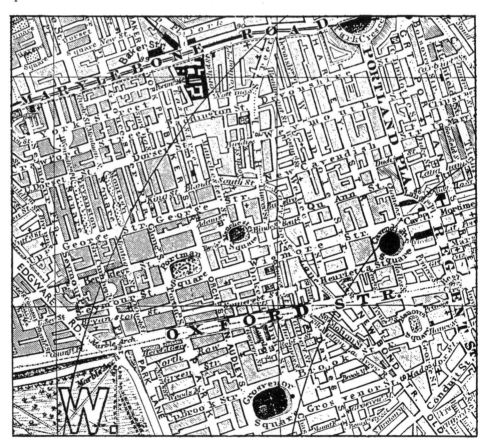

Map of London and the Baker Street area at the time of the Sherlock Holmes adventures

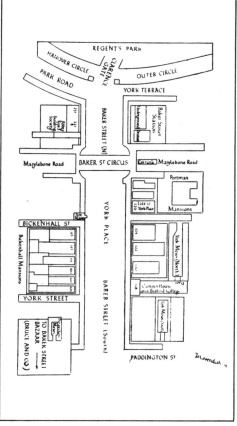

A view of 221b Baker Street? Holmes and Watson keep an eye on their home in 'The Adventure of the Empty House', *Strand*, 1903

The location of 221b Baker Street—a map drawn by Sherlockian Mr Ernest Short in 1950

Summing up, it may be said that the exegetists all agree that it was on the west side, not the east, of Baker Street that Sherlock Holmes lodged; and that is all the common ground to be discovered in this obdurate problem. What a misfortune it is that Holmes is himself no longer with us to turn his great brain to its elucidation.

ON THE WALL

Can you decipher this strange message discovered by Dr Watson on arriving home to find Holmes and Mrs Hudson absent and wondering what he should do about his tea!

```
T I N T H E C U T P B O A R
D I T S T A N T O T E T H A
T S T A Y S T A L L Y O T U
N E T T E D T O T K N O T W
```

The Case of the Baker Street Plans

Ellery Husted

The problem of 221b Baker Street has exercised the minds of Sherlockians everywhere, but probably no one has had such a strange experience as a result of trying to solve the mystery as the American Ellery Husted, the writer of this article. Mr Husted, a member of one of the scion societies known as The Five Orange Pips of New York, drew up a set of plans while serving with the American Navy during World War II. What happened to those plans when he sent them to another Sherlockian for his comments lead to an incident that would surely have brought a smile to the face of Sherlock himself. The article is reprinted from THE READER'S DIGEST *of April 1950.*

AFTER WAITING around Ford Island three weeks, my orders finally came: *Report Cincpac* (Admiral Nimitz, Commander in Chief Pacific) *Advanced Intelligence Headquarters, Guam. Passage via Air Transport. Proceed without delay.*

An hour's paper work, 15 minutes' packing, and I made it a minute before the plane took off. There was a two-day hop ahead, and I'd forgotten to pack a book. On my way through the hangar I saw on a chair a paper-backed volume with no visible owner. The cover said: *Six Adventures of Sherlock Holmes.* I stole it without shame.

After reading it twice, I wondered what I could do to make my monotonous trip less depressing. I pictured Sherlock Holmes and Dr. Watson seated comfortably before their fire at 221B Baker Street, and since I was an architect in peacetime it was natural to speculate as to what their rooms had looked like. Suddenly a thought burned through the cloud of my ennui. I retrieved the *Six Adventures* and prepared for another reading with reawakened eyes. Scattered through each of the stories were disconnected but explicit references to the physical arrangements of the famed rooms. I began to copy all references to them. When I had finished, and had sorted and assembled the architectural references, I found to my surprise that each fitted like a shaped piece into a picture puzzle. Then I reconstructed the plans and elevations of 221B. No line was drawn without confirmation from the text.

The complete work made a bulky package and on landing at Guam I was about to throw it away when I thought of my friend Dick Clarke, another Navy man and a member of 'The Five Orange Pips'. It might amuse him to receive this bit of literary archaeology. I put the papers in an envelope addressed to Clarke, gave them to a yeoman to send by air mail, and forgot them in the more serious business of war.

A splendid evocation of Holmes at home by Geoffrey Fletcher for *The Sphere*, 8 November 1957

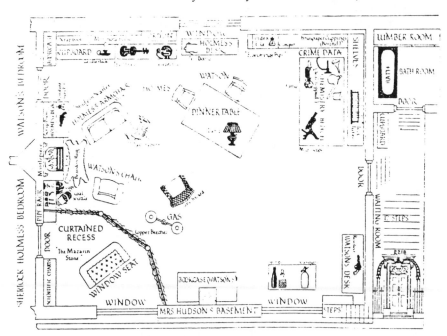

A detailed groundplan of Sherlock Holmes's main room at 221b
Baker Street by Mr Ernest Short

Some months later the war ended and I got my orders home. I was cheerfully destroying official papers when I was handed a large and familiar envelope covered with the ink of rubber stamps. It was my letter to Clarke come back to roost and I assumed that it had been sent off with too few stamps.

Next morning on the plane back to Pearl Harbour a blond young ensign in the seat ahead turned around and said, 'Your name's Husted?'

I nodded.

'And how's Dr. Watson?' he asked with a grin.

I considered the question for a moment and realized the ensign must have been a Cincpac censor. 'I suppose you censored that Baker Street letter.'

'Yeah. *And did it give us trouble.* They put the best brains in Guam on it, but nobody could make anything of it. It was obviously in code, but we couldn't break it, so we sent it to Pearl. They spent some time on it and sent it on to Washington, but it was no go. It came back to us, and we held it until the war was over.'

I laughed and said, 'You knew all about *me*. Why didn't you ask me about it?'

The ensign smiled. 'Yeah, we knew all about you, but it wasn't that easy. We checked your handwriting with the letter and it didn't agree. Too jerky. And you'll agree that all that stuff about 221B Baker Street sounded queer. On any basis the letter didn't make sense.'

I thought of the wavy handwriting caused by the undulations of air travel, of my mysterious disconnected passages lifted from the text, and especially of my enigmatic letter to Clarke:

Dear Dick: Tell your group of Peculiar Pips that 221B did exist, and that it has been resurrected by one who is not of you, but believes in you. I wish Holmes were with me to solve the riddle of the Empire. God bless you, and in the name of Holmes and Baker Street keep up the good fight.

Yours, Husted.

I could not but agree that Cincpac's alerted censors had had cause for their suspicions, and was ruminating pleasantly over the extent of the trouble I had probably caused when the blond head before me revolved again to say:

'And worst of all, my friend, Baker Street was the code name for the Office of Strategic Services Headquarters, London!'

The Sherlock Holmes Gazetteer

Sherlock Holmes and Dr Watson were, of course, inveterate travellers, and in the essays which follow three leading Sherlockians provide details about the various localities with which they are associated in England, Europe and America. Gavin Brend's 'The English Haunts of Sherlock Holmes' appeared in Coming Events in Britain, *October 1952; 'Sherlock Holmes on the Continent', by Michael C. Kaser, was in* The Baker Street Journal, *January 1956. The detailed maps which accompany each article are the work of another eminent Sherlockian, Dr Julian Wolff, M.D., of New York. Below is given a key to the abbreviations used for the story titles in the map references.*

KEY TO THE STORY TITLES

Abbe	Abbey Grange	Five	Five Orange Pips	Prio	Priory School
Bery	Beryl Coronet			RedC	Red Circle
Blac	Black Peter	Glor	Gloria Scott	Redh	Red-Headed League
Blan	Blanched Soldier	Gold	Golden Pince-Nez		
				Reig	Reigate Squires
Blue	Blue Carbuncle	Gree	Greek Interpreter		
Bose	Boscombe Valley Mystery			Resi	Resident Patient
		Houn	Hound of the Baskervilles		
Bruce	Bruce-Partington Plans			Reti	Retired Colourman
		Iden	Case of Identity		
Card	Cardboard Box			Scan	Scandal in Bohemia
Chas	Charles Augustus Milverton	Illu	Illustrious Client		
				Seco	Second Stain
		Lady	Lady Frances Carfax	Shos	Shoscombe Old Place
Copp	Copper Beeches	Last	His Last Bow		
		Lion	Lion's Mane	Sign	Sign of Four
Cree	Creeping Man	Maza	Mazarin Stone	Silv	Silver Blaze
Croo	Crooked Man	Miss	Missing Three-Quarter	Six	Six Napoleons
Danc	Dancing Men			Soli	Solitary Cyclist
Devi	Devil's Foot	Musg	Musgrave Ritual	Spec	Speckled Band
Dyin	Dying Detective	Nava	Naval Treaty	Stoe	Stockbrokers' Clerk
		Nobl	Noble Bachelor		
Empt	Empty House	Norw	Norwood Builder	Stud	Study in Scarlet
Engr	Engineer's Thumb			Suss	Sussex Vampire
Fina	Final Problem				

THOR	Thor Bridge	3STU	Three Students	VALL	Valley of Fear
3GAB	Three Gables	TWIS	Man with the Twisted Lip	VEIL	Veiled Lodger
3GAR	Three Garridebs			WIST	Wisteria Lodge
				YELL	Yellow Face

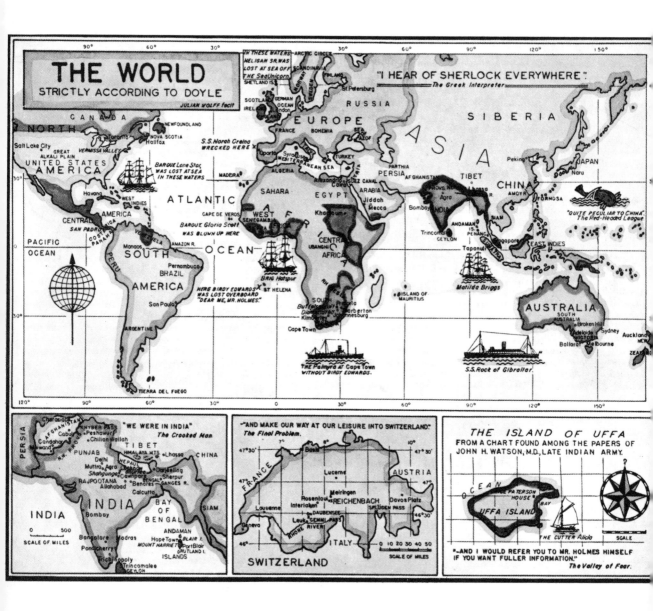

[80]

The English Haunts of Sherlock Holmes

Gavin Brend

Few Sherlockians have devoted more time and energy to studying the life of the Great Detective than Gavin Brend. Numerous articles in newspapers and magazines bear witness to his industry, and one of his books, MY DEAR HOLMES: A STUDY IN SHERLOCK (1951), is regarded as a classic of its kind. In this article, Mr Brend takes us on a tour of Holmesian England in a manner which once again demonstrates his extensive knowledge of the canon.

I

London

Iᴛ ɪs, of course, to Baker Street, that not particularly imposing shopping street in north-west London, that admirers of Sherlock Holmes first turn their steps. But it must be admitted that there is no agreement as to the exact location of Holmes's residence in Baker Street beyond the fact that it was on the west side of the thoroughfare—where, incidentally, an ominous gap in one of the terraces marks the spot where a bomb fell during the war. For all we know, however, the house may still stand; and the Holmes enthusiast can seek further consolation in the fact that he can still visit many of the places in London mentioned in Dr. Watson's narratives which can be more easily identified.

It is a curious fact that there appears to be only one recorded instance of a London pub being visited by the Master. This event is referred to in the case of 'The Blue Carbuncle' which introduces us to the Alpha Inn 'near the Museum . . . at the corner of one of the streets which runs down into Holborn'. This would appear to be the Plough Inn at the corner of Museum Street and Little Russell Street, Bloomsbury, since the stars in the constellation known as the Plough are called after the Greek letters and alpha is the largest and brightest of them all.

Near by is a landmark which I usually think of as 'Blue Carbuncle Corner' where Goodge Street runs into Tottenham Court Road. It was here that poor Henry Baker, after leaving the Alpha, bumped into a crowd of roughs and dropped his goose containing its precious treasure. We can follow the journey of the goose back to Mr. Breckinridge's shop in Covent Garden—though why a poultry seller should have a shop in London's leading vegetable market is not exactly clear.

We are in the fortunate position of being able to pin-point at least three incidents mentioned by Watson by the fact that they happened at street corners. The first has already been mentioned. The second is the corner of Bentinck and Welbeck Streets where, in 'The Final Problem', one of Moriarty's satellites made an attempt to run down Holmes by a furiously driven two-horse van which dashed round from Marylebone Lane and was gone in an instant. The resourceful Moriarty was not done yet, however, and a few moments later a brick descended from the roof of a house in Vere Street and was shattered to fragments at Holmes's feet. It would look as if this brick must have been thrown from the roof of Marshall & Snelgrove's, the well-known big store.

The third corner, featured in *The Sign of Four*, is the junction of Miles Street and Wandsworth Road (in those days known as Knight's Place). This was the scene of one of Holmes's few mistakes. He was using the dog Toby to track down the Andaman Islander who had obligingly trodden on some creosote. Unfortunately at Knight's Place the trail crossed that of a trolley which carried a large barrel of the same material, and this led the detective astray into a timber yard at Nine Elms.

Another landmark in *The Sign of Four* is the Wigmore Street Post Office, which, though modernised since then, was visited by Watson in the story. (He too put his foot in it, only this time it was not creosote but reddish coloured earth.) The Lyceum Theatre is now a dance hall, but the building is otherwise the same as it was when Holmes and his companions met Thad-

The London of Sherlock Holmes—a sketch of the Strand in the late 1880s by Joseph Pennell

deus Sholto's coachman 'at the third pillar from the left' in the course of the same episode.

We should find it difficult today to hire a boatman to row us across the Thames at Vauxhall. But we can today take a steamer down the river and follow the sensational pursuit of the *Aurora* in *The Sign of Four*, which started near the Tower and ended at Plumstead Marshes; or travel again Holmes's fog-bound journey (in the same story) through the London streets down to Brixton by way of Vauxhall, Wandsworth Road and Stockwell.

Mention should also be made of the three places which are connected with Watson's first introduction to Holmes. These are the Criterion Bar in Piccadilly Circus, where Watson encountered his former acquaintance 'young Stamford'; the Holborn Restaurant where they subsequently had lunch; and St. Bartholomew's Hospital (usually known as 'Barts') where Stamford ensured his place in history by introducing Holmes to his future biographer.

Space permits only a mere mention of some of the present-day London landmarks which are referred to in one or more of the cases: Scotland Yard, of course; the railway termini (Victoria, Paddington, Waterloo, Charing Cross, King's Cross and Euston) from which Holmes and Watson set off on so many momentous expeditions; Bow Street Police Station; Hyde Park; Hampstead Heath; Wandsworth Common; Covent Garden Opera House; the British Museum; the Haymarket Theatre; the London Library; and the College of Surgeons Museum.

Many more examples could be given, but let us end right in the centre of London. The case is 'The Noble Bachelor'. Inspector Lestrade tells Holmes that he has been dragging the Serpentine in a fruitless attempt to find the body of the missing Lady St. Simon. Holmes's reply is characteristically caustic: 'Have you dragged the basin of the Trafalgar Square fountain?'

II
Outside London

We do not know the birthplace either of Sherlock Holmes or of his almost equally famous companion Dr. Watson. For what it is worth, my own guess is that Holmes was born in London. Watson, I think, came either from Sussex or Hampshire. It is significant that on a blazing hot day in August, when Baker Street was like an oven, we find him yearning for 'the glades of the New Forest or the shingle of Southsea' ('The Cardboard Box'). He was also, however, familiar with the country around Horsham in Sussex. 'I know that country, Holmes. It is full of old houses which are named after the men who built them centuries ago' ('The Sussex Vampire').

Yet when the Baker Street epoch had ended it was not Watson but Holmes who retired to Sussex to a lonely villa 'on the southern slope of the Downs' (*The Lion's Mane*)—presumably somewhere between Brighton and Eastbourne.

It would appear that in those days crime flourished most extensively in the south of England. Seven of Holmes's cases are located in Surrey, six in Sussex and four each in Kent and Hampshire. There appears to be no definite evidence that he ever got farther north than Derbyshire. The story of this particular encounter with the 'cold bracing atmosphere of the Peak country' is told in 'The Priory School'. The school was situated near to 'Lower Gill Moor', a great lonely upland where 'the clover and the curlew are the only inhabitants.'

This Derbyshire visit gives Watson (or his creator, the late Sir Arthur Conan Doyle) a chance to exercise his admirable powers of description of the English countryside—in this case, the grand but austere hillsides of the north. By way of contrast, the south produces a picture which is softer and more mellow, as, for instance, this description of the Surrey heathlands in 'The Solitary Cyclist':

'A rainy night had been followed by a glorious morning . . . Holmes and I walked along the broad sandy road inhaling the fresh morning air and rejoicing in the music of the birds and the fresh breath of the Spring. From a rise of the road on the shoulder of Crooksbury Hill we could see the grim Hall bristling from amidst the ancient oaks, which, old as they were, were still younger than the building which they surrounded. Holmes pointed down the long tract of road which wound, a reddish-yellow band, between the brown of the heath and the budding green of the woods.'

The scene is set for another Sherlock Holmes adventure!

In the same way, 'The Missing Three Quarter' brings vividly before us the flat Cambridgeshire landscape, so flat that it offered Holmes no facilities to shadow Dr. Armstrong. Cornwall, with its rocky sinister coast, the grave of many seamen, is the appropriate scene of that strange story, 'The Devil's Foot'. For Norfolk and the enormous square-towered churches looking out

Isolated and mysterious—a picture of Dartmoor as featured in 'The Hound of the Baskervilles', Holmes's most famous case outside London

across the North Sea, we turn to 'The Dancing Men'.

Dartmoor in its sterner and wilder aspects is the eerie setting of that magnificent story *The Hound of the Baskervilles*. In a softer mood, with the autumn ferns turning brown, we return to Dartmoor in 'Silver Blaze'.

Outside London we cannot as a rule pinpoint with accuracy the exact places which Holmes visited. One exception to this general rule, however, is the Brambletye Hotel near East Grinstead in Sussex, where he stayed in connection with the case of 'Black Peter'.

Perhaps the most interesting landmark of all is Hill House Hotel at Happisburgh, near Norwich. Conan Doyle stayed there in 1903 at a time when this Norfolk hotel was kept by a family named Cubitt. The proprietor's son used to amuse himself by writing his signature in dancing men. Doyle, then and there, set to work on the story of 'The Dancing Men' and, when he left, his room was littered with drawings of the dancers. It will be recalled that Hilton Cubitt is the name of the central character in this tale. Similarly, 'Ridling Thorpe' in the story is a combination of two nearby villages, Ridlington and Edingthorpe. Mr. G. J. Cubitt, the original inventor of the dancing men, lives today in Aylesbury, Buckinghamshire. Hill House Hotel can still be visited, but the dancing men will, I fear, by now have danced their way into the distant past.

Map key

York *Houn*. Holdernesse *Prio*. Leeds *Houn*. 'May Day' *Card*. Bradford *Stud*. Tarleton *Musg*. New Brighton *Card*. Doncaster *SixN*. German Ocean *Danc*. The Peak *Prio*. Bangor *Prio*. Lower Gill Moor *Prio*. Mackleton *Prio*. Hallamshire *Prio*. Chesterfield *Prio*. Crewe *Spec*. Nottingham *Vall*. Derby *Vall*. North Walsham *Danc*. Ridling Thorpe *Danc*. Donnithorpe *Glor*. Langmere *Glor*. East Ruston *Danc*. Norwich *Danc*. Norfolk *Danc*. East Anglia *Danc*. Uppingham *Gold*. Leicester *Vall*. Walsall *Copp*. Aston *3Gar*. Birmingham *3Gab; 3Gar; Stoc; Glor*. Coventry *Soli; Five*. Worcestershire *Sign*. Cambridgeshire *Miss*. Cambridge *Miss; Gold*. Waterbeach, Oakington, Chesterton, Histon Newmarket *Shos*. The Cam, Trumpington *Miss*. Bedfordshire, Bedford, Tuxbury Old Park *Blan*. Boscombe Valley *Bosc*. Pershore *Sign*. Herefordshire *Bosc*. Harwich *Last*. Mossmoor, Little Purlington, Essex, Frinton *Reti*. Oxford *Miss; Empt; RedH*. Oxfordshire *Engi*. Stroud Valley *Bosc*. Gloucester *Houn*. Ross *Bosc*. Abergavenny *Prio*. River Severn *Bosc*. Bristol *Bosc*. Swindon *Bosc*. Berkshire *Engi*. Shoscombe *Shos*. Crendall *Shos*. Crane Water *Spec*. Reading *Bosc; SixN; Silv; Engi*. Windsor *Bruc*. Eton *Empt; RedH*. Pinner *Yell*. Eyford *Engi*. Wimbledon *Veil*. Middlesex *Yell; Twis*. East Ham *Vall*. Woolwich *Bruc*. Thames River *Sign; SixN; Bruc*. Gravesend *Twis; Sigv*. Margate *Seco; Veil*. Chatham *Gold*. Canterbury *Fina*. The Downs *Last; Lion*. Goodwin Sands *Five*. Tunbridge Wells *Vall; Blac*. Birlstone *Vall*. Marsham *Abbe*. Croydon *Card* Leatherhead *Spec*. Chislehurst *Abbe*. Esher *Wist*. Ripley *Nava*. Guildford *Wist*. Woking *Nava*. Aldershot *Copp; Croo*. Farnham *Soli*. Stoke Moran *Spec*. Abbas Parva *Veil*. Reigate *Reig*. Kent *Gold; Abbe; Twis*. Surrey *Sign; Twis; Reti*.

Charlington Heath *Soli*. Hampshire *Copp; Glor; Thor*. Alton *Houn*. Crooksbury Hill *Soli*. Andover *Iden*. Chiltern Grange *Soli*. The Weald *Vall*. Forest Row *Blac*. Lamberley *Suss*. Petersfield *Nobl*. Thor Mere *Thor*. Wilton *Spec*. Horsham *Suss; Five*. Winchester *Copp*. Sussex *Suss; Lion*. Hurlstone *Musg*. Southampton *Copp; Vall; Blan*. Fordingbridge *Glor*; Devonshire *Houn; Silv*. Folkestone Court *Houn*. Exeter *Silv*. New Forest *Card*. Netley *Stud*. Fareham, Portsdown Hill *Five*. Solent *Last*. Isle of Wight *Five*. Portsmouth *Stud; Last*. Southsea *Card*. Worthingdon *Resi*. South Downs *Last*. Lewes *Lion*. Fulworth *Lion*. Newhaven *Fina*. Eastbourne *Last*. Portland *Last*. King's Pyland *Silv*. Grimpen Mire *Houn*. Grimpen *Houn*. Tavistock *Silv*. Thorsley Parish *Houn*. Fernworthy *Houn*. Darmoor *Silv; Sign; Houn*. Long Down *Houn*. Coombe Tracey *Houn*. High Barrow Parish *Houn*. Plymouth *Devi; Silv*. Cornwall *Devi; Blac*. St. Ives *Devi*. Redruth *Devi*. Tredannick Wollas *Devi*. Beauchamp Arriance *Devi*. Falmouth *Glor*. Helston *Devi*. Mounts Bay, Poldhu Bay *Devi*. 'Gloria Scott *Glor*.

A Tour through Holmesian London

This tour, devised by the Sherlock Holmes Society of London, provides a guide to the major places in the city associated with the career of Sherlock Holmes. The itinerary can be covered on foot without much trouble in a single day, thus making it an ideal tour for visitors to London.

I—EAST OF BAKER STREET

Royal College of Surgeons
Dr. Mortimer's afternoon of 'pure amusement'
The Hound of the Baskervilles

Museum Street
Alpha Inn, patronised by Henry Baker
The Blue Carbuncle

Montague Street
Where Holmes had rooms when he first came to London
The Musgrave Ritual

Russell Square
Where the vicar of Ridling Thorpe stayed during the Jubilee
The Dancing Men

Montague Place
Miss Violet Hunter had rooms here
The Copper Beeches

Tottenham Court Road
Mr. Sutherland's plumber business
A Case of Identity

Morton and Waylight's, where Mr. Warren was a timekeeper
The Red Circle

The Jew broker's, where Holmes purchased his Stradivarius
The Cardboard Box

Goodge Street
Where Peterson lost the goose
The Blue Carbuncle

Regent Street	Area of Langham Hotel, where Captain Morstan, Count von Kramm and Hon. Philip Green stayed *The Sign of Four* *A Scandal in Bohemia* *Lady Frances Carfax*
Oxford Street	Capital and Counties Bank *The Priory School*
	Shop window with illustrious photographs *Charles Augustus Milverton*
Cavendish Square	Holmes stopped the cab *The Empty House*
Queen Anne Street	Watson had rooms of his own *The Illustrious Client*
Harley Street	Watson and Holmes walk back from their visit to Blessington *The Resident Patient*
	Suite of Dr. Moore Agar *The Devil's Foot*
Welbeck Street **Bentinck Street**	Where a two-horse van, furiously driven, nearly killed Holmes *The Final Problem*
Baker Street	The home of Sherlock Holmes

II—THE ROUTE TO SCOTLAND YARD

Grosvenor Square	Problem of the Grosvenor Square furniture van *The Noble Bachelor*
Brook Street	Dr. Percy Trevelyan's consulting room *The Resident Patient*
Claridge's Hotel	Patronised by Neil Gibson and Altamont *Thor Bridge* *His Last Bow*
Hanover Square	St. George's Church, where the St. Simon marriage was scheduled *The Noble Bachelor*
Regent Street	Holmes and Watson follow Stapleton in the cab *The Hound of the Baskervilles*

Conduit Street	Residence of Colonel Sebastian Moran *The Empty House*
Café Royal	Outside which Holmes was murderously assaulted *The Illustrious Client*
Piccadilly Circus	The Criterion Long Bar *A Study in Scarlet*
Haymarket	Where Josiah Amberley did not give his wife a treat *The Retired Colourman*
Pall Mall	The Diogenes Club *The Greek Interpreter*
Trafalgar Square	'Have you dragged the basin of the Trafalgar Square fountain?' *The Noble Bachelor*
The Admiralty	The naval centre of Great Britain *The Bruce-Partington Plans*
Whitehall	Where Mycroft Holmes worked *The Greek Interpreter* *The Bruce-Partington Plans*
Downing Street	Official residence of Lord Bellinger and Mr. H. H. Asquith *The Mazarin Stone* *His Last Bow* Lord Holdhurst's chambers *The Naval Treaty*
Charles Street	Where Percy Phelps worked *The Naval Treaty*
Scotland Yard	Where even the pick of a bad lot worked

III—NORTH TO THE STRAND

Kennington Road	Where Rose Spender's undertaker worked *Lady Frances Carfax*
Westminster Bridge Road	Bevington's the pawnbrokers *Lady Frances Carfax*
Big Ben	'Twenty-five to eight' *Lady Frances Carfax*
Westminster Pier	Holmes and Watson embark on their launch *The Sign of Four*

'We strolled about together'—Holmes and Watson in the streets of London in 'The Adventure of the Resident Patient', *Strand*, 1893

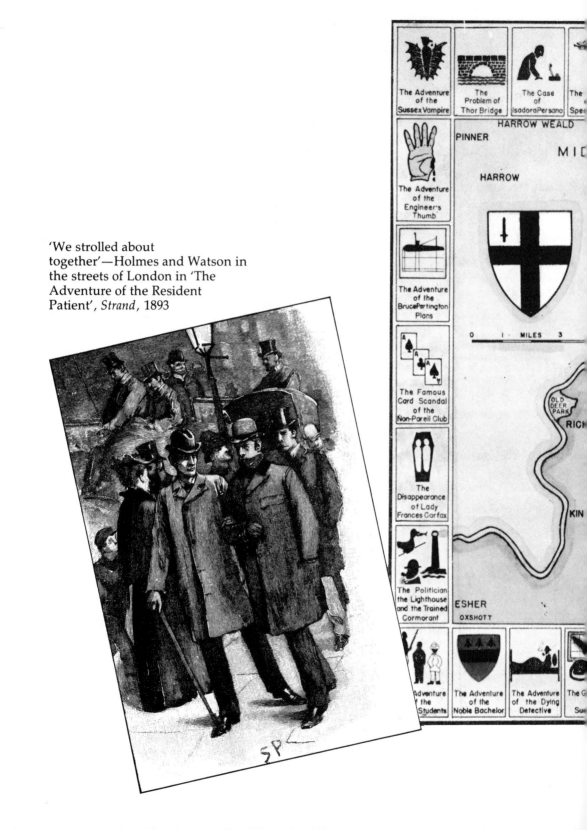

The Adventure of the Cardboard Box

The Five Orange Pips

The Yellow Face

The Red-headed League

The Adventure of the Creeping Man

°Camford

The Final Problem

The Sign of the Four

ESSEX

ESSEX

TRAFALGAR SQ.

STRAND

Charing Cross Station

CHARING CROSS

PALL MALL

CRAVEN ST.

CARLTON HOUSE TER.

THE MALL

NORTHUMBERLAND AVE.

Gt. Scotland Yard

WHITEHALL

WHITEHALL PL.

War Office

THAMES EMBANKMENT

RIVER THAMES

Admiralty

ST. JAMES PARK

Government Offices

WHITEHALL GAR.

Foreign Office

DOWNING ST.

New Scotland Yard

HAMPSTEAD HEATH

HAMPSTEAD

Manor House

Pentonville Prison

King's Cross Station

LLESDEN

KILBURN

ST. JOHN'S WOOD

St. Pancras Station

Euston Station

BARKING LEVEL

BROADMOOR

2218x

University

British Museum

Aldersgate Station

THAMES RIVER

Paddington Station

Covent Gdns. Mkt.

St. Bart's Hospital

Liverpool St. Sta.

West India Docks

BLACKWALL

Albert Dock

The Adventure of the Retired Colourman

PLUMSTEAD MARSHES

NOTTING HILL

Kensington Gardens

St. Pauls

Aldgate Sta.

KENSINGTON

HYDE PARK

Grosvenor Sq.

Hanover Sq.

Waterloo Br. & Sta.

The Tower

London Bridge

STEPNEY

ROTHERHITHE

THE POOL

Gloucester Road Station

WHITEHALL

WESTMINSTER

LAMBETH

Westminster Br.

BERMONDSEY

DEPTFORD REACH

ISLE OF DOGS

WOOLWICH

HAMMERSMITH

Hammersmith Bridge

Victoria Station

KENNINGTON

GREENWICH

HURLING-HAM

Vauxhall Bridge

The Oval°

Kennington Park

PECKHAM

BLACKHEATH

LEE

LEWISHAM

CAMBERWELL

CLAPHAM

BRIXTON

Clapham Junction°

For Don
WITH BEST WISHES
Julian, 5 FEB 1962
c. J.W., M.D. 1940

The Addleton Tragedy

STREATHAM

MARYLEBONE ROAD

SYDENHAM

BAKER STREET

PADDINGTON ST.

DEVONSHIRE ST.

HIGH STREET

WIMBLEDON

UPPER NORWOOD

Crystal Palace

DORSET ST.

WEYMOUTH ST.

HARLEY ST.

MANCHESTER ST.

WIMPOLE ST.

NORBURY

PENGE

BECKENHAM

CHISLEHURST

KING ST.

NEW CAVENDISH ST.

SURREY

MARSHAM

UPPER GEORGE ST.

WELBECK ST.

QUEEN ANNE ST.

ONDON

LOWER NORWOOD

KENT

MANCHESTER SQ.

DUKE ST.

CAV. SQ.

Watson, come! The game is afoot."
Adventure of the Abbey Grange.

WIGMORE STREET

WALLINGTON

CROYDON

OXFORD STREET

HENRIETTA ST.

"I have my eye on a suite in Baker Street..."
—A Study in Scarlet.

Wilson the Notorious Canary Trainer

The Adventure of the Six Napoleons

The Adventure of the Second Stain

The Adventure of the Mazarin Stone

The Adventure of the Blue Carbuncle

The Amsworth Castle Business

The Resident Patient

Huret the Boulevard Assassin

Northumberland Avenue	The Turkish Bath establishment *The Illustrious Client*
	Hotels where Sir Henry Baskerville, F. H. Moulton and wealthy Orientals stayed *The Hound of the Baskervilles* *The Noble Bachelor* *The Greek Interpreter*
Lowther Arcade	Where Mycroft Holmes meets Watson *The Final Problem*
Duncannon Street	The Post Office where Scott Eccles send off his telegram *Wisteria Lodge*
Charing Cross Hotel	Oberstein captured in the smoking room *The Bruce-Partington Plans*
Charing Cross Station	Mathews knocked out Holmes' left canine *The Empty House*
Craven Street	Stapleton stayed at the Mexborough Hotel *The Hound of the Baskervilles*
Strand	Watson leads a meaningless existence *A Study in Scarlet*
	Watson learns of the murderous attack on Holmes *The Illustrious Client*
Simpson's	'Something nutritious' *The Dying Detective*
Lyceum Theatre	Mary Morstan sets out on her unknown adventure *The Sign of Four*

Map key

CENTRAL. British Museum *Musg; Blue; Houn.* Covent Garden (Market) *Blue.* (Opera) *RedC.* Grosvenor Square 3 *Gab; Nobl.* Hanover Square *Nobl.* Lambeth *Sign.* London Bridge *Norw; Gree; Bruc; Twis.* London University *Stud;* St. Paul's Cathedral *Sign;* Victoria Station *Fina; Vall; Suss.* Waterloo Station *Nava; Spec; Houn; Five; Croo;* (Bridge) *Five.* Westminster *Lady;* (Bridge) Whitehall *Seco; Maza.*

NORTH. Euston Station *Blan.* King's Cross Station *Miss; Cree.* Manor House *Gree.* St. Pancras Station *Stoc; Shos.* Pentonville Prison *Blue.*

NORTH EAST. Aldersgate Station *Red.* St. Bartholomew's Hospital *Stud.*

EAST. Albert Dock *Card.* Aldgate Station *Bruc.* Barking Level *Sign;* also at *Sign* Blackwall, Plumstead Marshes, Greenwich,—see also *Engr;* at *Sign.*

West India Docks, Isle of Dogs, Deptford Reach, Pool of London; Tower of London *Sign*. Liverpool Street Station *Reti*. Woolwich *Bruc*. Gravesend *Twis; Sign*.

SOUTH EAST. Blackheath *Reti; Suss; Norw*. Chislehurst *Abbe*. Lee *Twis; Wist*. Marsham *Abbe*. Lewisham *Abbe; Reti*. Penge *Card*. Rotherhithe *Dyin*. Sydenham *Norw; Abbe*. Crystal Palace *Yell*.

SOUTH. Brixton *Sign; 3Gar; Lady; Blue; Stud*. Camberwell *Five; Sign; Iden*. Croydon *Stud; Lady; Vall; Card*. Kennington *SixN*. Oval *Sign*. Norwood *Norw; Sign*. Norbury *Yell*. Streatham *Sign; Bery*. Vauxhall Bridge *Sign*. Wallington *Card*. Clapham Junction *Gree*.

SOUTH WEST. Chiswick *SixN*. Esher *Wist*. Hammersmith *Suss; SixN*. Kingston-on-Thames *Illu*. Hurlingham *Illu*. Molesey *Empt*. Oxshott *Wist*. Richmond *Suss*. Old Deer Park *Suss*. Wandsworth Common *Gree*. Wimbledon *Veil*.

WEST. Gloucester Road Station *Bruc*. Hampstead *Chas; Vall; RedC*. Harrow *Spec*. Harrow Weald *3Gab*. Kilburn *Blue*. Kensington *Gree; Empt; Bruc; Wist; Norw; RedH; SixN*. Notting Hill *Bruc; Houn; RedC*.

NORTH WEST. Paddington *Bosc; Stoc; Engr; Silv*. Pinner *Yell*. St. John's Wood *Scan*. Willesden *Bruc*.

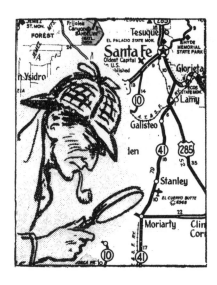

Sherlock Holmes
on the Continent

Michael C. Kaser

Michael C. Kaser is an American Sherlockian who has contributed numerous articles on the travels of Holmes and Watson to THE BAKER STREET JOURNAL, *from which this detailed examination is taken.*

'I T IS my business,' said Sherlock Holmes to the emissary of the Illustrious Client, 'to follow the details of continental crime.' His foreign correspondents, his newspaper clippings, his detailed files and his armchair were, however, his chief instruments of intelligence, and it was rare enough that he personally tracked his quarry overseas. Little is, in fact, known of his journeys abroad.

His European reputation was sufficient to attract many clients from across the Channel—among them such distinguished individuals as the kings of Scandinavia and Bohemia—but his own visits to the Continent were few and strictly professional. His journeys to Tibet, Iran, Arabia and the Sudan prove him to have been no mean traveller, and that for travel's sake. But his European journeys were for business, not pleasure, and in all his years of practice there are accounts of only infrequent trips to the Continent.

Holmes did go far afield at times, and we know that he was once in Odessa. It is perhaps a result of the impression he made upon the authorities that the Russians have done him the signal honor of translating his name directly in Russian script. Almost invariably the English 'H' is transcribed by 'G', as in 'guligan' for 'hooligan'. In the Ukraine, where Odessa is, the Russian 'g' is in fact usually softened into an 'h' and we can imagine Holmes sternly looking at the Tsarist customs inspector when he is having his passport details noted. 'Not Golmes, my man,' he must have snapped, 'Holmes!'—and chewing his pencil the official must have reluctantly put down 'Kholmes', for there is in Cyrillic a hard sound (X) like the Scottish 'ch' in 'loch'. Holmes's name apart, however, this 'kh' is never used for the English 'h', and 'Holmes' in Russian stayed unique until the Dean of Canterbury began his visits—for Hewlett Johnson is now also initialled 'Kh'.

Holmes and the faithful Watson set out on yet another journey—from 'The Adventure of the Naval Treaty', *Strand*, 1893

Holmes little knew the lasting effect he had upon the Russian language: he
never returned there, to our knowledge, and our detailed information is
confined to his journeys in France and Switzerland.

Of these, the first two (in 1891) are unquestionably the best known. Two
letters from Holmes to Watson, one from Narbonne and the other from
Nimes, supply the only clues to the first itinerary; but the second, which
ended in the death of Moriarty, is better documented. Holmes left Victoria
Station on the morning of the 25 April in the disguise of an Italian priest and
the company of Watson, but to avoid Moriarty's pursuit they left the train at
Canterbury. The possessor of a contemporary Bradshaw can check the
duration of his journey thence to Newhaven, but it is a sad commentary on
the present British railway services that he could have reached Newhaven in

time for the afternoon boat. It must have been 11 a.m. when he alighted from the continental express (he speaks of a 'premature lunch' at Canterbury); he had an hour's wait for his train, and it is likely that his route necessitated changes at Ashford, Hastings and Lewes. That he caught an afternoon, and not a night boat, for the crossing to Dieppe, is clear from their arrival 'that night' in Brussels. One must presume that it was, in fact, the early morning of the 26th, since a change in Paris (the interchange stations lie, however, close together) was required. He and Watson moved to Strasbourg via Luxembourg 'on the third day'—thus the 28th.

The kindness of Herr Martignoni of the Swiss Federal Railways Library has enabled me to follow the key sections of their journey in perfect detail. The keenness with which Holmes pursued Moriarty is clear from the fact that the departure to which Watson casually refers as 'the same night we had

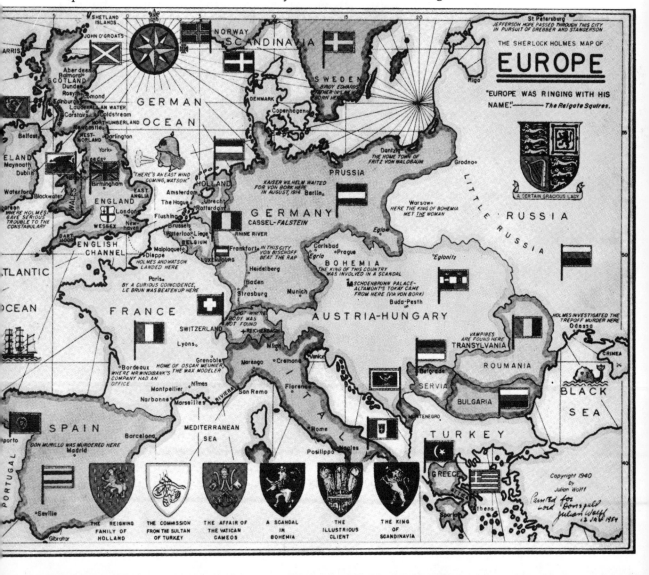

resumed our journey' was a departure in the small hours (3:55 a.m.), since there was no evening train on the 1890–91 winter timetable. They reached Geneva, via Colmar, Basel, Biel and Lausanne, at 3:18 the following afternoon (the 30th), and we know they passed the night at Geneva, probably at the Hotel de l'Ecu, the most patronised by literary Englishmen at that time. They did no more than change trains at Lausanne, but it is curious to note in passing that the Hotel National, where Watson stayed in 1896, is now a police station.

The night that Holmes and Watson spent in Geneva can be dated as that of 30 April without a shadow of doubt. The date is important, for the 'week' they spent in 'wandering up the valley of the Rhone' shrinks upon such investigation to no more than Thursday, 1 May, since by the 3rd they had reached Meiringen. When Watson writes of a 'week wandering up the valley', it is obviously a sarcastic reference to the easy pace of the train, for while from Geneva the slowest train of the day took eight and three-quarter hours, even the fastest took six hours to reach Leuk: today the journey is done in less than three hours. The line to Leukerbad, at the foot of the Gemmi Pass, had not been built, and obviously they must have left Leuk on 2 May. A study of the map Holmes must have used for his fateful journey—Blatt 17 of the *Topographische Karte der Schweiz*, in the revision of 1882—shows clearly the path from Leukerbad to the Gemmi and its bifurcation before the Daubensee. From the narrative, it is obvious that Holmes followed the right bank, since the rock dislodged in a presumed attempt on his life came from the *right*, and fell thence into the lake behind him. Moreover, the right bank path is shown on the map as the better one. They would have reached Kandersteg very late; with no train on the Leuk side and no cable car on the Kandersteg side as there is today, it is a full day's walk.

The railway from Kandersteg to Spiez was not built until much later, and the regular diligence service in that year did not operate until 1 June. They were perhaps able to hire a carriage and catch the 10:05 a.m. boat from Spiez which, via Interlaken, connected with the train leaving Brienz at 1 p.m.—Watson confirms that the journey was 'by way of Interlaken'. The pair thus arrived at Meiringen on 3 May at 1:25 p.m. and, as Watson records, they 'put up at the Englischer Hof, then kept by Peter Steiler, the elder.' No such hotel exists today, but there are Steiners (a slip of Watson's pen here) still tradesmen in Meiringen—one a tobacconist and another a haberdasher.

The events of the next day, recounted not only in 'The Final Problem' but also in the *Journal de Genéve* of 5 May, are too well known to relate. Holmes spent two years in the Orient, followed by a study of the coal tar derivatives in a laboratory in Montpellier.

Montpellier also saw Holmes upon his next journey, in connection with the disappearance of Lady Frances Carfax. The case can be dated as 1896, since it occurred between that of 'The Bruce-Partington Plans' (November 1895) and that of 'The Devil's Foot' (March 1897), and from internal evidence clearly did not take place during the winter. Holmes, finding himself unexpectedly free of the case concerning old Abrahams, joined Watson's pursuit at Montpellier and returned with him forthwith to London.

Such are the main details of Holmes's continental journeys. At first sight their concentration upon France and Switzerland appears no surprising restriction, since, for the average Englishman, French wines and Swiss mountains still represent the totality of the Continent. But a closer acquaintance than that of the average Englishman is to be inferred from references in other cases. Two of these references offer interesting paradoxes, the solution of which Watson does not explain in the published reports. Both relate in some manner to Switzerland.

The first occurs in the case just cited. Holmes refers to Baron Gruner's trial in Prague for the alleged murder of his wife at the Splügen Pass. But why, the reader asks, should a Prague court have had jurisdiction in a crime committed on the Swiss-Trentino (then, of course, Austrian) frontier? If the Baron appealed from the decision of the provincial court, the appeal would have been heard in Vienna, the imperial capital, and not in Prague. The best hypothesis is that the Baron had made an earlier attempt upon his wife's life in Prague.

The other paradox is somewhat deeper, and concerns 'The Adventure of the Three Gables'. It will be recalled that a successful attempt was made by the hirelings of Isadora Klein to steal the draft of a novel written, maligning her, by a former lover. After the young author's death in Rome, the text was dispatched among his personal effects to his mother's home in Harrow. It was from these trunks that the manuscript was burgled. The paradox arises in that Holmes noticed that some of the baggage bore the transit labels 'Milano' and 'Lucerne'. These are the stations at which baggage from Rome to London via the St Gotthard route would normally have been transferred. However, while baggage from Rome would correctly have had its immediate destination marked in Italian, that is, 'Milano', how could the Italian authorities have inscribed the next transfer point in French? They would surely have used either Italian ('Lucerna') or German ('Luzern'), for Lucerne is German-speaking.

It can only be concluded that between Milan and Lucerne the pieces so labeled had passed through a French-speaking intermediate transfer point and the relevant label had been deliberately removed. The reason is not far to seek. Mrs Klein's agents had succeeded in having the baggage directed to a locality in France where—perhaps by corruption of the railway staff—they were able to examine the trunks. France, and not French-speaking Switzerland, is indicated, since at that time (1902) the only direct connection between Milan and Switzerland lay through Lucerne. Either they were unable to open all the trunks or they had selected the wrong pieces for the diversion. In either case, the thieves would have had to return the bags to their original route (hence the addressing to Lucerne in French) to preclude suspicion and await delivery at Harrow, where the keys of the cases which they had been unable to inspect would be available for felony. It is impossible that Sherlock Holmes should have missed this obvious clue that the trunks had been tampered with en route, and it was this which must have led him to direct that they be examined and guarded.

Watson, in transcribing his account, implies with his customary unanalytical admiration that it was the purest unsupported deductive reasoning which indicated this precaution, but he missed the intermediate clue. We can almost hear Holmes mutter, as he read his friend's narrative, the remark that tradition has baselessly fathered on him: 'But it was elementary, my dear Watson, elementary!'

Map key

BRITISH ISLES. Aberdeen *Twis; Nobl.* Bangor *Prio.* Coldstream *Nava.* Darlington *Scan.* Eton *RedH; Empt.* Eyford *Engr.* Falmouth *Glor.* Leicester *Vall.* Maynooth *Empt.* Newcastle *Houn.* Oxford *RedH; Empt; Miss.* Pinner *Yell.* Reading *SixN.* Tunbridge Wells *Blac.* Waterford *Card.* York *Houn.*

FRANCE. Lyons *Reig.* Malplaquet *Reig.* Marseilles *Iden.* Montpellier *Stud; Empt; Lady.* Nimes *Fina.* Riviera *3Gab.*

BELGIUM. Brussels *Stoc; Fina.* Liège *Stud.* Waterloo *Abbe.*

HOLLAND. Amsterdam *Maza.* Hague *Iden.* Flushing *Last.* Rotterdam *Bosc.* Utrecht *Stud.*

GERMANY. Baden *Lady.* Berlin *Last.* Dantzig *Nava.* Heidelberg *3Gar.* Munich *Nobl.* Strasburg *Fina.*

BOHEMIA. Carlsbad *Scan.*

AUSTRIA-HUNGARY. Belgrade *Seco.* Buda-Pesth *Gree.* Schoenbrunn (Vienna) *Last.*

ITALY. Florence *Empt.* Marengo *Abbe.* Milan *3Gab.* Naples *SixN.* Posilippo *RedC.* Rome *3Gab; Wist.* San Remo *Stoc.* Vatican *Houn; Blac.* Venice *Sign.*

SWITZERLAND. Basle, Davos Platz, Geneva, Interlaken, Leuk, Meiringen, Rosenlaie, ect. *Fina.* Lausanne *Lady.* Lucerne *3Gab.*

SPAIN. Barcelona *Wist.* Madrid *Wist; Seco.*

GIBRALTAR. *Abbe.*

PORTUGAL. Oporto *Resi.*

DENMARK. Copenhagen *Stud.*

RUSSIA. Crimea *Croo; Blan.* Grodno *Houn.* Odessa *Stud; Scan.* Riga *Sign.* St. Petersburg (Lenningrad) *Stud.* Warsaw *Scan.*

GREECE. Athens *Gree.* Attica *RedH.* Sparta *Houn.*

TURKEY. *Blan.*

Sherlock Holmes Was An American!

Franklin Delano Roosevelt

Fans of Sherlock Holmes have come from all walks of life, but perhaps the most famous Sherlockian was Franklin Roosevelt, the thirty-second President of the United States. President Roosevelt was a member of the Baker Street Irregulars from 1942 until his death just before the end of World War II in 1945, and his most contentious contribution to Sherlockiana was his belief that the Great Detective was actually an American. He outlined this theory in a short item reprinted here from The Baker Street Journal *which, not surprisingly, was heatedly attacked as soon as it appeared.*

Now that I belong to the Baker Street Irregulars, I cannot restrain the impulse to tell you that since I have had to give up cruising on the Potomac I sometimes go off the record on Sundays to an undisclosed retreat. In that spot the group of little cabins which shelter the Secret Service Men is known as Baker Street!

'Sherlock Holmes' was the brand name of a popular make of cigars marketed in the first quarter of this century in America

As a result of my studies through Dr Watson's pages, I am inclined to revise a former estimate that Sherlock Holmes was a foundling. Actually he was born an American and brought up by his father or a foster father in the underground world, thus learning all the tricks of the trade in the highly developed American art of crime.

At an early age he felt the urge to do something for mankind. He was too well known in top circles in this country and, therefore, chose to operate in England. His attributes were primarily American, not English.

I feel that further study of this postulate will bring good results to history. Such discussion will go to show that interest in the whole field of Sherlock-iana is perennial.

William Gillette, the American actor, in his famous stage rôle
as Sherlock Holmes

Sherlock Holmes and American Presidents

During the American bicentennial celebrations in 1976, quiz-maker John Bennett Shaw devised this brain-teaser for his fellow-Sherlockians. It's now made available to a wider audience and the answers are to be found at the back of the book.

1. A character in 'The Yellow Face' bore the name of two US Presidents.

   _____

2. A large city in the eastern part of the United States has the same name as the 22nd President and was once the residence of the dreadful Drebber.

   _____

3. The barkeep of the Fighting Cock Inn had the same surname as the President, who won the election by one electoral vote after challenge and fraud.

   _____

4. If you know what Holmes did to a dead pig you will know the name of the 14th President.

   _____

5. Two presidents had the same last name, but one had a middle name which was the same as the surname of the Police Inspector in Surrey. ('Wisteria Lodge').

   _____

6. A key person in the formation of the alliance between Holmes and Watson had a name very much like the name of the alma mater and the depository of the library of the 31st President.

   _____

7. Well, maybe he, the 33rd President, was associated with a big city political boss whose name was almost like that of the convict leader in the 'Gloria Scott' mutiny, but he was a great decision making leader.

   (name both convict or boss and the President)

   _____

8. An oft remembered quotation from 'The Musgrave Ritual' reads 'He had a horror of destroying documents' and this cannot but make one think, regrettably of a recent President.

   _____

9. J. Neil Gibson was likened by Watson to what US President.

   _____

10. The name of one of the Worthington Bank Gang would describe President Taft physically in relation to the other Chief Executives.

    _____

11. The case 'The Noble Bachelor' can only remind one of a single US President.

    _____

12. A most fascinating character who seemed to worry about rain was mentioned in 'Thor Bridge': he had the same surname as the 13th President.

    _____

13. In 'The Crooked Man' a strange pet has the same name as the nickname of the most energetic US President.

    _____

14. One hopes this clue will give you the name of a great, perhaps the greatest, President.

    _____

15. A little _____ (the name of a President) was almost involved in a collision as mentioned in 'His Last Bow'.

    _____

16. The feelings of Alexander Holder toward Arthur Holder might cause one to recall the name of the 4th President.

    _____

17. When Jefferson sat down with the French to discuss the acquisition of vast property he might have used a common term that sounds much like the name of the most famous canonical professional detective.

    _____

18. The action that Holmes took with McMurdo (*The Sign Of Four*) could cause one to think of the name of the President who served before Taylor.

    _____

19. Selden might not have been attacked by the Hound had not Baskerville visited one whose profession carries the same name as the President who preceded Fillmore.

    _____

20. There is considerable debate whether Watson or Doyle was the _____ of the Holmes canon. And that reminds you of the name of the 21st President.

The Railway Journeys
of Mr Sherlock Holmes

J. Alan Rannie

*Sherlock Holmes's favourite mode of transport was by railway and the Adventures are full
of references to such journeys. During his day, of course, the railway was the last word in
transport, and the following essay does much to conjure up all the delights of steam travel.
Mr Rannie, a rail historian as well as a Sherlockian, published his article in* THE RAILWAY
MAGAZINE *of May, 1935.*

Now that so much scholarship is being expended on the life and times of
the immortal Mr. Sherlock Holmes and so many books are appearing that
deal with various aspects of his career, the time seems ripe for an investigation into his recorded journeys by rail. For this great detective was a notable
traveller and he flourished in an epoch when railways were still the last word
in land transport. Only once, when he emerged from retirement to assist his
country during the Great War, do we hear of his making use of a car with Dr.
Watson at the wheel; his true place was in a first-class compartment or in a
hansom cab. And what an epoch it was, the one in which he moved! A time
of single-wheelers and gas-lit, non-corridor coaches, of foot-warmers and
luncheon baskets, when broad-gauge expresses were still running out of
Paddington and the London Chatham & Dover had not yet become a legend
of the past.

Sherlock Holmes was indeed more than a casual traveller; he had all the
makings of a railwayist, and though his technical knowledge was usually
employed in connection with his professional problems, this was not always
the case. On one occasion, whilst on his way to investigate the mystery of
Silver Blaze, he is known to have timed a train, and though his method might
be considered inadeqauate by competent modern observers, he arrived at a
very reasonable result.

'We are going well,' said he, looking out of the window and glancing at his
watch. 'Our rate at present is fifty-three and a half miles an hour.'

'I have not observed the quarter-mile posts,' said I.

'Nor have I, but the telegraph posts upon this line are sixty yards apart and
the calculation is a simple one.'

And though it usually fell to Dr. Watson's lot to look up the trains, a task that he accomplished with commendable efficiency and despatch, there is abundant evidence that it was not from any lack of inability to wrestle with the intricacies of Bradshaw on Holmes's part.

As an example of the good use to which the detective put his railway lore, we may consider the following passage from 'The Norwood Builders'.

'There are some points about that document, Lestrade, are there not?' said he, pushing them over.

The official looked at them with a puzzled expression. 'I can read the first few lines, and these in the middle of the second page and one or two at the end, those are as clear as print,' said he, 'but the writing in between is very bad, and there are three places where I cannot read it at all.'

'What do you make of it?' said Holmes.

'Well, what do you make of it?'

'That it was written in a train; the good writing represents stations, the bad writing movement, and the very bad writing passing over points. A scientific expert would pronounce at once that this was drawn up on a suburban line, since nowhere save in the immediate vicinity of a great city could there be so quick a succession of points. Granting that his whole journey was occupied in drawing up the will, then the train was an express, only stopping once between Norwood and London Bridge'.

There is also the whole story of 'The Bruce-Partington Plans', the scene of which is largely laid upon the Inner Circle. We read that the body of the victim was found near Aldgate station where trains run 'from West to East, some purely Metropolitan, some from Willesden and other outlying junctions.' An interesting point of departure for an inquiry into now forgotten train services is here suggested, and another curious point is that the train from which Holmes concluded that the body had fallen 'had now been broken up', which seems an unusual practice in connection with an Underground train, even though it must have consisted of steam-hauled rolling-stock, complete with gas-bags on the roof. At a later stage we are taken to Gloucester Road, where trains are often held up in the open 'owing to the intersection of one of the larger lines.' Here is a note which will find its response in the experience of most of us, though purists might cavil at the diagnosis of the trouble, and it is interesting to read in THE RAILWAY MAGAZINE for November, 1934, that the London Passenger Transport Board is proposing to do away with the delays, after so many years, by constructing a flying junction at this point.

Although he must have lived within a very short distance of Baker Street station, there is little evidence that Holmes made extensive use of the Underground. That Dr. Watson had been in a third-class carriage thereon is, indeed, implied in *A Study in Scarlet*, and when they went to Harrow to visit the Three Gables it is fair to assume that they travelled by Metropolitan. Incidentally, an electric locomotive bearing the detective's name is sometimes to be seen at Baker Street station.

Holmes and Watson, railway travellers, with a huge pile of
luggage—from 'The Final Problem', *Strand*, 1893

The suburban journeys which the two friends are known to have taken
were many. Beckenham, Chislehurst, Croydon, Norbury, Streatham, and
Woolwich were all outside the range of convenient horse transport, and even
so it took $\frac{3}{4}$ hour to reach Beckenham from London Bridge, and the train to
Woolwich is described as being very slow. An unusually high proportion of
Holmes's clients seems to have come from the southern Home Counties, and
rather longer journeys into Kent, Surrey, Sussex, and Hants are correspond-
ingly frequent. Either the grim reputation of the London Chatham & Dover

Preparing to travel, a Sidney Paget illustration for 'The Hound of the Baskervilles', *Strand*, 1902

or the superior location of Charing Cross caused him to choose the last-named station as a starting point for Chatham in the affair of 'Yoxley Old Place', though it meant starting at 6 a.m. and the journey, presumably by the North Kent line, was 'long and weary'. Forest Row was another objective, as also a station 'south of Horsham', whilst in 'Shoscombe Old Place' we are introduced to a 'Halt-on-demand' station in the same neighbourhood. The case of the 'Solitary Cyclist' took Watson to Farnham, and he found that there were two trains from Waterloo at 9.13 and 9.50 a.m., which seems to argue a very frequent service for the date and distance involved. And they were both at Leatherhead in connection with 'The Speckled Band' Waterloo being again the point of departure. There were also a journey of Holmes's to Aldershot and no fewer than three trips to Winchester, one of which will have to claim our attention later.

Before dealing with the longer journeys of the famous pair, it may be well to mention some of their general characteristics. That they invariably went first class has already been mentioned, and we can hardly imagine it otherwise. On the solitary occasion when Watson was compelled to travel third to suit the penurious instincts of the Retired Colourman, he lodged quite a bitter complaint. When, however, we reflect that it was on an Essex branch line of the Great Eastern and probably, therefore, in a six-wheeler of light construction and bare of upholstery, we pampered moderns may feel more inclined to sympathise.

We are glad to note that the timetable in use at 221b Baker Street was Bradshaw's Guide, though the easy alternative of the A.B.C. would have served the turn of the two friends so well and might have proved a snare. By a fortunate series of coincidences a convenient train was nearly always available; the sole exception recorded is in the adventure of the 'Norfolk Squire', when the Great Eastern was at fault in not providing an evening train to North Walsham, though it did well for them the following day by enabling them to dine in Baker Street after leaving that comparatively distant spot at 3.40 p.m. Holmes habitually wore a travelling-cap with ear-flaps and covered his legs with a rug in wintry weather. For the first part of each journey he was apt to be immersed in piles of newspapers, and he would use much of the remainder for going over aloud the details of the case so far as they were already known, partly for the edification of the good doctor, but partly also to clear his own mind. It would seem that there were seldom any other passengers in the compartment; perhaps friendly guards saw to that! But there were also times when both would look out of the window. Watson had a genuine appreciation of scenery and would at times wax quite romantic about it. (He was once told somewhat sternly to 'cut out the poetry.') Holmes, on the other hand, looked at it with a professionally biased eye. The peaceful countryside near Aldershot, as seen from the London & South Western main line, suggested a charming picture of rural domesticity to Watson, but a potential scene of lonely helplessness in face of violent crime to Holmes. And the chimney-pots of South London, whose unloveliness depressed the doctor when the Portsmouth train which they had boarded at Woking was running into Waterloo, were set off in the eyes of the detective by the sight of the board schools rising like beacons of progress in their midst.

The question as to whether Holmes had any favourite railway is one which cannot be answered with certainty. There is indeed a quality about the references to the Great Western which seems to be lacking in the case of other lines, but this may be due to the predilections of Watson, who once lived near Paddington and had patients amongst its staff. That he disliked the shorter southern lines is obvious though in no way remarkable, and that he did not care over-much for the Great Eastern is proved, amongst other things, by the fact that he used King's Cross on his only recorded trip to Cambridge, (in 'The Missing Three-Quarters') though the journey appears to have been a rather lengthy one. Another point of doubtful significance is that Euston seems to take rather more than its fair share of work in connection with calls to the North; it was used, for instance, for journeys to Bedfordshire and Derbyshire, though it is not possible to be sure that St. Pancras would have served better in either case. But, be that as it may, there is no mention of the Midland in the pages of Watson, and the Great Northern does not occur except in the instance already given. Yet we always have to remember that we have records of only a small proportion of Holmes's problems, and those that must have reached him from the industrial North are not frequently selected for inclusion by his biographer.

The North Western was used for the run to Birmingham in the case of 'The Stockbroker's Clerk', a circumstance which will not surprise us when we reflect that the Great Western was still obliged to perform the journey *via* Oxford and was at a disadvantage to the tune of over 18 miles. 'We have here a clear run of seventy minutes,' Holmes remarked when they were 'well started'—surely from Willesden to Blisworth—and the train characteristically rolled into New Street at the very moment when the detective had finished his analysis of the case.

In the adventure of 'The Priory School', Euston figures again. It will be remembered that 'a return ticket from Mackleton in the North of England' was found in the pocket of the insensible Dr. Huxtable, who had left home so early that he was in Baker Street before noon. In seeking to locate his home station, one's thoughts turn first to the Potteries route to Manchester, which may then have boasted an early fast service to town. But the references to the Chesterfield Road and the prestige of the Duke of Holdernesse lead one away from Congleton and Macclesfield to the region of Chatsworth, and one wonders whether Buxton would not be a better guess. The story belongs to the early years of the present century, when the Buxton and Ashbourne line was already open, so this identification is not incompatible with an arrival at Euston, which was certainly the station from which Holmes, Watson and Dr. Huxtable set out for the scene of their investigations.

The journeys to the West are full of incident and colour. When called to Ross in connection with 'The Boscombe Valley Mystery', our travellers used the 11.15 a.m. from Paddington. They duly lunched at Swindon—for this was in the days when the Swindon Hotel Company still exercised its right of holding up all trains for ten minutes whilst the passengers refreshed themselves in its dining-rooms. Watson was charmed with the scenery of the

Golden Valley as they descended the bank to Stroud, and by the 'broad, gleaming Severn' at Gloucester, before they reached Ross a little before four o'clock.

The disappearance of Silver Blaze took them to Tavistock, and as the story is included in the *Memoirs*, which appeared in 1892, they rightly chose the Great Western route in preference to that of the South Western, which may still have depended on somewhat precarious running-powers beyond Lydford. This was the occasion on which Holmes timed the train, and it is pleasant to reflect that this was certainly a broad gauge journey. They returned by the 'midnight express' and must have passed through Bristol in both directions.

When we turn to the great epic of *The Hound of the Baskervilles*, which is dated 1889, we are on slightly more difficult ground. Watson, Dr. Mortimer and the Baronet started merely from 'the station,' but the writer likes to think that the platform on which the 'tall, austere figure of Holmes' could be seen 'standing motionless and gazing after us, when we had left it far behind' was No. 1 at Paddington. Nor does the fact that the murderer, Stapleton, cried out to his cab-driver to be driven to Waterloo when he discovered that Holmes was following him, really upset this hypothesis. Granted that both parties were bound for Dartmoor, we know that when Stapleton first bought the Hound, he brought it down by the North Devon line—presumably the South Western between Exeter and Lydford—and walked it for a great distance across the moor. And what could be more natural than that he should continue to avoid observation by adopting a route which was not the natural one to the nearest station to Baskerville Hall?

The description of Watson's journey must be given in his own words: 'The journey was a swift and pleasant one, and I spent it in making the closer acquaintance of my two companions and in playing with Dr. Mortimer's spaniel. In a very few hours the brown earth had become ruddy, the brick had changed to granite, and red cows grazed in well-hedged fields where the lush grasses and more luxuriant vegetation spoke of a richer, if a damper, climate. Young Baskerville stared eagerly out of the window, and cried aloud with delight as he recognised the familiar features of the Devon scenery . . .

'"I'm as keen as possible to see the moor," he said.

'"Are you? Then your wish is easily granted, for there is your first sight of the moor," said Dr. Mortimer, pointing out of the carriage window.

'Over the green squares of the fields and the low curve of a wood, there rose in the distance a grey, melancholy hill, with a strange, jagged summit, dim and vague in the distance, like some fantastic landscape in a dream.

'The train drew up at a small wayside station, and we all descended. . . . Our coming was evidently a great event, for station-master and porters clustered round us to carry out our luggage . . . It was a sweet, simple country spot,' and surely, so the writer thinks, in the neighbourhood of Ivybridge or Yelverton.

But is this wayside station to be identified with the station of Coombe Tracey, at which Lestrade arrived with the warrant when the 'London Express came roaring into the station' a week or two later at 5.40 p.m.? This station was apparently equally convenient for Baskerville Hall, but Coombe Tracey seems to have been a small town, and the evidence inclines towards the supposition that we are dealing with two distinct localities.

We may conclude our survey by mentioning three problems which seem incapable of entirely satisfactory elucidation.

The story of Silver Blaze has already been referred to. It ends with a journey back from the Winchester Races, which had a real existence in those days, in a comfortable Pullman car. So far, so good, for the last Pullman—apart from recent developments—was not withdrawn from the Bournemouth route until a short time before the war. But when Holmes remarks that they are approaching Clapham Junction and should be in Victoria in less than ten minutes we begin to prick up our ears. We have to choose between four possible explanations. Either Holmes himself suffered a temporary lapse of memory, or Watson has incorrectly reported his words, or again some unknown factor may have induced them to change at Clapham, or the Brighton and the South Western may have been acting in somewhat closer collaboration than was usual in those pre-grouping days, and diverting a proportion of Bournemouth trains to the West End. It may be added that a study of the track connections at Clapham Junction, as they at present exist, inclines one against this last explanation.

The adventure of 'The Engineer's Thumb' affords a more intriguing mystery. The victim of the outrage was instructed to travel by the last train 'to Eyford in Berkshire. It is a little place near the borders of Oxfordshire, and within seven miles of Reading. There is a train from Paddington which would bring you in there at about 11.15.' The intelligent reader has just attuned his mind to the idea of Pangbourne or Streatley when he reads that the Engineer had to change stations as well as trains at Reading. This can only have been from Great Western to South Eastern, since Reading West was as yet unborn. And the mystery only deepens when we learn that he was able to return by an early morning train to Paddington, which brought him to Dr. Watson's consulting room, in charge of the guard, a little before seven o'clock. The writer confesses that he finds this particular piece of topography entirely baffling.

And now for 'The Final Problem', which takes us beyond the confines of these islands. It was April, 1891, and Holmes, disguised as an aged Italian priest, was obliged to flee before Professor Moriarty for his very life. He was joined by the faithful Watson at Victoria just before the departure of the Continental express. This train left at about 9.45 a.m. and was booked to stop at Canterbury, a procedure which must have been more usual in those days than it subsequently became. As Moriarty had appeared at Victoria just as the express 'shot clear of the station', Holmes wisely decided to alight at

Holmes sees Watson off by train in 'The Adventure of the Naval Treaty', *Strand*, 1893

Canterbury, leaving the luggage, which had been registered through to Paris, to continue its career unchecked. They had hardly got out, and Watson 'was still looking rather ruefully after the rapidly disappearing luggage van', when Holmes plucked his sleeve and pointed up the line.

'"Already, you see," said he.

'Far away from among the Kentish woods there arose a thin spray of smoke. A minute later a carriage and engine could be seen flying along the open curve that led to the station. We had hardly time to take our places behind a pile of luggage when it passed with a rattle and a roar, beating a blast of hot air into our faces. "There he goes," said Holmes, as we watched the carriage swing and rock over the points.' The block sections on the Chatham & Dover line must have been short in those days.

The next part of Holmes's plan of escape took the form of a cross-country journey to Newhaven, to be followed by a crossing to Dieppe. In the absence of detailed information we may assume that they crossed the town to Canterbury West and proceeded *via* Ashford, Hastings and Lewes, a distance of some 72 miles. Even with good connections, this may well have occupied the greater part of four hours, and as we know that the journey did not commence until an hour after Moriarty's special had passed, the travellers cannot have reached Newhaven before tea-time. We are further led to suppose that there would have been time for a meal previous to embarkation. Anyone who is in a position to prove that there was a late afternoon boat from Newhaven in the spring of 'ninety-one[1] would be shedding light in dark places, for there is a grave difficulty in the way of supposing that they waited for the ordinary night service. Watson states that they made their way to Brussels that night and even the most liberal construction of these words is inconsistent with an arrival at Dieppe in the small hours of the morning. The length and complexity of a journey from Canterbury to Newhaven are as nothing when compared with a cross-country trip from Dieppe to Brussels, and it is unlikely that Holmes would have ventured into Paris and risked a departure from the Gare du Nord, which Moriarty was believed to have been watching. Nor indeed would even this course have fitted in with Watson's chronology, unless we postulate a 5 o'clock boat from Newhaven, and the whole subject bristles with difficulties.

There is, of course, the theory that when Watson wrote Newhaven and Dieppe he should have written Folkestone and Boulogne, but the following remark by Holmes has the ring of conviction and seems out of keeping with the short journey over the Elham Valley line. 'The question now is whether we should take a premature lunch here, or run our chance of starving before we reach the buffet at Newhaven.' It would besides have been dangerous to pass through Calais by train or even to have appeared at Boulogne itself.

The most feasible explanation seems to the present writer to be that Watson, whose mind was subsequently to be disturbed by many days of continuous and exciting travel, and by grief at the loss of his friend, has allowed one of these days to slip from his memory altogether. Upon this supposition, the words 'we made our way to Brussels that night' should be amended to allow of a crossing by the night boat from Newhaven and, after a few wretched hours of slumber at Dieppe, the consumption of the whole of the following day in a journey to Brussels through Serqueux, Amiens, Tergnier, St. Quentin and Maubeuge.

From Brussels onwards all is plain sailing. By way of Strasbourg, Basle and Geneva, the Belgian, German and Swiss railways conducted the great detective to meet the crisis of his fate, and his apparent end, in the gorge of Reichenbach.

But we know that he was to return, and if in some of the later stories the railway references show a falling off in clarity and interest, they leave all the more scope for our imagination. It may be, indeed, that Holmes still lives as an octogenarian amongst his beehives on the Sussex Downs, and that he is still able to enjoy an occasional visit to town, to attend a concert or exchange reminiscences at Scotland Yard, equipped with a monthly return ticket and travelling upon the Southern Electric.

[1] The service ceased to be a 'tidal' one some months previously.

London Transport and Sherlock Holmes join forces. Special symbol adopted when LT named a train 'Sherlock Holmes' in October 1953

The Great Holmes Joke

Bernard Darwin

The game of detecting the detective has, as already demonstrated, delighted Sherlockians since Ronald Knox wrote his pioneering essay more than fifty years ago. But there are other admirers of the Great Detective who believe that far too much is read into the Adventures and that they should be taken at face value, mistakes and all. Such enthusiasts are known as 'Fundamentalists', and one of their leading spokesmen is Bernard Darwin who has protested more than once, 'I grow a little tired of this ingenious game which these clever people play with one another.' So, to provide the reader new to the world of Sherlockiana a view from the other side of the canon, so to speak, I have included here one of Mr Darwin's most pungent discourses on the matter which first appeared in JOHN O'LONDON'S WEEKLY, 19 February, 1954.

A FEW years ago there were in the State of Tennessee some gentlemen who, a little late in the day perhaps, came across *The Origin of Species* and were much shocked by it. These simple souls were called fundamentalists and I am beginning to think that I too am a fundamentalist in regard to Sherlock Holmes.

For a number of years some extremely clever people have been amusing themselves with irreverent speculation. They have remarried the sorrowing widower Watson; they have suggested that Holmes took a harmless professor of mathematics and foisted on him the character of the Napoleon of crime in order to excuse his own failures. Dates can prove anything; the good doctor was no chronologist and they are doubtless right in holding that Moriarty could not be devising murder at Birlstone Manor years after he had fallen over the precipice.

But the curious thing is that I do not seem greatly to care. I grow a little tired of this ingenious game which these clever people play with one another. It does me no harm, to be sure, unless by making me feel almost as stupid as poor dear old Watson. Moreover, I will readily admit that I used to take a deep interest in whether Holmes was at Oxford or Cambridge. I was delighted by the brilliant use in favour of Cambridge of the bull-terrier that bit Holmes on his way to chapel.

But now I have had enough of this great Holmes joke. I want to go back to the simple and sublime jokes which are the stories themselves. Just as the gentlemen of Tennessee believed, no doubt, in the exact order of creation as set out in Genesis, so I believe in the exact order of the stories as they originally came to us. I want no more meddling with the sacred writings.

If I need any excuse for this guileless faith of mine it is that I first read the

stories at a most impressionable time of life. I must have been about seventeen when 'The Scandal in Bohemia' and 'The Red-headed League' burst on the world. To buy the *Strand Magazine* was an extravagance not always possible; it was cheaper to waylay the newspaper boy who brought it to the house library. If one could get the first look at it one could just finish the story before the bell began to ring for Chapel, and with this object privateers went through the yard and far down the High Street to cut off the boy.

I do not say that we accepted the stories with entire seriousness. I am sure that even as we thrilled we laughed at their absurdities, but it was with a very tender, almost a reverent laughter. And so to-day in reading them we breathe again the airs of our youth, and are very sensitive on their behalf.

This same fundamental quality in my belief makes me immovably confident that the earlier stories surpassed those that followed them. In his preface to the complete edition of the short stories Sir Arthur Conan Doyle expressed the hope that now that the reader could take them in any order he chose he would not find that 'the end shows any conspicuous falling off from the modest merits of the beginning.'

I wish I could agree with that characteristically modest remark but I cannot; the old friends are the ones to which I constantly turn. Not to some of them, I own; I do not care two pins for Miss Mary Sutherland and the flat-footed little love affair that failed, but think of 'Boscombe Valley' and 'The Red-headed League' and 'The Five Orange Pips'. Think above all of 'The Speckled Band'. I remember that in those days at school when we were very fond of making lists in order of affection, whether of books or cricketers or what not, we were all agreed on one point: 'The Speckled Band' was *the* best of the stories, nor have I ever found reason to change that view.

I protest that I am not narrow-minded. Down at any rate to the return of Holmes there are some really fine specimens. Notably 'The Dancing Men', with the dark creeping shadow that squats before the tool-house door to inscribe its ruthless hieroglyphics. 'The Six Napoleons', too, works up to an admirable climax with Holmes producing the black pearl and Watson and Lestrade breaking into spontaneous clapping. But no, no, the springtime was best.

It is to those early stories that we go for some familiar sentence to be whispered over again with a never failing joy. 'You see it, Watson,' he yelled. 'You see it?' That is great, but for myself I prefer 'Have you never—' said Sherlock Holmes bending forward and sinking his voice—'have you never heard of the Ku Klux Klan?' All the horror and mystery of all the secret societies in the world were concentrated in that sentence.

Conan Doyle was a master of what may be called atmospherics. He had at least something of Dickens's unique gift of suggesting by means of a storm the tremendous events to come. In 'The Five Orange Pips', for instance, from which I have just been quoting, there is a fine admonitory thrill in the wind that screamed and the rain that beat against the window! It set Watson to thinking of 'the great elemental forces which shriek at mankind through the bars of his civilization.' Naturally that warning could never be quite so terrible again. In 'The Golden Pince-Nez' the wind once more howled down Baker Street and the rain lashed the windows; once more Watson mused on the great elemental forces and it was all very capital, but not quite what it had been.

I must allow one honourable exception in favour of the later stories in this matter of atmosphere. The story of the Bruce-Partington Plans begins in a splendidly sinister fog, its greasy, heavy, brown swirl drifting past us and condensing in oily drops upon the window panes. It is not comparable with the fog at the beginning of *Bleak House*, but still it is an undeniably good fog, full of formidable possibilities.

Perhaps what I have been saying amounts to no more than this, that I am a hide-bound Conservative and a lazy reader, who loves to go back and back again to his oldest friends. Be it so. I admit the impeachment. To me Holmes will always be at his best in his more primitive days, before he had become too famous. He did not make a mock of poor Watson then; he did not say in answer to an innocent suggestion: 'We must not let him think that this Agency is a home for the weak-minded.' Just put me down at the Hereford Arms at Ross or the Crown at Stoke Moran and I shall be perfectly happy.

MYSTERY CODE

When the police found the spy's body in a remote country mansion, they also discovered the entrance to a secret passageway in the building. Clutched in the dead man's fingers was the following message. Given that the letters of the alphabet have been numbered in 1,2,3 sequence (but *not* starting with A), that H is worth twice Z and that R is worth twice E, can you crack the mystery code?

2.16.13 21.9.24 2.23 2.16.13
3.22.12.13.26.15.26.23.3.22.12 24.9.1.1.9.15.13
20.17.13.1 10.13.16.17.22.12 2.16.3
14.17.26.13.24.20.9.11.13

The Adventures of Picklock Holes

'Cunnin Toil'

The immediate success which the Sherlock Holmes Adventures enjoyed once they began appearing in the STRAND *from 1891 quickly led to the Great Detective being parodied by other writers—the inevitable fate of any popular literary figure. The earliest known Sherlockian parody cycle appeared, not surprisingly, in* PUNCH *in the winter of 1893. 'The Adventures of Picklock Holes' by 'Cunnin Toil' were the work of the well-known humorist R. C. Lehmann, and featured a detective who either created the evidence in his cases himself or else hired a criminal for the occasion. The story selected appeared in the issue of 7 October 1893. (Also illustrated here are two other important early parodies: 'Sherlaw Kombs', created by Robert Barr for* THE IDLER *(1894), and 'Fetlock Jones', Mark Twain's contribution to the genre who featured in* A DOUBLE-BARRELLED DETECTIVE STORY, *published in 1902.)*

EVERYBODY must remember the apparently causeless panic that seized the various European governments only a few years ago. It was the dead season. Members of Parliament were all disporting themselves on the various grouse-moors which are specially reserved for that august legislative body in order that there may be no lack of accuracy in the articles of those who imagine that the 12th of August brings to every M.P. a yearning for the scent of heather and the sound of breech-loading guns. Suddenly, and without any warning, a great fear spread through Europe. Nobody seemed able to state precisely how it began. There were, of course, some who attributed it to an after-dinner speech made by the German Emperor at the annual banquet of the Blue Bösewitzers, the famous Cuirassier regiment of which the Grand Duke of SCHNUPFTUCHSTEIN is the honorary commanding officer. Others again saw in it the influence of M. PAUL DEROULÈDE, while yet a third party attributed it with an equal assumption of certainty to the fact that Austria had recently forbidden the import of Servian pigs. They were all wrong. The time has come when the truth must be known. The story I am about to tell will show my extraordinary friend, PICKLOCK HOLES, on an even higher pinnacle of unmatchable acumen than that which fame has hitherto assigned to him. He may be vexed when he reads my narrative of his triumphs, for he is as modest as he is inductive; but I am determined that, at whatever cost, the story shall be made public.

It was on one of those delightful evenings for which our English summer is famous, that HOLES and I were as usual sitting together and conversing as to the best methods of inferring an Archbishop from a hat-band and a Commander-in-Chief from a penny-whistle. I had put forward several plans which appeared to me to be satisfactory, but HOLES had scouted them one after another with a cold impassivity which had not failed to impress me, accustomed though I was to the great man's exhibition of it.

'Here,' said HOLES, eventually, 'are the necessary steps. Hat-band, band-master, master-mind, mind-your-eye, eye-ball, ball-bearing, bear-leader, Leda and the Swan, swan-bill, bill-post, post-cart, cart-road, road-way, Weybridge, bridge-arch, arch-bishop. The inference of a Commander-in-Chief is even easier. You have only to assume that a penny-whistle has been found lying on the Horse-Guards' Parade by the Colonel of the Scots

Right, Mark Twain's 'Fetlock Jones'; *below*, 'Sherlaw Kombs', created by Robert Barr

Guards, and carried by him to the office of the Secretary of State for War. Thereupon you sub-divide the number of drummer-boys in a regiment of Goorkhas by the capital value of a sergeant's retiring pension, and—'

But the rest of this marvellous piece of concise reasoning must remain for ever a secret, for at this moment a bugle-call disturbed the stillness of the summer night, and HOLES immediately paused.

'What can that mean?' I asked, in some alarm, for Camberwell (our meeting place) is an essentially unmilitary district, and I could not account for this strange and awe-inspiring musical demonstration.

'Hush,' said HOLES, with perfect composure; 'it is the agreed signal. Listen. The great Samovar diamond, the most brilliant jewel in the turquoise crown of Hungary, has been lost. The Emperor of AUSTRIA is in despair. Next week he is due at Pesth, but he cannot appear before the fierce and haughty Magyars in a crown deprived of the decoration that all Hungary looks upon as symbolical of the national existence. A riot in Pesth at this moment would shake the Austro-Hungarian empire to its foundations. With it the Triple Alliance would crumble into dust, and the peace of Europe would not be worth an hour's purchase. It is, therefore, imperative that before the dawn of next Monday the diamond should be restored to its wonted setting.'

'My dear HOLES,' I said, 'this is more terrible than I thought. Have they appealed to you, as usual, after exhausting all the native talent?'

'My dear POTSON.' replied my friend, 'you ask too much. Let is suffice that I have been consulted, and that the determination of the question of peace or war lies in these hands.' And with these words the arch-detective spread before my eyes those long, sinewy, and meditative fingers which had so often excited my admiration.

Our preparations for departure to Hungary were soon made. I hardly know why I accompanied HOLES. It seemed somehow to be the usual thing that I should be present at all his feats. I thought he looked for my company, and though his undemonstrative nature would never have suffered him to betray any annoyance had I remained absent, I judged it best not to disturb the even current of his investigations by departing from established precedent. I therefore departed from London—my only alternative. Just as we were setting out, HOLES stopped me with a warning gesture.

'Have you brought the clue with you?' he asked.

'What clue?'

'Oh,' he answered, rather testily, 'any clue you like, so long as it's a clue. A torn scrap of paper with writing on it, a foot-print in the mud, a broken chair, a soiled overcoat—it really doesn't matter what it is, but a clue of some kind we must have.'

'Of course, of course,' I said, in soothing tones. 'How stupid of me to forget it. Will this do?' I continued, picking up a piece of faded green ribbon which happened to be lying on the pavement.

'The very thing,' said HOLES, pocketing it, and so we started. Our first visit on arriving at Pesth was to the Emperor-King, who was living *incognito* in a small back alley of the Hungarian capital. We cheered the monarch's heart, and proceeded to call on the leader of the Opposition in the Hungarian Diet. He was a stern man of some fifty summers, dressed in the national costume. We found him at supper. HOLES was the first to speak. 'Sir,' he said, 'resistance is useless. Your schemes have been discovered. All that is left for you is to throw yourself upon the mercy of your King.'

The rage of the Magyar was fearful to witness. HOLES continued, inexorably—'This piece of green ribbon matches the colour of your Sunday tunic. Can you swear it has not been torn from the lining? You cannot. I thought so. Know then that wrapped in this ribbon was found the great Samovar diamond, and that you, you alone, were concerned in the robbery.'

At this moment the police broke into the room.

'Remove his Excellency,' said HOLES, 'and let him forthwith expiate his crimes upon the scaffold.'

'But,' I ventured to interpose, 'where is the diamond? Unless you restore that—'

'POTSON,' whispered HOLES, almost fiercely, 'do not be a fool.'

As he said this, the door once again opened, and the Emperor-King entered the room, bearing on his head the turquoise crown, in the centre of which sparkled the great Samovar, 'the moon of brilliancy,' as the Hungarian poets love to call it. The Emperor approached the marvellous detective. 'Pardon me,' he said, 'for troubling you. I have just found the missing stone under my pillow.'

'Where,' said HOLES, 'I was about to tell your Majesty that you would find it.'

'Thank you,' said his Majesty, 'for restoring to me a valued possession and ridding me of a knave about whom I have long had my suspicions.' The conclusion of this speech was greeted with loud '*Eljens*,' the Hungarian national shout, in the midst of which we took our leave. That is the true story of how the peace of Europe was preserved by my wonderful friend.

The Bound of the Haskervilles

Peter Todd

The longest running series of parodies were THE ADVENTURES OF HERLOCK SHOLMES, *written by Charles Harold St John Hamilton, known to the world as Frank Richards, creator of the guzzling fat boy, Billy Bunter. In all, Hamilton wrote a hundred tales about Sholmes and his friend Jotson under the Todd pen-name, which appeared in a number of boy's magazines including* THE GEM, THE MAGNET *and* THE PENNY POPULAR. *The first series were published in* THE GREYFRIARS HERALD, *halfpenny magazine which began publication in 1915 and died unceremoniously eighteen issues later. Sholmes, though, was already established and moved happily on to new homes. Copies of those early* HERALDS *are now among the most sought after items of Sherlockiana, and I'm pleased to be able to reprint one of the best tales from this period—'The Bound of the Haskervilles'—complete with a selection of drawings by Lewis R. Higgins, who illustrated the series.*

Chapter One

THE story of the disappearance of Sir Huckaback Haskerville, and the strange events that followed, has never been fully told. It is my privilege, as the faithful companion and chronicler of Herlock Sholmes, to give the story to the public for the first time.

It was Sholmes, it is needless to say, who solved the mystery that had baffled the police for three weeks. It is only just that my amazing friend should be given, even at this late date, the credit that is his due.

The disappearance of Sir Huckaback, the head of one of the oldest familes in Slopshire, had created a sensation. There were whispers of family dissensions that had preceded it. Society held that Lady Haskerville was to blame. What seemed certain was that the unhappy baronet, after hot words at the breakfast-table, had rushed forth from his ancestral halls, and plunged to his death in the deep chasm in the heart of Haskerville Park. From those gloomy depths he had never emerged.

Strange stories were told of that yawning chasm in Haskerville Park. Tradition had it that a certain ancestor of the Haskervilles, who had sided with King Charles in the Civil Wars, had escaped the soldiers of the Parliament by a desperate leap across the yawning gulf. From this tradition the place was known locally as 'The Bound of the Haskervilles.' A certain resemblance was given to the story by the fact that this ancient Haskerville had had a considerable reputation as a bounder in the Royal Court before the wars.

Be this as it may, there could be little doubt that his descendant had perished in those gloomy depths. His footsteps had been traced to the edge of the chasm, and there were no returning footprints. Where his ancestor, pursued by Cromwell's Ironsides, had bounded to safety, if local tradition was to be relied upon, Sir Huckaback had plunged into his doom.

The grief of Lady Haskerville was terrible. For several days she was not seen at the theatre or the cinema. I was not surprised when, one morning, as I sat at breakfast with Herlock Sholmes in our rooms at Shaker Street, Lady Haskerville was announced.

Sholmes made a slight gesture of impatience. He was very busy at this time upon the case of the missing Depaste diamonds, and had no mind for other work. But his face relaxed at the sight of Lady Haskerville. Even the clever work of her Bond Street complexion specialist could not hide the pallor of her beautiful face.

A strong scent of frying fish came from the open window!

Stretched upon the floor was the gigantic form of Dr. Grimey Pylott. b ut it was coiled a huge ra t esna e.

Herlock Sholmes and Jotson on the trail of 'The Bound of the Haskervilles', in Peter Todd's story illustrated by Lewis R. Higgins for *The Greyfriars Herald*, 4 December 1915

Dr Grimey Pylott, in the grip of a huge rattlesnake, is about to be rescued by Herlock Sholmes in 'The Freckled Hand', *Greyfriars Herald*, 11 December 1915

'Mr. Sholmes,' she exclaimed, clasping her hands, 'you will help me! I have come to you as a last resource. The police are helpless.'

Sholmes smiled ironically.

'It is not uncommon for my aid to be called in when the police have proved to be helpless.' he remarked. 'But really, my dear Lady Haskerville—pray sit down—really, I cannot leave the case I am engaged upon.'

'Mr. Sholmes, to save me from despair!'

I glanced at Sholmes, wondering whether his firmness would be proof against this appeal. My friend wavered.

'Well, well,' he said. 'Let us see what can be done. Pray give me the details, Lady Haskerville. You may speak quite freely before my friend Jotson.'

'I am convinced that Sir Huckaback still lives,' said Lady Haskerville, weeping. 'But he will not return. Mr Sholmes, it was my fault; I admit it. Oh, to see him once more, and confess my fault upon my knees! The bloaters were burnt!'

'The bloaters?' queried Herlock Sholmes.

'It was a trifling quarrel,' said Lady Haskerville tearfully. 'Sir Huckaback's favourite breakfast dish was the succulent bloater. I have never cared for bloaters; my own taste ran rather in the direction of shrimps. Mr. Sholmes, we loved each other dearly; yet upon this subject there was frequently argument. On the morning of Sir Huckaback's disappearance there were words—high words. Sir Huckaback maintained that the bloaters were burnt. I maintained that they were done perfectly. Mr. Sholmes, to my shame I confess it, I knew that the bloaters were burnt!' She sobbed.

Sholmes' clear-cut face was very grave.

'And then?' he asked quietly.

'Then, Mr. Sholmes, Sir Huckaback rose in wrath, and declared that if he must eat burnt bloaters he would not remain at Haskerville Park. I was angry, too; I was not myself at that moment. In my haste I said that if he persisted in his obnoxious predilection for bloaters, I never desired to look upon him again. He gave me one terrible look, and vanished. Too late I called to him; he did not hear, or he would not heed. I hoped he would return. In spite of the difference in our tastes, I loved him dearly. But he did not come back. Search was made. The police were called in. The track of his boots was found, leading down to the yawning abyss in the park known as the Bound of the Haskervilles. There he had disappeared.'

Lady Haskerville trembled with emotion. My own eyes were not dry. The grief of this beautiful woman moved me deeply. Sholmes was unusually gentle.

'But I cannot believe that he is dead,' continued Lady Haskerville, controlling her emotion. 'Mr. Sholmes, he is keeping away from me. He has taken my hasty words too, too seriously; and that he will never give up bloaters I know only too well. I feel that he is living yet, in some quiet and serene spot where he may be able to enjoy his favourite breakfast-dish undisturbed. He must be found, Mr. Sholmes, or my heart will be broken. This dreadful doubt must be set at rest.'

'It is quite certain that the footprints leading to the chasm were really Sir Huckaback's?' asked Sholmes.

'Yes, that is certain: his footprints were well known. He took number eleven in boots.'

Herlock Sholmes caressed his chin thoughtfully for a moment. Then he rose to his feet.

'Your car is outside, Lady Haskerville?'

'Yes, Mr. Sholmes. You will come with me?' she exclaimed eagerly.

'We will come,' corrected Herlock Sholmes. 'My friend Jotson will, I am sure, give up his patients for one day.'

'Willingly!' I exclaimed.

Ten seconds later we were in the car, whirling away at top speed for the ancient home of the Haskervilles, in the heart of Slopshire.

Chapter Two

'So that is the celebrated Bound of the Haskervilles!' said Herlock Sholmes thoughtfully.

We arrived at Haskerville Park, and my friend had proceeded at once to the scene of the supposed suicide of the baronet. Following the tracks in the grassy sward, which had not been disturbed, we had arrived at the border of the yawning abyss.

Sholmes stood regarding it thoughtfully. I watched, in wonder, striving to guess the thoughts that were passing in that subtle brain. He had stopped for a few minutes in the house to use the telephone. 'Why? I could not guess. Now we were upon the scene of the disappearance. Three weeks had passed since Sir Huckaback had reached that fatal verge. What did Sholmes hope to discover there?

'He turned to me at last with his inscrutable smile.

'Do you feel inclined for a stroll, Jotson?' he asked.

'Anything you like Sholmes.'

'Come, then.'

We started off along the edge of the abyss. A quarter of a mile's walk brought us to the end, and we walked round it, and along the other side. Sholmes took a pair of powerful glasses from his pocket, and scanned the smiling countryside. In the distance the smoke of a cottage rose above the trees.

He started off again, and I followed him in wonder. When we reached the cottage it was easy to learn that the occupant was at a meal, for the strong scent of frying fish came from the open window.

Sholmes knocked at the door.

It was opened by a man in rough attire, wearing very large, heavy boots. He looked suspiciously at Sholmes.

'What's wanted?' he asked gruffly.

Sholmes smiled.

'You are Sir Huckaback Haskerville?' he replied tranquilly.

The man staggered back.

I could not repress a cry of astonishment.

'Sholmes!'

'It is false!' exclaimed the cottager. 'Sir Huckaback Haskerville is dead.'

'My dear Sir Huckaback,' said Sholmes quietly, 'it is useless to deny your identity. But I have come as a friend, not as an enemy. Her ladyship has repented. She confesses her fault. In future, I am assured, she will utter not a single word that could wound your feelings upon the subject of bloaters. Sir Huckaback, be generous. Return to her ladyship, and relieve her breaking heart.'

He wavered.

'Come!' said Sholmes, with a smile. And, after a brief hesitation, the baronet assented.

The wealthy American, Mr Squawk, comes to seek the assistance of Herlock Sholmes in 'The Case of the American Millionaire', *Greyfriars Herald*, 22 January 1916

Sholmes, who speaks American like a native, nodded. As on many previous occasions, his gifts as a linguist stood him in good stead. "Pray give me a few details, Mr. Squawk," he remarked. "You may speak quite freely."

*   *   *

'Sholmes, I am on tenterhooks!' I exclaimed, as the express bore us Londonwards. 'You astonish me anew every day. But this—'

He laughed as he lighted a couple of cigarettes.

'The fact is, Jotson, I am pleased myself,' he said. 'Yet is was very simple.'

'But the police—'

He shrugged his shoulders.

'The police knew that old story of the Bound of the Haskervilles,' he said. 'Yet they never thought of the obvious deduction. The baronet had determined to disappear. By leaving the unmistakable track of number eleven boots to the verge of the chasm he gave the desired impression. A certain ancestor of Sir Huckaback originated the tradition of the Bound of the Haskervilles by clearing that chasm at a single jump. Why should not that trait have descended to the present baronet? That was the theory I worked upon, Jotson. I was perfectly prepared to find that, instead of having fallen into the abyss, Sir Huckaback had repeated the performance of his ancestor by clearing it. Consequently, I searched for him on the other side.

'Wonderful!'

Sholmes smiled.

'I wished to ascertain, Jotson, whether Sir Huckaback had ever shown any trace of inheriting the peculiar bounding powers of his ancestor. I called up his college at Oxford. In five minutes I had learned all I wished to know. Sir Huckaback's reputation, in his college days, was that of the biggest bounder at Oxford. Have you any cocaine about you, Jotson? Thanks!'

And Herlock Sholmes remained in a comatose condition till we arrived at Shaker Street.

ODDS AND ENDS

Enter the initial letter of the odd-man-out in the box at the end of each row and together they will spell out a fictional detective reading downwards.

AUSTRIA HOLLAND MUNICH BELGIUM ☐

NOVEL POEM DRAMA AUTHOR ☐

TULIP IVY CROCUS DAFFODIL ☐

MERSEY THAMES GANGES SEVERN ☐

GRANITE QUARTZ FLINT ROCK ☐

SIX ELEVEN TEN FOUR ☐

TROUT HERRING PLAICE MACKEREL ☐

The Adventure of
the Two Collaborators

J. M. Barrie

Sir Arthur Conan Doyle undoubtedly read many of the parodies of his creation, but apparently most admired one written by his friend J. M. Barrie, author of Peter Pan. *The parody was produced as a direct result of the failure of a play entitled* Jane Annie, *on which Barrie and Doyle had collaborated in 1893. Reminiscing later about the story, called* The Adventure of the Two Collaborators, *Conan Doyle wrote in his* Memories and Adventures *(1924): 'It was really a gay gesture of resignation over the failure we had encountered with a comic opera for which he undertook to write the libretto. I collaborated with him on this, but in spite of our joint efforts the piece fell flat. Whereupon Barrie sent me a rollicking parody on Holmes written on the fly leaf of one of his books . . . [it was] the best of all the numerous parodies.'*

IN bringing to a close the adventures of my friend Sherlock Holmes I am perforce reminded that he never, save on the occasion which, as you will now hear, brought his singular career to an end, consented to act in any mystery which was concerned with persons who made a livelihood by the pen. 'I am not particular about the people I mix among for business purposes,' he would say, 'but at literary characters I draw the line.'

We were in our rooms in Baker Street one evening. I was (I remember) by the centre table writing out 'The Adventures of the Man without a Cork Leg' (which had so puzzled the Royal Society and all the other scientific bodies of Europe), and Holmes was amusing himself with a little revolver practice. It was his custom of a summer evening to fire round my head, just shaving my face, until he had made a photograph of me on the opposite wall, and it is a slight proof of his skill that many of these portraits in pistol shots are considered admirable likenesses.

I happened to look out of the window, and perceiving two gentlemen advancing rapidly along Baker Street asked him who they were. He immediately lit his pipe, and, twisting himself on a chair into the figure 8, replied:

'They are two collaborators in comic opera, and their play has not been a triumph.'

I sprang from my chair to the ceiling in amazement, and he then explained:

My dear Watson, they are obviously men who follow some low calling. That much even you should be able to read in their faces. Those little pieces of blue paper which they fling angrily from them are Durrant's Press Notices. Of these they have obviously hundreds about their person (see how their pockets bulge). They would not dance on them if they were pleasant reading.'

A remarkable photograph of Sir Arthur Conan Doyle and his wife
on a visit to Hollywood and meeting Douglas Fairbanks Snr

I again sprang to the ceiling (which is much dented), and shouted: 'Amazing! but they may be mere authors.'

'No,' said Holmes, 'for mere authors only get one press notice a week. Only criminals, dramatists and actors get them by the hundred.'

'Then they may be actors.'

'No, actors would come in a carriage.'

'Can you tell me anything else about them?'

'A great deal. From the mud on the boots of the tall one I perceive that he comes from South Norwood. The other is as obviously a Scotch author.'

'How can you tell that?'

'He is carrying in his pocket a book called (I clearly see) 'Auld Licht Something'. Would any one but the author be likely to carry about a book with such a title?'

I had to confess that this was improbable.

It was now evident that the two men (if such they can be called) were seeking our lodgings. I have said (often) that my friend Holmes seldom gave way to emotion of any kind, but he now turned livid with passion. Presently this gave place to a strange look of triumph.

'Watson,' he said, 'that big fellow has for years taken the credit for my most remarkable doings, but at last I have him—at last!'

Up I went to the ceiling, and when I returned the strangers were in the room.

'I perceive, gentlemen,' said Mr Sherlock Holmes, 'that you are at present afflicted by an extraordinary novelty.'

The handsomer of our visitors asked in amazement how he knew this, but the big one only scowled.

'You forget that you wear a ring on your fourth finger,' replied Mr Holmes calmly.

I was about to jump to the ceiling when the big brute interposed.

'That Tommy-rot is all very well for the public, Holmes,' said he, 'but you can drop it before me. And, Watson, if you go up to the ceiling again I shall make you stay there.'

Here I observed a curious phenomenon. My Friend Sherlock Holmes *shrank*. He became small before my eyes. I looked longingly at the ceiling, but dared not.

'Let us cut the first four pages,' said the big man, 'and proceed to business. I want to know why—'

'Allow me,' said Mr Holmes, with some of his old courage. 'You want to know why the public does not go to your opera.'

'Exactly,' said the other ironically, 'as you perceive by my shirt stud.' He added more gravely, 'And as you can only find out in one way I must insist on your witnessing an entire performance of the piece.'

It was an anxious moment for me. I shuddered, for I knew that if Holmes went I should have to go with him. But my friend had a heart of gold. 'Never,' he cried fiercely, 'I will do anything for you save that.'

'Your continued existence depends on it,' said the big man menacingly.

'I would rather melt into air,' replied Holmes, proudly taking another chair. 'But I can tell you why the public don't go to your piece without sitting the thing out myself.'

'Why?'

'Because,' replied Holmes calmly, 'they prefer to stay away.'

A dead silence followed that extraordinary remark. For a moment the two intruders gazed with awe upon the man who had unravelled their mystery so wonderfully. Then drawing their knives . . .

Holmes grew less and less, until nothing was left save a ring of smoke which slowly circled to the ceiling.

The last words of great men are often noteworthy. These were the last words of Sherlock Holmes: 'Fool, fool! I have kept you in luxury for years. By my help you have ridden extensively in cabs, where no author was ever seen before. *Henceforth you will ride in buses!'*

The brute sank into a chair aghast.

The other author did not turn a hair.

Sherlock Holmes' 'death'

From Dr David Lunn

Sir, I have a confession to make. My great grandfather, Sir Henry Lunn, founder of the travel business, was the man who murdered Sherlock Holmes. The story, based on little more than family tradition—but one that can be traced back through three generations—is that Conan Doyle and my great grandfather were walking together between Grosse Scheidegg and Meiringen, when Conan Doyle started talking about his wish to get rid of Holmes in order to devote more time to psychical research. "But how can I do it?" he asked. "Throw him over the Reichenbach Falls", replied my great grandfather. "What are they?" "I'll show you", and he did.

Fans of Sherlock Holmes may well wonder if it was the business of a travel agent to send anyone, least of all the best of detectives, to his death. Joking apart, however, there is a bit of circumstantial evidence to support the story: the fact that it was Conan Doyle who persuaded Sir Henry's son, Arnold, then a materialist and sceptical about psychical research, to investigate it fully—advice which led eventually to my grandfather's conversion to, and lifelong defence of, Roman Catholicism. This fact, which does at least establish the connexion between the two families, is recorded in my grandfather's book, *Come What May*, but the story behind it has never, as far as I know, appeared in print.

Yours faithfully,
DAVID LUNN,
58 Granby Hill,
Bristol.

Another theory about Holmes's 'death', from *The Times*,
10 December 1976

[*133*]

HOLMES SWEET HOLMES

Across

5 A Holmes investigation? (4)
7 At original location (anag. of UNIT IS) (2,4)
9 The cinema's 1959 Dr Watson (5,6)
11 Diamonds in the fridge? (3)
12 Tied (7)
15 Following a heavenly path? (2,5)
17 Trades vehicle (3)
19 Sherlock's hat (11)
20 Home to Holmes! (6)
21 Police informer (4)

Down

1 Discerns by sleuthing (7)
2 Deduce (5)
3 Instrument played by Holmes (6)
4 A typical Sherlock Holmes tale (6,5)
6 Acoustic equipment (5)
8 Hounded Doyle family! (11)
10 Accepts into the priesthood (7)
13 Drug taken by Holmes (7)
14 Disconnected, loose (6)
16 221B —— Street (5)
18 County of the 8Down home (5)

The Rivals of Sherlock Holmes

Peter Haining

ASIDE from the parodies of Sherlock Holmes, the Great Detective was soon being more seriously challenged for the public's attention by a plethora of private detectives whose creators intended them to take on the Master at his own game—and beat him. Some were such poor imitators that they disappeared as suddenly as they had appeared, mourned by no one; but others—the more original and exciting figures—survived the inevitable comparisons and indeed became widely popular. Time, however, has treated very few of them as well as Holmes, as the detective-story historian Hugh Greene has remarked, 'The rivals of Sherlock Holmes have remained for too long in the shadow of the Master. Some were honest men; some were crooks; all were formidable. From Holborn to the Temple in the east to Richmond in the west, they dominated the criminal underworld of late Victorian and Edwardian London.' In a modest attempt to set the record straight, I have compiled the following brief Who's Who of the most important of these rivals from England, Europe and America. Most of the novels featuring these characters which are listed in the individual entries are still available at the larger public libraries or through book-dealers specialising in detective fiction.

Sexton Blake: *Detective Weekly*, 20 January 1934

BLAKE, Sexton.   Sometimes referred to as 'the most famous Englishman in the world', Sexton Blake was created in 1893 as an imitation of Sherlock Holmes, complete with similar features (he was tall, had a hawk-like profile and smoked a pipe) and an address in Baker Street. Despite this (or maybe because of it), Blake quickly developed his own following—particularly among younger readers of *The Union Jack*, where his adventures were published until they became separate paperbacks called the *Sexton Blake Library*. More than 4,000 stories were written about him by a string of writers. A prolific magazine writer named Harry Blythe (1852–98) is credited with having created Blake along with his assistant, Tinker, and their long-suffering landlady, Mrs Bardell. The last Sexton Blake story was published in 1963.

BROWN, Father Paul(?).   This quietly spoken, gentle Roman Catholic priest is widely held to be one of the three greatest detectives in literature (Holmes and Poe's C. Auguste Dupin are the other two). Created by the journalist and poet G. K. Chesterton (1874–1936), Father Brown first appeared in 1911 and immediately established himself as unique for he saw his main purpose as being to convert criminals to a more Christian way of life rather than simply bringing them to justice. Although there has always been something of a mystery about Brown's Christian name, it is reliably believed he was based on an Essex clergyman named Father John O'Connor whom Chesterton knew well. Books: *The Innocence of Father Brown* (1911), *The Wisdom of Father Brown* (1914), *The Scandal of Father Brown* (1927), *The Father Brown Omnibus* (1951).

CARRADOS, Max.   A remarkable blind detective who lost his sight as a young man but subsequently developed his other senses to such a degree that he became more than a match for criminals. Carrados has an assistant named Parkinson who acts as his 'eyes', and a seemingly inexhaustible supply of money which enables him to take on cases without requiring a fee. He first appeared in 1914, the creation of Ernest Bramah (1868–1942), a reclusive English author who went to great lengths to conceal details of his life. Books: *Max Carrados* (1914), *The Eyes of Max Carrados* (1923), *Max Carrados Mysteries* (1927), *The Bravo of London* (1934).

CARTER, Nick.   The series of tales featuring Nick Carter are the longest running in the whole detective story genre. First launched in 1886 on his career of crime busting, the young, resourceful Nick is still at large today, but now an older, more sophisticated man serving as a secret agent and with an eye for the women. He was created by a New York magazine publisher named Ormond G. Smith (1860–1933) though his first adventures were written under commission by a freelance author named John Russell Coryell (1848–1924). Thereafter the series was taken up by a string of writers, of whom the most prolific was Frederic Van Rensselaer Day (1861–1922), who is said to have written in excess of a thousand episodes. Despite his change of character, Nick has never lost his physical strength or his mastery of disguise.

NICK CARTER

NICK CARTER IN VARIOUS DISGUISES

DETECTIVE LIBRARY

The Only 5 Cent Detective Library Published.

Entered According to Act of Congress, in the Year 1891, by Street & Smith, in the Office of the Librarian of Congress, Washington, D. C.
Entered as Second-class Matter at the New York Post Office, N. Y., August 8, 1891.   Issued Weekly. Subscription Price, $2.50 per Year.

No. 1.   STREET & SMITH, Publishers,   NEW YORK.   31 Rose St., N. Y. P. O. Box 2734.   5 Cents.

Nick Carter, Detective.
By A Celebrated Author.

Far left, Max Carrados; *left*, Nick Carter; *below*, Father Brown

AREFUL AIM AT

CLAY, Colonel. The Mysterious colonel, a master of disguise and able to transform himself from young man to old veteran with consummate ease, is regarded in crime history as the first detective rogue 'hero'. He appeared in 1897, the creation of a Canadian named Grant Allen (1848–99) who gained considerable notoriety in Victorian times because of his outspoken discussion of sexual matters in his novel, *The Woman Who Did* (1895). He was also a friend of Sir Arthur Conan Doyle, who actually completed one of Allen's novels, *Hilda Wade*, which he had left unfinished at his death. Book: *An African Millionaire* (1897).

CLEEK, Hamilton. Beginning his career as a criminal known as 'The Vanishing Cracksman', Cleek later changed sides to become the scourge of villains, helping Scotland Yard solve many of their most difficult cases. His strange attribute is a rare facial skin condition which allows him to change his features at will and which earned him the title of 'The Man of the Forty Faces'. Created in 1910 by an English-American writer named Thomas W. Hanshew (1857–1914), Cleek is often joined in his adventures by a small boy with the unlikely name of Dollops. Books: *The Man of Forty Faces* (1910), *Cleek of Scotland Yard* (1914), *Cleek's Greatest Riddles* (1916).

Colonel Clay: 'An African Millionaire', 1897.

Hamilton Cleek: 'Cleek of Scotland Yard', 1914

HEWITT, Martin.   Hewitt was the first detective to be created in the wake of Sherlock Holmes's triumphant appearance. Like Holmes, he was published in the *Strand* and his cases were illustrated by Sidney Paget, the first of these in 1894. A former lawyer's clerk turned private detective, Hewitt operated from an office in London and his cases were chronicled by a journalist named Brett. Although he uses similar methods to Holmes, systematically examining all the clues in the case, Hewitt has none of the charisma of the Master, yet still proved enormously popular with the reading public. His creator was Arthur Morrison (1863–1945), a campaigning journalist whose attacks on the terrible conditions in London's East End led to a number of important social reforms. Books: *Martin Hewitt, Investigator* (1894), *The Chronicles of Martin Hewitt* (1895), *The Adventures of Martin Hewitt* (1896), *The Red Triangle* (1903).

KENNEDY, Craig.   Known as 'The American Sherlock Holmes', Kennedy appeared in 1912 and is regarded as one of the first and most popular scientific detectives. He is like Holmes in that he has a profound knowledge of chemistry and is also a master of disguise. Created by Arthur B. Reeve (1880–1936), who studied to become a lawyer but instead turned to journalism, Craig Kennedy is accompanied by a Watson-like chronicler named Walter Jameson and often gives assistance to the hard-pressed Inspector Barney O'Connor of the New York Police Department. Books: *The Silent Bullet* (1912), *The War Terror* (1915), *The Social Gangster* (1916), *The Panama Plot* (1918), *Craig Kennedy Listens In* (1923).

Martin Hewitt:
'The Lenton Croft Robberies'
Strand, 1894

"From somewhere in the depths of that great hotel came a wailing cry."
Craig Kennedy: 'The Death Cry',
Weird Tales, 1935

LUPIN, Arsène.   A bold and handsome rogue, Lupin is known as 'The Prince of Thieves' and is a constant thorn in the flesh of the French police until, tiring of the criminal life, he becomes a private detective. Created in 1907 by a former court reporter and playwright, Maurice Leblanc (1864–1941), Lupin is a man of many identities and aliases as he plots and carries out one audacious crime after another under the noses of the authorities. He is often helped in these adventures by a gang of ruffians and small urchins. His only real equal in the realms of crime fiction is probably the English master-criminal, Raffles. Books: *The Exploits of Arsène Lupin* (1907), *Arsène Lupin versus Holmlock Shears* (1908), *The Confessions of Arsène Lupin* (1912), *The Memoirs of Arsène Lupin* (1925).

NIKOLA, Dr.   A sinister and ruthless master-criminal who for a time enjoyed the same kind of notoriety among readers as did Professor Moriarty. Dr Nikola was created by Guy Boothby (1867–1905), an Australian-born writer who moved to England in 1894 and produced almost fifty novels in the remaining eleven years of his life. Following Nikola's appearance in 1895, a major advertising campaign was mounted by his publishers and pictures of him by the popular artist Stanley Wood were 'splashed all over London', to quote one contemporary report. He was allegedly based on a real man, Dr McGregor Reed, who had stood unsuccessfully for election to both the United States Senate and the House of Commons and lived to be 91. Books: *A Bid for Fortune* (1895), *Doctor Nikola* (1896), *The Lust of Hate* (1898), *Dr Nikola's Experiment* (1899), *Farewell Nikola* (1901).

RAFFLES, A. J.   Considered by several authorities as the greatest cracksman in the literature of roguery, Raffles is a mixture of gentleman, criminal and thrill-seeker who, with his faithful companion and chronicler Bunny Manders, has become one of the immortals of crime fiction. His masterly planning and ice-cool nerve enable him to move freely among the gentry from whom he steals, while his distinguished bearing and charming personality completely disarm the officers of the law. Raffles was created in 1899 by E. W. Hornung (1866–1921), a writer of outstanding imagination who was also a friend of Conan Doyle and married his sister, Constance. The adventures of the cracksman have been filmed several times, with Ronald Colman and David Niven respectively in the title rôle, and the series has also been continued since Hornung's death by Barry Perowne (1908–   ) in the popular British magazine, *The Thriller*, and latterly in *Ellery Queen's Mystery Magazine*. Books: (By Hornung) *The Amateur Cracksman* (1899), *The Black Mask* (1901), *Mr Justice Raffles* (1909). (By Perowne) *Raffles After Dark* (1933), *Raffles v. Sexton Blake* (1937), *Raffles Revisited: New Adventures of a Famous Gentleman Crook* (1974).

Top, Dr Nikola: 'The Lust of Hate', 1898; *left*, Raffles: 'The Thriller', 1933; *right*, Arsene Lupin: 'The Black Pearl', 1934; *bottom right*, Rouletabille: 'The Mystery of the Yellow Room', 1907

ROULETABILLE, Joseph.   A precocious young French amateur detective who makes his entrance in *The Mystery of the Yellow Room* (1907), the first 'Locked room mystery' in which a seemingly impossible crime is committed inside a sealed chamber. Rouletabille's cases are described by his chronicler, a man named Sainclair, who is invariably baffled by the young man's powers of insight. He was created by the prolific French journalist and mystery writer, Gaston Leroux (1868–1927), whose most famous work is *The Phantom of the Opera* (1911), which has been filmed several times. Books: *The Mystery of the Yellow Room* (1907), *The Perfume of the Lady in Black* (1909).

THORNDYKE, Dr John.   Without doubt the most painstaking of sleuths, Dr Thorndyke, who is both a forensic scientist and a lawyer, has been described as 'the greatest medico-legal detective of all time'. Certainly his ability to deduce evidence from the tiniest clues, combined with his deep knowledge of a whole range of subjects from anatomy to Egyptology, enables him to bring formidable skills to bear on his cases. Thorndyke made his first appearance in 1907 and was created by R. Austin Freeman (1862–1943), an accomplished medical man himself who was forced to abandon his practice as a surgeon due to failing health brought about by years spent in Africa. Dr Thorndyke is well served in all his cases by his two assistants, Christopher Jervis, who recounts the adventures, and Nathaniel Polton, his ingenious butler, driver and laboratory assistant. A particular feature of the Thorndyke series is the illustrating of the tiny clues which invariably help the Doctor solve the mystery and thereby giving the reader an equal chance of drawing the same conclusions ahead of him. (A typical example is shown here.) Books: *The Red Thumb Mark* (1907), *John Thorndyke's Cases* (1909), *The Singing Bone* (1912), *Dr Thorndyke's Casebook* (1923), *A Certain Dr Thorndyke* (1927), *Dr Thorndyke Intervenes* (1933), *The Best Dr Thorndyke Detective Stories* (1973).

VAN DUSEN, Professor Augustus S. F. X.   Known as 'The Thinking Machine', Professor Van Dusen solves his cases by pure logic, rarely stirring from the Boston college where he lectures. All the evidence and clues relating to the crime in which he is interested are assembled by his aide, a reporter named Hutchinson Hutch, and he then applies his powers of deduction to solving the mystery. Van Dusen is unlike virtually all the other famous detectives in that he is small, almost dwarfish, pale and thin, and peers constantly from behind thick glasses. He was created in 1906 by a remarkable American named Jaques Futrelle (1875–1912) a one-time theatrical manager and journalist who died heroically during the sinking of the *Titanic*. Books: *The Chase of the Golden Plate* (1906), *The Thinking Machine* (1907), *The Thinking Machine on the Case* (1908), *The Best Thinking Machine Detective Stories* (1973).

Professor Van Dusen: 'The Thinking Machine', 1907

Dr Thorndyke, assistants, and an important clue: 'The Blue Diamond Mystery', *Pearson's Magazine*, 1923

From The Diary of Sherlock Holmes

Maurice Baring

Although a great many writers have attempted to create new Adventures of Sherlock Holmes as they might have been told by Dr Watson, very few indeed have tried to put themselves into the shoes of the Great Detective himself. The first, and arguably still the best of such pastiches, is the item which follows by Maurice Baring, published in THE EYE-WITNESS *of 23 November 1911. This peep into Holmes's diary reveals two unsuccessful cases which Holmes evidently feels are more interesting than his usual triumphs. . . .*

Baker Street, January 1.—Starting a diary in order to jot down a few useful incidents which will be of no use to Watson. Watson very often fails to see that an unsuccessful case is more interesting from a professional point of view than a successful case. He means well.

January 6.—Watson has gone to Brighton for a few days, for change of air. This morning quite an interesting little incident happened which I note as a useful example of how sometimes people who have no powers of deduction nevertheless stumble on the truth for the wrong reason. (This never happens to Watson, *fortunately*.) Lestrade called from Scotland Yard with reference to the theft of a diamond and ruby ring from Lady Dorothy Smith's wedding presents. The facts of the case were briefly these: On Thursday evening such of the presents as were jewels had been brought down from Lady Dorothy's bedroom to the drawing-room to be shown to an admiring group of friends. The ring was amongst them. After they had been shown, the jewels were taken upstairs once more and locked in the safe. The next morning the ring was missing. Lestrade, after investigating the matter, came to the conclusion that the ring had not been stolen, but had either been dropped in the drawing-room, or replaced in one of the other cases; but since he had searched the room and the remaining cases, his theory so far received no support. I accompanied him to Eaton Square to the residence of Lady Middlesex, Lady Dorothy's mother.

While we were engaged in searching the drawing-room, Lestrade uttered a cry of triumph and produced the ring from the lining of the arm-chair. I told him he might enjoy the triumph, but that the matter was not quite so simple as he seemed to think. A glance at the ring had shown me not only that the stones were false, but that the false ring had been made in a hurry. To deduce the name of its maker was of course child's play. Lestrade or any pupil of Scotland Yard would have taken for granted it was the same jeweller who had made the real ring. I asked for the bridegroom's present, and in a short time I was interviewing the jeweller who had provided it. As I thought, he had made a ring, with imitation stones (made of the dust of real stones), a week ago, for a young lady. She had given no name and had fetched and paid for it herself. I deduced the obvious fact that Lady Dorothy had lost the real ring, her uncle's gift, and, not daring to say so, had had an imitation ring made. I returned to the house, where I found Lestrade, who had called to make arrangements for watching the presents during their exhibition.

I asked for Lady Dorothy, who at once said to me:

'The ring was found yesterday by Mr. Lestrade.'

'I know,' I answered, 'But which ring?'

She could not repress a slight twitch of the eyelids as she said: 'There was only one ring.'

I told her of my discovery and of my investigations.

'This is a very odd coincidence, Mr. Holmes,' she said. 'Some one else must have ordered an imitation. But you shall examine my ring for yourself.' Whereupon she fetched the ring, and I saw it was no imitation. She had of course in the meantime found the real ring.

But to my intense annoyance she took it to Lestrade and said to him:

'Isn't this the ring you found yesterday, Mr. Lestrade?'

Lestrade examined it and said, 'Of course it is absolutely identical in every respect.'

'And do you think it is an imitation?' asked this most provoking young lady.

'Certainly not,' said Lestrade, and turning to me he added: 'Ah! Holmes, that is where theory leads one. At the Yard we go in for facts.'

I could say nothing; but as I said good-bye to Lady Dorothy, I congratulated her on having found the real ring. The incident, although it proved the correctness of my reasoning, was vexing as it gave that ignorant blunderer an opportunity of crowing over me.

January 10. — A man called just as Watson and I were having breakfast. He didn't give his name. He asked me if I knew who he was. I said, 'Beyond seeing that you are unmarried, that you have travelled up this morning from Sussex, that you have served in the French Army, that you write for reviews, and are especially interested in the battles of the Middle Ages, that you give lectures, that you are a Roman Catholic, and that you have once been to Japan, I don't know who you are.'

The man replied that he *was* unmarried, but that he lived in Manchester, that he had never been to Sussex or Japan, that he had never written a line in his life, that he had never served in any army save the English Territorial force, that so far from being a Roman Catholic he was a Freemason, and that he was by trade an electrical engineer—I suspected him of lying; and I asked him why his boots were covered with the clayey and chalk mixture peculiar to Horsham; why his boots were French Army service boots, elastic-sided, and bought probably at Valmy; why the second half of a return ticket from Southwater was emerging from his ticket-pocket; why he wore the medal of St. Anthony on his watch-chain; why he smoked Caporal cigarettes; why the proofs of an article on the Battle of Eylau were protruding from his breast-pocket, together with a copy of the *Tablet*; why he carried in his hand a parcel which, owing to the untidy way in which it had been made (an untidiness which, in harmony with the rest of his clothes, showed that he could not be married) revealed the fact that it contained photographic magic lantern slides; and why he was tattooed on the left wrist with a Japanese fish.

'The reason I have come to consult you will explain some of these things,' he answered.

'I was staying last night at the Windsor Hotel, and this morning when I woke up I found an entirely different set of clothes from my own. I called the waiter and pointed this out, but neither the waiter nor any of the other servants, after making full enquiries, were able to account for the change. None of the other occupants of the hotel had complained of anything being wrong with their own clothes.

'Two gentlemen had gone out early from the hotel at 7:30. One of them had left for good, the other was expected to return.

All the belongings I am wearing, including this parcel, which contains slides, belong to someone else.

'My own things contained nothing valuable, and consisted of clothes and boots very similar to these; my coat was also stuffed with papers. As to the tattoo, it was done at a Turkish bath by a shampooer, who learnt the trick in the Navy.'

The case did not present any features of the slightest interest. I merely advised the man to return to the hotel and await the real owner of the clothes, who was evidently the man who had gone out at 7:30.

This is a case of my reasoning being, with one partial exception, perfectly correct. Everything I had deduced would no doubt have fitted the real owner of the clothes.

Watson asked rather irrelevantly why I had not noticed that the clothes were not the man's own.

A stupid question, as the clothes were reach-me-downs which fitted him as well as such clothes ever do fit, and he was probably of the same build as their rightful owner.

January 12.—Found a carbuncle of unusual size in the plum-pudding. Suspected the makings of an interesting case. But luckily, before I had stated any hypothesis to Watson—who was greatly excited—Mrs. Turner came in and noticed it and said her naughty nephew Bill had been at his tricks again, and that the red stone had come from a Christmas tree. Of course, I had not examined the stone with my lens.

An Encounter in Central Park

Basil Rathbone

The total number of films made from the Adventures of Sherlock Holmes from the early years of this century until the present time now runs into several hundreds. (There were over a hundred silent films alone, for example.) Naturally, there has been considerable debate as to which actor portrayed the Great Detective most realistically and accurately on the screen. A large number of people award the honour to British actor Basil Rathbone, who made a famous series of twelve pictures as Holmes for Universal Pictures in the 1930s. Rathbone's classic features and resonant voice, combined with his precise acting style, certainly made him an ideal Holmes, and he was well supported by the fine character actor Nigel Bruce as Dr Watson. Rathbone was also something of an expert on the stories, and in April 1954 wrote the following short item about perhaps the most extraordinary encounter anyone who believes in the world of Sherlock Holmes might hope to have.

GOODBYE, my friend. I am glad to have had this opportunity to talk with you.'

He rose from the park bench beside me and lit a cigarette. A thin wisp of smoke was caught by a gust of cold wind and quickly disappeared into oblivion. A few dead leaves rustled by, turning over and over mechanically, and then lay still for a moment, as if to listen to his parting words . . . "Never regret anything you have attempted with a sincere affection. Nothing is lost that is born of the heart.'

The distant sound of children playing mingled inexplicably with excerpts from Schubert's Ninth Symphony . . . not so inexplicably, perhaps, since a recording of this great work had so often accompanied my personal studies in preparation for the play that had just closed . . .

It is my custom to take long walks in Central Park whenever the weather permits. The autumn of 1953 had been more beautiful than any I can remember for many years. Day after day, and week after week, a soft sunlight had enveloped the city with many varying colours. The air was crisp and invigorating. The trees shed their leaves with a calm and patient resignation; then stood naked and strong to sleep peacefully in the promise of spring. It was indeed difficult to associate the perils of our times with one's instinct to accept, without reservation, Robert Browning's unique expression of faith, 'God's in his heaven, all's right with the world.'

One afternoon in mid-November I paused in my walk to sit down on a park bench and empty my mind of everything but the pervading beauty about me. It may be that I dozed off. Of this I cannot be certain. There was still the sound of children playing; of this I am sure: and together with the

Schubert Ninth there was woven a delicious pattern of half-forgotten memories through my reveries. Suddenly I had a feeling that someone was looking at me. I opened my eyes slowly and with caution, to become aware of a man seated on the bench beside me. He was not looking directly at me, but with a sidelong glance that could have been disregarded had I so wished. It was a quizzical look from a face I seemed to remember. Since my instinct is always to enter into conversation with anyone who indicates the slightest interest in me (a normal curiosity and an expression of one's ego prevailing on such occasions) I turned slightly toward him. 'What a day!' I said. To which he replied with a long-drawn-out and somewhat hesitant 'Ye-e-s-s!'

He not only intrigued my curiosity and my ego, but he also startled in me a vague sense of remembrance. Where have I seen that face before? I thought to myself. He was a large man, at least six feet tall, immaculately dressed in clothes that had obviously been well cared for; for their style indicated that they had been tailored in the early part of the century. He wore a 'bowler' hat of a kind I had not seen since I was a very little boy, and soft-topped button boots. From a round, well-tanned face there twinkled two pale-blue eyes that seemed to belie his age, for there was no question in my mind that he was very old.

Without looking my way he said suddenly, 'Is your name Rathbone?'

'Yes,' I replied.

He turned to me and held out his hand.

'How do you do? My name is Watson. *John* Watson.'

Taking his hand, I ventured, 'What a curious coincidence!'

'Coincidence?'

'Yes.'

'Why?' And his whole face took part in a most provocative smile.

'Well, it's an unusual name . . . and . . .'

'Not at all,' he interrupted. 'There are 15 John Watsons in the New York telephone book.'

'. . . and associated for me,' I continued, 'and many others, I imagine, with the famous Dr John Watson, who chronicled the adventures of Sherlock Holmes.'

'I knew him well,' said my companion, softly.

'Who? . . . Sherlock Holmes!'

He nodded his head in a firm assent. 'We-e-l-l,' I said, without looking up.

During the pause that followed, I found myself wondering just how far the game would go before one of us became bored and decided to go home.

'Of course I knew Dr Watson even better,' he went on. And at this he laughed heartily. Then suddenly he turned, and quite seriously he added: 'I don't expect you to believe me. Why should you?'

To which *I* replied, instinctively and with equal sincerity: 'One is more inclined to believe than to disbelieve the unusual.'

Again the voices of children playing to the accompaniment of the Symphony . . . the rustle of leaves as a soft breath of wind brushed gently across my face . . . I heard his voice again.

'I saw your play a few nights ago. I'm sorry it had to come off.'

'Did you like it?' I turned to him.

In the pause that followed, I noticed that the laughter had left his eyes, and his mouth assumed a petulance that surprised me.

'You shouldn't ask questions like that,' he said at last.

'Why not? It seems natural enough to me.'

'It wasn't what you said. It was the way you said it.'

'I'm sorry, sir, but I don't understand.'

Without looking at me he continued. 'Forgive me. I'm a very old man. Even as a young man I was a slow thinker. In my old age I am virtually at a standstill.' A smile crept slowly back into his eyes. 'I hope you will forgive me if I don't answer your question, for two reasons. We could *both* be hurt, under the circumstances, by almost anything I might say.' He paused again for a moment. Then it seemed to me he went on with some difficulty.

'The tone in your voice suggested to me your need for consolation. But I am afraid I would find it difficult to talk to you about anything so extremely personal to us both . . . I was educated in a school and at a time that gave early priority to self-discipline. One sought for consolation within one's self rather than from others. To be truthful with one's self was one's only criterion of success. If you have been truthful with yourself in this play, you have been successful with it.'

I felt no desire to interrupt him in any way whatsoever. A deep peace of understanding, and of gratitude to him, consumed my whole being.

'For my part,' he continued, 'I find your theatre of today too much concerned with the problems that emanate from a major world revolution that first showed its purpose and direction in 1914, and will probably continue for another fifty years. Of course, at my age, it is impossible for me to adjust myself to an era of atomic energy and purely material progress . . . and which has so little time for autumn leaves, the scent of a rose, and the eternal promise of spring. Your theatre is earth-bound, my friend. It lacks reverence for the unknown, and the simplest and most beautiful of all human relationships—love.'

I could resist it no longer: I had to look at him. And I was much disturbed to see that the petulant quality had crept back into his mouth, and to hear an odd harshness in his voice. 'In my young days I wanted to be a writer, a great writer,' he said. And as he continued his mouth lost its petulance and his voice grew soft again.

'But I had to compromise with myself because I needed money . . . and I was associated for many years with a man of incredible talents. I was devoted to him, but he absorbed me completely. I don't think I ever quite found myself . . . Never compromise, my friend, if it's humanly possible. And never regret anything you have attempted with a sincere affection. Nothing

Basil Rathbone—best of all the screen Sherlock Holmes

is lost that is born of the heart.'

He rose slowly to his feet. His back was turned to me. A huge back, with slightly stooping shoulders. He lit a cigarette. I closed my eyes. I didn't want to look at him again for fear it might not be true. I sat very still for quite some time. . . .

Yes, there it was again—the laughter of children, the soft wind on my face, the rustle of leaves, and that ever-recurring theme from the Schubert Ninth. When I opened my eyes—only minutes had passed, surely!—the sky to the west was multi-coloured from the setting sun, and one little cloud hung like a pink feather from some gigantic flamingo.

Douglas Wilmer, a well-known British actor, was an impressive Holmes in the BBC Television presentation of 'The Illustrious Client' in 1964

Mycroft Holmes: Private Detective

J. Randolph Cox

Although he appeared only briefly in four of the Sherlock Holmes stories, Mycroft Holmes, his elder brother, has long attracted the interest and study of Sherlockians. A number of theories have been advanced about his life—including the claim that he was a superior detective to Sherlock!—but perhaps the most intriguing of all these essays is that which follows. For it links Mycroft with one of his brother's most famous rivals. It appeared in THE BAKER STREET JOURNAL *of October, 1956.*

AROUND the corner from Whitehall, where the British Foreign Office is located, is Pall Mall, the site of the unique and little-known Diogenes Club. And just opposite to the Diogenes Club are the rooms which once belonged to Sherlock Holmes's older brother, Mycroft. Very little is known about Mycroft outside of what Sherlock himself told Watson in 'The Greek Interpreter', and the observations of Watson in both this and the later adventure of 'The Bruce-Partington Plans'. We know that he was seven years older than Sherlock, that he was by far the better of the two in powers of observation, and that occasionally he *was* the British Government. Beyond this we know very little, except for a few statements about his physical appearance and his lack of ambition and energy.

But was he always lacking in ambition and energy? I think not. Wasn't he able to muster enough to forego his usual habits and travel to his brother's rooms, to say nothing of the trip back, when the occasion warranted it? What he was able to do then he must have been able to do in his younger days before he obtained his high position in the British government. And what was he before his brain was put to work for the government? It must certainly have been something that would call attention to his capabilities in such a way as to make the government call on him.

My theory is that he had set himself up as a private consultant, much as his brother did. But where is the record of such a business? Or is there a record at all?

There is such a record, but until now it has been thought by everyone to be fiction. The early cases of Mycroft Holmes are neatly filed away in four volumes which were published shortly after Watson began his biography of Sherlock. These early episodes are in the guise of a series of short stories

Martin Hewitt—Mycroft
Holmes in disguise? An
illustration by Sidney Paget of
Hewitt at work in 'The Case of
the Dixon Torpedo', *Strand*,
1894

Mycroft Holmes greeting
his younger brother in
'The Adventure of the
Greek Interpreter', *Strand*,
1893

Mycroft Holmes and his chronicler, Professor Mustie, illustrated by Enid Schantz, for 'The Resources of Mycroft Holmes' by Charlton Andrews (1973)

Christopher Lee, the only actor to have played both Sherlock Holmes and his brother Mycroft on the screen. Lee was Mycroft in

'The Private Life Sherlock Holmes' 19 (*left*) and Sherlock 'Sherlock Holmes an the Deadly Necklace 1962 (*right*

about a former law clerk named *Martin Hewitt*.

I first suspected it when I noticed a slight resemblance between Sidney Paget's drawing of Mycroft in *The Strand* and the Paget drawings in the Ward, Lock edition of *Martin Hewitt, Investigator*. But there is more to this than a mere physical resemblance. Observe the similarity between the mental capacities of the young 'Hewitt' and the older Mycroft:

'This is one of the twenty thousand tiny things that few people take the trouble to notice, but which it is useful for a man in my position to know.'[1]
'He has the tidiest and most orderly brain, with the greatest capacity for storing facts, of any man living.'[2]

The two of them were both able to retain the smallest details, although Hewitt's abilities were less accomplished than Mycroft's, due, it is to be realized, to his youth and inexperience.

There is hardly any problem in proper chronology, as far as a relationship between the two sets of tales, since Watson first heard of Mycroft in 1889 or 1890 and the only positive date listed in the Hewitt books[3] is 1879. Hewitt's biographer, a journalist named Brett, says in 'The Affair of the Tortoise' that the events occurred 'some time before my acquaintance with him began—in 1879, in fact.' Thus 'Hewitt', or Mycroft, was working before Sherlock met Watson and set up headquarters in Baker Street. The last case young Hewitt had worked on for the law firm of Crellan, Hunt, and Crellan took place, according to 'The Lenton Croft Robberies', 'fifteen or twenty years back.' *Martin Hewitt, Investigator* came out in 1894, which would place his beginnings as a private investigator between 1874 and 1879.

'The Affair of the Tortoise' is evidently not Hewitt's first case, since Inspector Nettings seems to know Hewitt by reputation rather than otherwise. ('Perhaps you can spot something we have overlooked, and You're not instructed to act for any one in the case, are you?'). He must have had a few successes before the events in this particular case, and he therefore began his career as an investigator two or three years prior to 1879. It is hard to tell whether the inspector's tone of voice is serious or not in the above quotations. If he isn't in a particularly serious mood it might give the impression that Hewitt had only had a very few cases before the one concerning the tortoise.

During Hewitt's career he is always depicted as being rather young. Brett describes him in 'The Lenton Croft Robberies' as 'a young clerk in the employ of Messrs. Crellan.' This was in 1874, when Mycroft was twenty-seven and his brother Sherlock was twenty, and was about to make his own choice of a career. Late in 1874, then, or early in 1875, Martin Hewitt began his work as a private detective. Several of the episodes in the Hewitt tetralogy occurred before Brett appeared on the scene, which was probably in 1880 or even 1881. It couldn't have been later than this for several reasons. The episodes concerning Brett are about as numerous as those that don't, and it is difficult to say which occurred before his time and which were merely ones he did not hear about until later. Hewitt and Brett were never as close as Sherlock Holmes and Dr. Watson, and he may have preferred to handle most of his cases alone.

Since the time of Mycroft's government service could not have begun much later than 1885[4] he could not have been acquainted with Brett for a shorter period than four or five years, or for much more than that either.

The statement by Hewitt, 'You have known something of me and my doings for some years,'[5] doesn't necessarily mean that Brett had been concerned with all of these 'doings'. Brett speaks of their acquaintance having lasted 'many years', but nowhere does he say that most of those years encompassed his private detective profession. It becomes apparent that in none of the stories are the two very close friends, and it is not until much later that Hewitt trusts him enough to let him write anything about his affairs. Therefore, the time during which Brett knew him as a detective was relatively short, even supposing that he had nothing to do with most of the cases recorded.

Sometime in 1885, then 'Martin Hewitt' closed his office and turned to Whitehall and the Foreign Office. What made him take this step isn't certain. Perhaps his success in such affairs as 'The Case of the Dixon Torpedo' and the intrigue of the 'Red Triangle' episodes made him decide in favor of a government career, or it might even have been patriotism. The rest is easily figured out from the two stories in the Canon about Mycroft and his brother. The government realized from his past record that here was a man with a mind capable of sorting out and interpreting their data. 'They began by using him as a short-cut, a convenience; now he has made himself an essential.'[6]

And shortly before the Bruce-Partington affair he evidently gave his old friend, Brett, permission to publish the reminiscences of his earlier exploits. This was agreed to only on the condition that Brett give him another name in place of his own. The reason for this was perhaps the same which led him to found the Diogenes Club, that strange league who 'some from shyness, some from misanthropy' had no wish for the company of their fellows. Sherlock himself was inclined to be unsociable at times, and his brother was even more so. After his retirement as a private detective he withdrew to the company of men who shared his opinions on the proper places to be sociable. Yet he attained the fame he refused to allow Brett to give him in earlier life when he was introduced to Dr. Watson and took his place in the saga of another great man named Holmes.

[1] 'The Case of Mr. Foggatt', *Martin Hewitt, Investigator*. London: Ward, Lock & Co.
[2] 'The Bruce-Partington Plans'.
[3] Barring the *Adventures of Martin Hewitt*, which I have failed to unearth in any condition.
[4] He apparently had been working for the British Government several years at the time of GREE.
[5] BRUC
[6] GREE.

'You Know My Methods, Apply Them!'

Fifteen questions devised by John Bennet Shaw as a qualifying examination for would-be American Sherlockians. The answer to each question or statement is the title of one of the sixty cases in the canon. (Answers are to be found at the back of the book.)

1. The specialist in internal medicine recognized at once that the patient suffered from a liver related ailment.

   _____

2. A terribly deformed boldily member which, if very painful and if the podiatrist failed to help, one might attribute to diabolical causes.

   _____

3. The psychiatrist decided early in the interview that the patient suffered from some form of amnesia.

   _____

4. If Holmes's actions in this case were for real, Watson would summon a coroner.

   _____

5. If a beloved and very ill pet did this you would fear it was too late for the veterinarian.

   _____

6. A prosthodontist would be most likely to think of this case-history.

   _____

7. This boil, even if artificially coloured, would concern a dermatologist.

   _____

8. The very appearance of this patient would cause most members of the medical profession to think he might have been the victim of malpractice.

   _____

9. The injured hydrologist went to a plastic surgeon for help.

   _____

10. If this were the only way you could get about, you would consult an orthopaedist.

_____

11. This person would consult a plastic surgeon.

_____

12. A remains, badly mangled, brought to a pathologist for examination would make one think of this Watsonian tale.

_____

13. This case mentioned the part of one's anatomy that early on would concern both an obstetrician and a pediatrician.

_____

14. Which of Watson's titles causes one to think of an ophthalmologist.

_____

15. If a famous French statesman hurries obviously in great pain to a urologist you might assume he suffers from this.

_____

Original drawing by Sidnet Paget for the climactic moment of 'The Hound of the Baskervilles', _Strand_ 1902

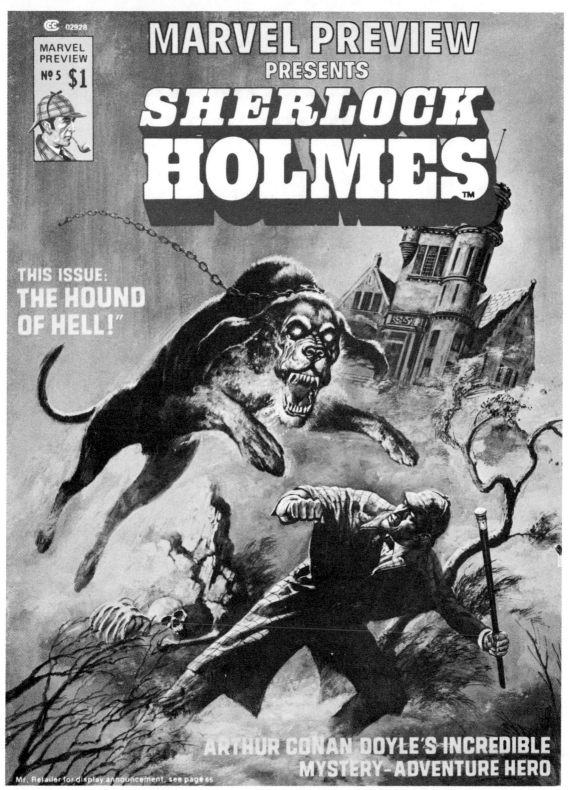

The same dramatic moment from 'The Hound of the Baskervilles'
more than seventy years later—Ken Barr's superb cover illustration for the Marvel Comic's version of the story

From A Detective's Notebook

P. G. Wodehouse

P. G. Wodehouse was a Sherlock Holmes enthusiast, although he confessed to being continually amused by the amazing theories put forward about the life of the Great Detective. On the hundredth anniversary of the birth of Sir Arthur Conan Doyle he set out to top them all in this essay for PUNCH *of 20 May, 1959.*

WE were sitting round the club fire, old General Malpus, Driscoll the QC, young Freddie ffinch-ffinch and myself, when Adrian Mulliner, the private investigator, gave a soft chuckle. This was, of course, in the smoking-room, where soft chuckling is permitted.

'I wonder,' he said, 'if it would interest you chaps to hear the story of what I always look upon as the greatest triumph of my career?'

We said No, it wouldn't, and he began.

'Looking back over my years as a detective, I recall many problems the solution of which made me modestly proud, but though all of them undoubtedly presented certain features of interest and tested my powers to the utmost, I can think of none of my feats of ratiocination which gave me more pleasure than the unmasking of the man Sherlock Holmes, now better known as the Fiend of Baker Street.'

Here General Malpus looked at his watch, said 'Bless my soul,' and hurried out, no doubt to keep some appointment which had temporarily slipped his mind.

'I had at first so little to go on,' Adrian Mulliner proceeded. 'But just as a brief sniff at a handkerchief or shoe will start one of Mr. Thurber's bloodhounds giving quick service, so is the merest suggestion of anything that I might call fishy enough to set me off on the trail, and what first aroused my suspicions of this sinister character was his peculiar financial position.

'Here we had a man who evidently was obliged to watch the pennies closely, for when we are introduced to him he is, according to Doctor Watson's friend Stamford, "bemoaning himself because he could not find someone to go halves with him in some nice rooms which he had found and which were too much for his purse." Watson offers himself as a fellow

An illustration from a rare piece of Sherlockiana: 'Sherlock Holmes in Peril of Death' (1902) a novel by Dutchman Owen Glens 'adapted from the play by Conan Doyle and William Gillette'. This picture shows Professor Moriarty in his underground office and was drawn by A. Rovers

Another A. Rovers illustration from 'Sherlock Holmes in Peril of Death', showing Holmes questioning Moriarty at gunpoint

lodger, and they settle down in—I quote—"a couple of comfortable bedrooms and a large sitting-room at 221B Baker Street."

'Now I never lived in Baker Street at the turn of the century, but I knew old gentlemen who had done so, and they assured me that in those days you could get a bedroom and sitting-room and three meals a day for a pound a week. An extra bedroom no doubt made the thing come higher, but thirty shillings must have covered the rent, and there was never a question of a man as honest as Doctor Watson failing to come up with his fifteen each Saturday. It followed, then, that even allowing for expenditure in the way of Persian slippers, tobacco, disguises, revolver cartridges, cocaine and spare fiddle-strings, Holmes would have been getting by on a couple of pounds or so weekly. And with this modest state of life he appeared to be perfectly content. In a position where you or I would have spared no effort to add to our resources he simply did not bother about the financial side of his profession. Let us take a few instances at random and see what he made as a "consulting detective." Where are you going, Driscoll?'

'Out,' said the Q.C., suiting action to the word.

Adrian Mulliner resumed his tale.

'In the early days of their association Watson speaks of being constantly bundled off into his bedroom because Holmes needed the sitting-room for interviewing callers. "I have to use this room as a place of business," he said, "and these people are my clients." And who were these clients? "A grey-headed, seedy visitor, who was closely followed by a slipshod elderly woman," and after these came "a railway porter in his velveteen uniform." Not much cash in that lot, and things did not noticeably improve later, for we find his services engaged by a stenographer, an average commonplace British tradesman, a commissionaire, a City clerk, a Greek interpreter, a landlady ("You arranged an affair for a lodger of mine last year") and a Cambridge undergraduate.

'So far from making money as a consulting detective, he must have been a good deal out of pocket most of the time. In *A Study in Scarlet* Inspector Gregson says there has been a bad business during the night at 3 Lauriston Gardens off the Brixton Road and he would esteem it a great kindness if Holmes would favour him with his opinions. Off goes Holmes in a hansom from Baker Street to Brixton, a fare of several shillings, dispatches a long telegram (another two or three bob to the bad), summons "half a dozen of the dirtiest and most ragged street Arabs that ever I clapped eyes on," and gives each of them a shilling, and finally, calling on Police Constable Bunce, the officer who discovered the body, takes half a sovereign from his pocket and after "playing with it pensively" presents it to the constable. The whole affair must have cost him considerably more than a week's rent at Baker Street, and no hope of getting it back from Inspector Gregson, for Gregson, according to Holmes himself, was one of the smartest of the Scotland Yarders.

'Inspector Gregson! Inspector Lestrade! These clients! I found myself thinking a good deal about them, and it was not long before the truth dawned upon me that they were merely cheap actors, hired to deceive Doctor Watson. For what would the ordinary private investigator have said to himself when starting out in business? He would have said "Before I take on work for a client I must be sure that that client has the stuff. The daily sweetener and the little something down in advance are of the essence," and would have had those landladies and those Greek interpreters out of that sitting-room before you could say "blood-stain." Yet Holmes, who could not afford a pound a week for lodgings, never bothered. Significant?'

On what seemed to me the somewhat shallow pretext that he had to see a man about a dog, Freddie ffinch-ffinch now excused himself and left the room.

'Later,' Adrian Mulliner went on 'the thing became absolutely farcical, for all pretence that he was engaged in a gainful occupation was dropped by himself and the clients. I quote Doctor Watson: "He tossed a crumpled letter across to me. It was dated from Montague Place upon the preceding evening and ran thus:

DEAR MR. HOLMES,—I am very anxious to consult you as to whether or not

I should accept a situation which has been offered me as a governess. I shall call at half past ten to-morrow if I do not inconvenience you.

Yours faithfully,

VIOLET HUNTER."

'Now, the fee an investigator could expect from a governess, even one in full employment, could scarcely be more than a few shillings, yet when two weeks later Miss Hunter wired "PLEASE BE AT THE BLACK SWAN HOTEL AT WINCHESTER AT MIDDAY TO-MORROW", Holmes dropped everything and sprang into the 9.30 train.'

Adrian Mulliner paused and chuckled softly.

'You see where all this is heading?'

I said No, I didn't. I was the only one there, and had to say something.

'Tut, tut, man! You know my methods. Apply them. Why is a man casual about money?'

'Because he has a lot of it.'

'Precisely.'

'But you said Holmes hadn't.'

'I said nothing of the sort. That was merely the illusion he was trying to create.'

'Why?'

'Because he needed a front for his true activities. Sherlock Holmes had no need to worry about fees. He was pulling in the stuff in sackfulls from another source. Where is the big money? Where has it always been! In crime. Bags of it, and no income tax. If you want to salt away a few million for a rainy day you don't spring into 9.30 trains to go and see governesses, you become a master criminal, sitting like a spider in the centre of its web and egging your corps of assistants on to steal jewels and naval treaties.'

'You mean . . .'

'Exactly. He was Professor Moriarty.'

'What was that name again?'

'Professor Moriarty.'

'The bird with the reptilian head?'

'That's right.'

'But Holmes hadn't a reptilian head.'

'Nor had Moriarty.'

'Holmes said he had.'

'And to whom? To Watson. So as to get the description given publicity. Watson never saw Moriarty. All he knew about him was what Holmes told him. Well, that's the story, old man.'

'The whole story?'

'Yes.'

'There isn't any more.'

'No.'

I chuckled softly.

The Head of The Family

John Gardner

P. G. Wodehouse's mention of Professor Moriarty leads us conveniently to a fresh look at the 'Napoleon of Crime'—undoubtedly the most fascinating character in the Adventures after Holmes and Watson. Sherlockians have had great fun over the years theorising about him, and best-selling author John Gardner has written a splendid novel, THE RETURN OF MORIARTY (1974), in which the criminal genius escapes his supposed death at the Reichenbach Falls. Gardner also wrote the following intriguing article about Moriarty in which he visualises him as a kind of nineteenth-century 'Godfather' ruling the London underworld. It appeared in THE DAILY TELEGRAPH colour magazine of 29 November 1974.

MENTION the name of Professor James Moriarty to anyone who has even a nodding acquaintance with Sir Arthur Conan Doyle's Sherlock Holmes, and a picture is immediately conjured—the tall, gaunt, scholarly figure threatening Holmes in his Baker Street rooms; the fight on the ledge at the Reichenbach Falls; a vast army of criminals ready to do his bidding; the clop of horses' hooves in the streets, and the rumble of hansoms; gaslight casting eerie shadows; the thick yellow fogs, 'London particulars', creeping up from the river; sinister figures lurking in alleys and passageways; robbery, murder, extortion, violence; the sly tongue of the confidence man, the quick fingers of the pickpocket, the wheedling of the beggar and the wiles of the whore: the whole wretched, dingy, yet compulsive aura of the nineteenth-century underworld.

Professor Moriarty is, in fiction, the apotheosis of organised evil—even though *The Goon Show* borrowed his name for a comic and ludicrous villain. Yet Conan Doyle, through Holmes's faithful chronicler, John H. Watson, tells us very little of the man or his world. Perhaps this is the fascination—the shadowy figure, once a mathematical genius, author of the treatise on the Binomial Theorem and *The Dynamics of an Asteroid*, who fell from grace to become 'the Napoleon of crime . . . the organiser of half that is evil and nearly all that is undetected in this great city.'

Holmes himself is reported to have said of the Professor (in *The Final Problem*), '. . . his agents are numerous and splendidly organised. Is there a crime to be done, a paper to be abstracted, we will say, a house to be rifled, a man to be removed—the word is passed on to the Professor, the matter is organised and carried out. The agent may be caught. In that case money is found for his bail or his defence. But the central power which uses the agent

'The Napoleon of Crime' and his visiting card

is never caught—never so much as suspected.' The description has a strangely modern ring to it.

In view of it, Moriarty would undoubtedly have spent the bulk of his time within the underworld of his era: and here we come to the link which joins that world to the underworld of our own time, for the sprawling regiment of nineteenth-century villains referred to themselves, collectively, as The Family. In 1841 an article in *Tait's Magazine* spoke of '"The Family" . . . The generic name for thieves, pickpockets, gamblers, house-breakers *et hoc genus omne*.' The term was certainly still in use at the end of the century, and villains spoke of each other as family men and family women.

With the ripe crop of novels and factual works which, in recent years, has sprung up around our contemporary structure of organised crime, the analogy becomes instantly recognisable. Doyle's Moriarty could only have been the Victorian equivalent of the twentieth-century criminal Godfather. His influence certainly had its starting point in the whirling vortex of the nineteenth-century underworld.

The essential satisfaction for hundreds of Holmesian *aficionados* is to plot the course of Holmes's life and to come up with answers to many of the imponderables set by the author. The life and times of James Moriarty is perhaps the greatest of these imponderables, and the literary and academic game of clothing the Napoleon of Crime with flesh, blood and environs, still continues. It is a dangerous game, for Sherlockian experts are ready to chop down any theory which does not quite fit the knowledge one can glean from the Holmes Canon.

In *The Return of Moriarty* I set out both to entertain and to play this game—in the form of a novel—by claiming access to the evil Professor's coded journals, so providing information never available before: throwing up new facts and presenting further imponderables.

Briefly, one sees the fictional Moriarty as a ruthless criminal leader of high intellect and advanced organisational talents—a man determined to rule his chosen universe. This is, of course, the picture we have from the Holmes stories. But, with a certain impertinence, one is forced to alter, or at least slightly shift, facts, in order to make it work within the framework of the Godfather theory.

It is the first essential that Professor Moriarty should not die during the struggle at the Reichenbach Falls, as Holmes claimed. This is not a new idea. The Holmesian scholar William S. Baring-Gould has written, 'For three long years . . . Watson and the world thought Holmes also lay dead beneath the dark and swirling waters of the Reichenbach; but Holmes in 1894 was very much alive. . . . Why not Moriarty? . . . anyone familiar with the history of evil in the world since 1894 has little difficulty in seeing that Professor James Moriarty was taking advantage of a long period of social unrest to consolidate and expand his undisputed position as the Napoleon of crime. . . .'

At least one Holmesian addict has evolved the theory that the Professor did die, his place in the underworld being taken by his brother, Colonel James Moriarty.

My own findings are more sinister, claiming that no physical struggle, as such, ever took place at the Reichenbach Falls; nor was Moriarty, the Victorian Godfather, that same Professor James Moriarty once lionised in academic circles; nor indeed was he the military brother, Colonel James. The truth is centred in another close source—the Professor's youngest brother (another James), thought by many to have been a station master in the West of England.

It would seem that the genius Professor Moriarty was totally involved in his academic calling, as Colonel James was involved in his military career. The black sheep of the Moriarty clan was the youngest—that member of the family who loathed the success of his two older brothers, and certainly envied his eldest brother with a pathological obsession: a man who from his earliest years was determined to make a name for himself among the denizens of vice and crime.

From Holmes, through Watson, we learn that the brilliant Professor Moriarty was forced to resign the Chair of Mathematics at one of the smaller universities. With the added evidence of my fictional Moriarty Journals the facts are now plain.

In envy, hatred, and on the crest of obsessional ambition, the youngest brother was determined to make use of his famous brother's name and rank by discrediting him and eventually taking on his physical presence by subtle disguise, thereby becoming the most respected and feared figure in the criminal underworld.

There is not space here to give the full details of Moriarty s ingenious and vile plot, nor the later intrigue which took place at the Reichenbach Falls. What is now certain is that his mastery of crime covered the last decades of the nineteenth century and continued well into the first years of the twentieth.

But what sort of underworld would he have ruled?

The picture we have of the London underworld during the first half of the nineteenth century is one of a perpetual war waged between the respectable middle and upper classes, and the great horde of criminals, many of them specialist technicians, who lived in the Rookeries—those swamped, fetid and congested areas of the outer perimeter of the metropolis. From the Rookeries these parasites would emerge to perpetrate their villainy, only to disappear again into the warrens of courts, alleys and cellars of the tightly-packed, rogue-infested hives such as the great St Giles's Rookery around Holborn—known as the Holy Land—or the Devil's Acre around Pye Street; and a dozen more, including the terrain of Whitechapel and Spitalfields which contained such unlovely byways as Flower and Dean Street, and Dorset Street—at one time known as the most evil street in London.

Throughout the century there was a national obsession with law and order—as well there might be, for the contrast between the glittering West End, and the impoverished East, was horrifyingly marked. This sense of two distinct communities—one a natural prey of the other—appears constant throughout Victoria's reign. However, one cannot be blind to the fact that the more prosperous were not the only victims: the poor suffered deplorably at the hands of criminals, for dog ate dog unscrupulously in the sinks and stews of the cities.

Yet the whole period was one of gradual, and massive, progress. Great changes made themselves felt at all levels. Legal, penal and social reform, a more effective police force, the cutting of new roads through the Rookeries—all played a part in bringing the crime rate down by the end of the century. But the criminal, while adept at altering his techniques, is basically conservative in outlook; so the underworld of the Eighties and

The famous 'death struggle' at the Reichenbach Falls as depicted
by Sidney Paget

Nineties still clung to past ways. While London's underworld became more diffuse towards the end of the century, its business methods altered little. The argot of the criminal, for instance, appears to be not so different in the Eighties and Nineties from that of the Fifties. In the same way, the specialists of nineteenth-century crime are still easily identifiable with their counterparts in our own time.

As ever, the fences—the receivers of stolen property—played a major part in the life force of criminal activities. Almost anything could be disposed of through the small back-street pawnbrokers, the market traders, the hordes of middlemen and the few really big fences, who were often the instigators of large robberies.

The most trivial items were stolen and sold: food and trifles filched by servants, clothes, even handfuls of hay had ready buyers. There was a particularly large traffic in stolen clothing—often provided by 'skinners', who were usually women working the 'kinchen-lay'—stealing from children. The 'skinners' lured young boys and girls into alleys or other quiet places to strip them of their clothes, leaving them naked and, as often as not, in shocked terror.

The most colourful fence to emerge during the first half of the century was the great and legendary Ikey Solomons who lived, in a house full of secret trapdoors and hidden rooms, in the heart of Spitalfields. Solomons was almost certainly Dickens's model for Fagin in *Oliver Twist*, and when he was finally arrested two coachloads of stolen goods were removed from his home on the first visit, while the officers had to return at least twice before the place was cleared of loot.

Working hand in glove with the fences were, of course, the cracksmen and sneak-thieves. They still operate today with as much verve as they did in Victorian London—as Shaw Taylor (known to our villains as 'Whispering Grass') demonstrates weekly on television's *Police Five*. In Moriarty's day both the cracksman and sneak-thief were very high in the criminal hierarchy. The latter, often known as a 'snoozer', was a particularly cunning operator who would plan his jobs with great care, posing as a respectable businessman, staying at good hotels, mixing with his fellow guests in order to pick the best victims before stealing from them as they slept.

One of the most famous cracksmen of the age was Charlie Peace, whose career well illustrates the skill and technique of the Victorian burglar. Unhappily, Peace turned to murder as well as theft, but his methods were most sophisticated and the tools of his trade included a collapsible ladder and a false arm. He was also a past-master in disguise and is even credited with visiting Scotland Yard to study the notices offering a reward for his arrest. Peace came to his end, on the gallows, in 1879.

Cracksmen certainly took their profession very seriously, using ingenious methods and careful perparation. Nowhere is this more clear than in the train robbery of 1855. This was probably the most sensational theft of the century, having an obvious parallel with the Great Train Robbery of 1963. In all, over £12,000 in gold and coin—a most considerable sum at the time—was stolen from a shipment en route from London to Paris.

The conspirators, Pierce and Agar—both professional cracksmen—and Tester, a railway clerk, spent over a year preparing for the crime, going to great lengths to get information, to bribe the guard of the London to Folkestone passenger train on which the bullion was carried, and to provide themselves with duplicate keys to the three Chubb safes used for transporting it.

The crime itself was carried out with flair. Pierce and Agar boarded the train with bags containing lead shot sewn into special pockets and gained access to the guard's van through the corrupted guard, Burgess. The safes were unlocked, the gold removed and the lead substituted so that the theft would not be discovered until the safes reached France.

Colonel Moran, Moriarty's scheming associate, another Paget illustration

Some of the gold was removed, in one of the cases, by Tester at Redhill, the remainder was actually taken on to Ostend by Pierce and Agar.

The culprits were eventually caught in the classic manner, being informed on by Agar's mistress.

If the Victorian was not safe from burglary in his own home, the streets were also full of hazards. By far the largest number of criminals worked in the streets. Many of them were pickpockets, and the problem is with us today, as the warning signs on the London Underground tell us. It is doubtful if the Victorian Londoner needed warning, for the artful mobs-men, toolers and dippers, together with their stickman accomplices, were everywhere among the crowds. It is, perhaps, indicative of their proliferation that Havelock Ellis in his book *The Criminal*, published in 1890, illustrates his chapter on criminal slang with a passage describing events in a pickpocket's life, in the dipper's own words.

'I was jogging down a blooming slum in the Chapel,' he says, 'When I butted a reeler, who was sporting a red slang. I broke off his jerry, and boned the clock, which was a red one, but I was spotted by a copper, who claimed me. I was lugged before the beak, who gave me a six doss in the Steel. The week after I was chucked up I did a snatch near St Paul's, was collared, lagged and got this bit of seven stretch.'

The translation follows: 'As I was walking down a narrow alley in Whitechapel, I ran up against a drunk, who had a gold watch guard. I stole his watch, which was gold, but was seen by a policeman, who caught me and took me before the magistrate, who gave me six months in the Bastille (the House of Correction, Coldbath Fields). When I was released I attempted to steal a watch near St Paul's, but was caught again, convicted, and sentenced to seven years' penal servitude.' The streets were dangerous in other ways also, because of footpads, demanding with menaces and the protection racket—all still very familiar to us. The bovine, bullying rampsmen—tearaways—were not very selective in whom they attacked. But prostitutes suffered much from the protection gangs, such as the Old Nicol Street and Hoxton Market mobs, and at least one of the murders so often cited as a preliminary to the Jack the Ripper killings was perpetrated by one of these gangs.

On Easter Monday, 1888, a middle-aged prostitute, Emma Smith, returning home in the small hours after a night in the public houses, was set upon and robbed by four men in Osborn Street, Spitalfields. She later died from wounds inflicted with a sharp spike. The assailants could only have made a few pence from their night's work, yet they were typical of their kind.

Demanding with menaces and general footpadding were common enough crimes in the badly lit streets, and in mid-century law-abiding Londoners went in real terror from garotters who would choke their victims insensible before fleecing them.

Even in daylight one was not safe, for the unwary were always at the mercy of the macers, magsmen and sharps—the tricksters and frauds, swindlers and cheats, the forerunners of every cheapjack and con man on our own streets, doorsteps and in the files of the Criminal Records Office.

It is surprising that even today swindles which were already old in the 1880s are still very much in use. One can still see innocents in London streets crowding round the three card man, while the long firm fraud—by which villains obtain goods on credit, sell them and decamp—was as recognisable in the 1870s as it is to our present-day police officers.

There were other villains: the forgers, the shofulmen—coiners—and the screevers, the writers of false character references and testimonials. Their heyday was in the last century when anything which could be faked—from documents to bank notes to coins and jewellery settings—was duplicated in small crude dens or elaborate workshops equipped with moulds, presses, engraving tools and electro-plating devices.

Whatever its cause, vice has always drawn crime and Victoria's London reeked of it. In mid-century it was estimated that there were over 80,000 prostitutes working in the city—good money for the cash-carriers (nineteenth-century ponces), the minders and madams—words which, like racket, mob and pig, have not altered with time. Many of these women doubtless doubled as skinners and pickpockets' accomplices; certainly women predominated among the 'palmers'—adroit shoplifters, often working in pairs, one to distract, the other to steal.

These, then, were the various criminal types with whom, and through whom, a man like Moriarty would have worked.

While frustration, hideous poverty, the ruthless class system, with its imbalance of wealth and power, undoubtedly all contributed to the vast criminal activity within the Victorian urban community, one cannot disregard the ever-present traits of lust and greed which seem, in every age, to operate in favour of the criminal, throwing willing victims in the path of villainy.

If the fictional Moriarty, with his particular qualities, had existed he might easily have formed a criminal union which could have brought some order within the corrupt chaos of crime.

One can see him, as Holmes suggested in *The Final Problem*, sitting 'motionless, like a spider in the centre of its web, but that web has a thousand radiations, and he knows well every quiver of each of them.'

The imaginative mind cannot fail to see how this double strand of fact and fiction can be weaved, knowing well that a criminal society, built on organised lines in the nineteenth century could have survived, leaving a backlash that might have been with us today. Or perhaps it is.

The Colonel Moran Quiz

A three-part quiz, devised in the spirit of Professor Moriarty's henchman, Colonel Moran, by William E. Dunning of The Brothers Three of Moriarty, an American scion society, to test your knowledge of Holmesian titles, personalities and dates. The answers appear at the end of the book.

Sherlock Holmes by the Numbers

Supply complete canonical story titles that contain the following numbers (the first, not from the canon, has been filled in as an example):

The	7	% Solution		3	
	6			3	
	5			2	
	4			3/4	
	3			0	

The Age of his Hans Sloan (and Others)

The ages of several personalities who appear in the canon are clearly specified. Supply the ages of the following persons (at the time they appear in the stories):

Irene Adler (SCAN) _____

Cartwright (HOUN) _____

Jeremiah Hayling (THUM) _____

John Horner (BLUE) _____

Patience Moran (BOSC) _____

Neville St Clair (TWIS) _____

Significant Dates

The following years are significant items in various stories (not, however, chronological dates of the adventures). Identify them by source and meaning.

1607 ....

1742 ....

1858 ....

1860 ....

1878 ....

The arrest of Colonel Moran, from 'The Adventure of the Empty
House', *Strand*, 1903

Re: Vampires

William Leonard

Without giving the contents away, there is little I can say by way of introduction to this item beyond that it is my favourite piece of Sherlockian speculation and first appeared in THE BAKER STREET JOURNAL CHRISTMAS ANNUAL OF 1957. *After reading it I have to confess that I've never been able to see Sherlock Holmes and Professor Moriarty in quite the same light as before . . .*

Iₙ 1897, Bram Stoker compiled a collection of horrifying notes, clippings, diaries and other memoranda, and published them under the title *Dracula*. They told the fantastic story of Count Voivode Dracula, king of vampires, and his diabolical plot, in the summer and early autumn of 1890, to transplant himself and a few of his long-extinct kinfolk to London, that great cesspool into which all the loungers and idlers of the Empire are irresistably drained, but which never before had been cursed by vampires. Vampires, the book explained, are the Un-Dead who had shuffled off the mortal coil, but, instead of resigning themselves to eternity and the cold, cold ground, endure through the ages by nourishing their unholy bodies on the blood of living humans.

The victims, if they have lost enough plasma to a vampire before they themselves succumb to anaemia, in turn become vampires themselves, and the legions of the Un-Dead are swelled from generation to generation. Surely, this was a threat more dire than any Professor James Moriarty ever planned and it is impossible to believe Count Dracula's unearthly evil could have penetrated to within a stone's throw of Baker Street without stirring Sherlock Holmes.

When I brought this strange situation, nearly two years ago, to the attention of Sherlockian Professor Jay Finley Christ, at that time a smooth-cheeked youth, he calmly countered with the declaration (as if he had known it all the time) that Moriarty and Dracula were the same man. Now I'm a fundamentalist, when it comes to the Sacred Writings; I believe every word in them is the truth, and the contradictions are the mysteries of our faith. So I set out to disprove this latest heresy of Mr Christ, who delights in foraging outside the precincts of the sixty Adventures—and I ended with a disconcerting semi-substantiation of his theory about the man he has called Moriarty-Dracula with a hyphen.

The appalling events related by Bram Stoker in *Dracula* took place over the six months from May to November, 1890. And there is an almost suspicious silence on the part of the Canon about the career of Sherlock Holmes through almost all of those very months. Watson himself says: 'The very intimate relations which had existed between Holmes and myself became to some extent modified. He still came to me when he desired a companion in his investigations, but these occasions grew more and more seldom, until I find that in the year 1890 there were only three cases of which I retain any record.' Yet most Baker Street Irregulars believe that 1890, the last full year before the tussle at the Reichenbach Falls, represented a period in which Holmes was at the peak of his powers.

There is only one Adventure recorded for the six-month period in which Count Dracula was attempting to invade London. It is that of 'The Red-Headed League', which took place 4 and 5 October, 1890. This story opens with the most abrupt introduction in all the canon. There is not a word of preliminary reminiscence, not even a brief sample of the parlour tricks of deduction which furnish delightful prefaces for most of the tales. Watson comes to the point in the very first sentence: 'I had called upon my friend, Mr Sherlock Holmes, one day in the autumn of last year, and found him in deep conversation with a very stout, florid-faced, elderly gentleman with red hair.' If Holmes had spent the preceding days or weeks in a hellish game of chess with the king of the vampires, this unusually terse opening might well have been designed to conceal every hint of the struggle. But 'The Red-Headed League' and its dates do not, as a matter of fact, conflict with the movements on 4 and 5 October of the man who manoeuvered the campaign against the vampire—and who may have been Sherlock Holmes in a some-what thin disguise.

Count Dracula, you will recall, had himself and two lady vampire compan-ions shipped to Whitby, on the Yorkshire coast, in a collection of boxes containing the unconsecrated earth in which they had been buried centuries before in Transylvania. There the trio of Un-Dead preyed upon one unhappy young lady until her distraught friends enlisted the aid of a Dr John Seward who, perplexed by the case, called in a mysterious Dr Adolph Van Helsing, ostensibly from Amsterdam. Of the brave little band upon whom Count Dracula centered his attention, none excepting Dr Seward had ever heard of Van Helsing before, and none penetrated his inscrutability in all the months they worked with him.

Several participants in the Dracula adventure describe Van Helsing in their journals, and he *could* be Sherlock Holmes—poised head; hard, square chin; long, straight nose with sensitive nostrils; brows that knit deeply over a problem. Van Helsing is supposed to be a much more elderly man than

Were Professor Moriarty and Count Dracula one and the same person? Moriarty as seen by Sidney Paget (*below*) and Christopher Lee (*left*) as Dracula in 'Count Dracula' (1970), the film he believes to be most faithful to Bram Stoker's original story

Holmes, but the assumption of old age was one of Holmes's best tricks when he assumed a disguise.

This Van Helsing's methods also are those of Sherlock Holmes, and at no time does he betray any acquaintance with medicine, although he is supposed to be a doctor. One of his associates comments that 'the professor's actions were certainly odd and not to be found in any pharmacopoeia.' He is as expert a housebreaker as Holmes; he is as secretive about his moves until he is good and ready to divulge their purpose. He maintains an exaggerated pose of broken English except in moments of stress, when he speaks in flowing prose of complete clarity—and at times his conversation sounds like the voice of the Master himself beside the fire on Baker Street; as for instance when he says: 'You do not let your eyes see nor your ears hear, and that which is outside your daily life is not of account to you. . . Do you not think that there are things which you cannot understand, and yet which are; that some people see things that others cannot?'

While the man's physical appearance, his presentation of arguments, his secrecy, his calm confidence, bear striking resemblances to Sherlock Holmes, one cannot conclude on those grounds alone that the mysterious Alphonse Van Helsing was Sherlock Holmes in disguise. A sound reason for the disguise exists, however, apart from its purpose of mystifying Moriarty-Dracula. The ladies involved in the vampire adventure were all Victorianly fragile creatures from whom the gentlemen admittedly endeavored at every turn to hide the awful facts of life—or should I say of Un-Death? One of them, in addition, was in such poor health that every male whose diary or notes went into Bram Stoker's book felt constrained to opine at one time or another that any shock might cause her death.

Further ground for the belief that Holmes participated in the overthrow of Count Dracula exists in the fact that the movements of the monster were recorded thoroughly in the Press, although he was not, of course, identified as a vampire. There were stories about his outrages in the *Dailygraph* of 8 August, 1890, the *Pall Mall Gazette* of 18 September, and the *Westminster Gazette* of 25 September. Excerpts from these newspapers are included in the Dracula volume, and anyone familiar with the existence of Holmes's library of scrap books will find it impossible to believe that he could have been ignorant of the case. One remembers him saying of Moriarty at a later date: 'With that man in the field, one's morning paper presented infinite possibilities. Often it was only the smallest trace, Watson, the faintest indication, and yet it was enough to tell me that the great malignant brain was there, as the gentlest tremors of the edges of the web remind one of the foul spider which lurks in the center. Petty thefts, wanton assaults, purposeless-outrages—to the man who held the clue all could be worked into one connected whole.' Clearly, it would have been impossible for Holmes to have overlooked or ignored Count Dracula.

Parenthetically, while on the subject of the public Press, if Sherlock

Could Sherlock Holmes have been Van Helsing, the Vampire Hunter? *Above left*, Peter Cushing as Van Helsing in 'Horror of Dracula' (1958); *right*, a Sidney Paget portrait of the Great Detective from 'The Adventure of the Resident Patient', *Strand*, 1893

Holmes were at work on 'The Adventure of the Transylvanian Vampire' in the summer of 1890, that might clear up a minor, semi-canonical mystery. 'The Lost Special', which appeared in the *Strand* Magazine under the signature of Watson's literary agent, has been offered for subsumption into the canon beause it contains a letter written to *The Times* 'over the signature of an amateur reasoner of some celebrity at that date.' Those in favour of accepting 'The Lost Special' as a Holmes adventure claim that our Sherlock was the unidentified man who wrote the message attempting to deal in a critical and semi-scientific manner with the matter of a disappearing railway train. Another school of thought asserts that such half-hearted methods were not those of Sherlock Holmes, and that Holmes would not have been content, like a Nero Wolfe, to file a suggestion without budging from Baker Street. But if Sherlock Holmes were deeply involved in the Dracula campaign in July, 1890, that might well explain his inability to run up to Kenyon Junction to look into the affair of the lost special.

As for Dracula being Moriarty himself, as Professor Christ suggests, there is certainly the argument of a striking physical resemblance between them. Both are extremely tall, thin, pallid, grey-haired—Dracula with 'lofty domed forehead', Moriarty with 'forehead doming out in a white curve'.

Permit me, in conclusion, to quote just two eminent authorities on the subject of Moriarty-Dracula:

The first, Jay Finley Christ, has written: 'It is true that Dr Watson never mentioned the count, but that hardly proves that Mr Holmes was not involved in the case. There were many things which Dr Watson did not know. For instance, when Mr Holmes mentioned Professor Moriarty in 'The Final Problem,' Watson never had heard of the man. Mr Holmes himself had just met the professor that same day, and the professor had complained, "You crossed my path on the 4th of January, and now, through your continual persecution, I am in positive danger of losing my liberty." Here was a clue for Dr Watson, but he muffed it.'

'Moriarty and Dracula were two names for the same man. Mr Holmes had been after him for over three months and began to catch up with him in January. Moriarty-Dracula knew this all the time, but Watson didn't get it. If he had, he probably would have told the world about it before Bram Stoker got round to it in 1897. Stoker's account didn't dispose of the Count, either, for they used a metal dagger instead of a stake of holly, and it didn't knock him out.'

On the other hand, we have the opinion of an amateur reasoner of some celebrity at that date, who consulted his card index, found vampires in Transylvania following in somewhat unalphabetical order after Victor Lynch, Venemous lizard, Vittoria, Vanderbilt and Vipers, and declared:

'Rubbish, Watson, rubbish! What have we to do with walking corpses who can only be held in their grave by stakes driven through their hearts? It's pure lunacy. . . Are we to give serious consideration to such things? This agency stands flatfooted upon the ground and there it must remain. The world is big enough for us. No ghosts need apply.'

Well, as I say, I'm a fundamentalist in these things, but I'm not certain yet that Professor Moriarty isn't still roaming about waiting for the right man to come along with that stake of holly.

Shady Mr. Holmes

J. P. W. Mallalieu

As a final piece of conjecture on the characters of Holmes and Watson, here is a highly irreverent portrait of the two men. The author, Sir William Mallalieu, a former MP and Minister of State, was also an author and journalist who contributed humorous essays to several publications, including THE SPECTATOR *in which this article first appeared on 27 February 1953.*

JOHN H. WATSON, MD, was clearly a bad lot. His father, I suspect, was a heavy drinker, I know that his elder brother died of drink, and there is evidence that Dr. Watson shared the family failing. Although his pension of 11s. 6d. a day was barely enough for necessities he was to be found lounging about in expensive bars. Indeed, it was while he was 'standing at the Criterion Bar'—no doubt waiting for someone to offer him a drink—that he met Stamford, and through Stamford, Sherlock Holmes, and thus landed himself in the *Study in Scarlet*. At the beginning of *The Sign of Four* we find him throwing his weight about in Baker Street on courage derived from the bottle of Beaune he had swallowed with his lunch.

True, in later years, when gossip about his habits became widespread, he tried to create the impression that he was or had been a hearty, athletic type who played Rugger for Blackheath, but I doubt that he ever played the game. When Cyril Overton, the Cambridge Rugger Captain and England's first reserve, arrived in Baker Street looking for a Missing Three-Quarter, Watson had never even heard of him. Worse, he makes Overton say things about Rugger which no one who knew or played the game could ever say. 'Stevenson is fast enough,' Watson reports Overton to have said when discussing possible substitutes for the missing winger, Staunton, 'but he couldn't drop from the twenty-five line, and a three-quarter who can't either punt or drop isn't worth a place for pace alone.' Twaddle! A wing three-quarter virtually never gets a chance to drop a goal, and as for dropping out from the twenty-five, if Stevenson can't do it, let someone else try.

No. I am satisfied that when Big Bob Ferguson, 'the finest three-quarter Richmond ever had,' came to consult Holmes about Vampires in Sussex, he was not thinking of Watson as a player when he said to him, 'You don't look

The Real Sherlock Holmes? A shadow portrait
allegedly taken in Baker Street, London, in
1951, the year of the Festival of Britain

quite the man you did when I threw you over the ropes into the crowd at the
Old Deer Park.' What actually happened on that famous afternoon was that
Watson, befuddled as usual with Beaune, strayed from the crowd on to the
field, where he interfered with the play and had to be thrown out by
Ferguson.

Yes, Watson was a bad lot. I've known that for a long time. But now I am
beginning to have serious suspicions even about Holmes. I have always
thought that his performance in 'The Five Orange Pips' was lamentable—he
allowed an innocent and defenceless man to walk out of 221b to certain death
when he could easily have saved him by offering him the sofa for the
night—assuming that the sofa was temporarily unoccupied by Lestrade.
Further, his activities in the matter of Silver Blaze were, to say the least of it,
questionable. You will remember that, instead of returning the missing

favourite at once to its owner, he allowed it to remain concealed until the very day of the Wessex Plate, no doubt so that he could have plenty of time to place his own bets. Worse, in the race itself, Desborough, the second favourite, piled up a big lead and then fell right away for no apparent reason to give Silver Blaze—and Holmes—a comfortable win. The fact that Silas Brown, the trainer of Desborough, had had a private and painful interview with Holmes some days before the race speaks for itself.

Now a still more sinister light has been shed on Holmes' sporting activities by Mr. Red Smith, who was recently invited by the *New York Herald Tribune* to make some investigations. Mr. Smith runs through the familiar history of Silver Blaze and emphasises its more sinister aspects. He also makes what to me is an entirely new point. When the Wessex Plate had been run, and Colonel Ross, the owner of Silver Blaze, was begging Holmes to tell him what had been happening to the horse in the past few days. Holmes replied: 'As I stand to win a little on this next race I shall defer a lengthy explanation.' Nothing remarkable about that? Just look at the phrasing! Holmes does not say, 'I've got a bet on the next race' or 'I am risking some money on the next race.' Instead he says 'As I stand to win a little on this next race.' There was no risk. Holmes knew. It was not for nothing that he spent so much time in Baker Street experimenting with dope and syringes.

Mr. Wilson also sheds new light on Holmes' connection with 'Wilson, the notorious canary-trainer.' How, asks Mr. Red Smith, could a canary-trainer become notorious if he stayed with canaries? Wilson clearly branched out, just as Hirsch Jacobs, who began by training pigeons, branched out, until he became America's leading horse-trainer. Wilson became notorious because he allowed Holmes to dope the horses with which, at a quite early stage, he had replaced his canaries.

Mr. Smith's most devastating indictment of Holmes, the sportsman, however, is over his handling of the Case of the Missing Three-Quarter, to which I referred earlier, Holmes first extracted an admission from the Cambridge captain that Cambridge had no chance of winning without Godfrey Staunton. That done, he carefully refrained from finding Staunton until the match was over. Twice, while dawdling through the investigation, he made sly remarks to Watson, e.g. 'You must admit that it is curious and suggestive that this incident should occur on the eve of this important match and should involve the only man whose presence seems essential to the success of the side'; and, 'Amateur sport is free from betting, but a good deal of outside betting goes on among the public, and it is possible that it might be worth someone's while to get at a player, as the ruffians of the turf might get at a race-horse.'

Worth someone's while, eh? comments Mr. Red Smith.

After these suggestive reflections, Holmes takes himself off to Cambridge, and realises at once that Dr. Leslie Armstrong holds the key to the mystery. But instead of tracking the doctor efficiently he follows him on a bicycle, knowing well enough that in the flat countryside of Cambridgeshire the doctor will spot him. Why did he not at once adopt the elementary dodge of squirting the doctor's brougham with aniseed and following the trail with a dog? Because, says Mr. Smith, Holmes was too busy at the Post Office sending and receiving telegrams.

It is only when the result of the match is known and Oxford have won—just how much did Holmes 'stand to win' on that one?—that Holmes finally puts his finger on the Missing Three-Quarter. Having found him, sobbing his heart out over the dead body of his beautiful young wife, did Holmes offer Staunton any consolation or any suggestions about how the news of the marriage could be kept from Lord Mount James? He did not. He was in a hurry to collect his winnings. 'Come Watson,' he said, and passed from that house of grief, telegrams rustling in his pockets.

Mr. Smith's revelations put many things about Holmes in a new light. Do you remember in *The Sign of Four* how Holmes arrives at the closely guarded Pondicherry Lodge and is refused admittance by McMurdo, not the boss who put Fear into the Valley, but the ex-professional boxer? But the moment Holmes reminds him that he was the amateur who fought three rounds with him on McMurdo's benefit-night the door is swung open welcomingly. A likely story! Any professional boxer who on his benefit-night of all nights is made a fool of by a ruddy amateur waits only for the moment when he can kick that amateur's seat. He certainly does not disobey orders to do him a favour. I now suspect that Holmes and McMurdo had gone into partnership to frame boxing-matches for their joint advantage. I further suspect that the late Professor Moriarty, so far from being the arch-criminal depicted by Holmes, was in fact employed by various sporting bodies to clean up the turf, the ring and other sources of Holmes's income, and that this was the reason why the poor man was flung to his death at the falls of Reichenbach.

CRYPTIC CROSSWORD

Across

7 The red room mystery? (1, 5, 2, 7)
9 Watson's pre-occupation? (6)
10 Professed enemy of 21Dn (8)
11 Ruin—of 21Dn at Reichenback? (8)
13 An authorative middle name? (5)
15 A street irregular starts moving (5)
17 Guide ox (5)
19 Five hundred mats, smuggled possibly (5)
20 & 21Dn Sleuth from Hemsker School (8, 6)
24 Scene of fire: two King Cole requests (4–4)
26 French waiter excitedly rang about company (6)
28 Dreadfully low place conceived by 23Dn (3, 6, 2, 4)

Down

1 Some industrial evidence in which fingerprints are found (4)
2 20Ac's brother asserts farm ownership (7)
3 Creature lifts the plate (6)
4 Fruit is a problem for the foot (5)
5 District in which to share a flat? (4)
6 Yard detective confused lad with 17Ac (8)
8 Tolerated point to do up (5)
12 Mangle the said band (5)
14 Dismissed party to excel (5)
16 Honest saint has article in right (8)
18 6Dn's side-kick and actor John (7)
21 See 20Ac
22 Swedish coin, OK—ran out (5)
23 Ye old gnarled author (5)
25 Turnham Green sin?! (4)
27 Makeshift boat craftily hidden (4)

A View of Sherlock Holmes From New Scotland Yard

Sir Robert Mark

Sir Robert Mark, the former Commissioner of Police for London, delivered this perceptive and interesting policeman's view of the Great Detective at the annual dinner of the Sherlock Holmes Society in January 1974. In it, Sir Robert shows himself to be no mean Sherlockian.

IT is generally regarded in police circles as improper or unethical to comment publicly on the characteristics or achievements of a detective not belonging to one's own Force. Indeed so far as Scotland Yard is concerned that reticence has been complete to the considerable advantage of those senior detectives who on retirement with the occasional help of the needy journalist have attempted heights of biographical fiction not unworthy of Conan Doyle himself. They and their mentors have been responsible for the now happily vanishing legend of the Big Five, a legend unthinkable in the days of Holmes himself. Indeed were he alive I have no doubt that he would unhesitatingly deduce that the adjective 'Big' in no way related to status or intellectual capacity. I imagine the feet would have come most readily to mind. And as usual he would have been right. The legend of the Big Five is dying, not just because it is so obviously ill-founded but because it lacked the imaginative and cultural skill of a single gifted author or biographer. The police have never had a Boswell or a Watson and even their tactful reticence cannot conceal that not everyone of the literary aspirants who retires from the Force can really have caught the Great Train Robbers single-handed. The unending stream of pensioned detectives who never forgot a face or who smashed this or that hydra-headed gang real or imaginary is so predictable as to ensure for each only a brief and dubious glory. As one of Mr Holmes's contemporaries put it—when everybody is somebody then no one's anybody.

It is interesting when you think about it that of all the policemen who since 1829, when the Metropolitan Force was founded, have sought fame in literature not one has achieved it or is now remembered. This is surely in stark contrast to Sherlock Holmes who can rightly be said to have established

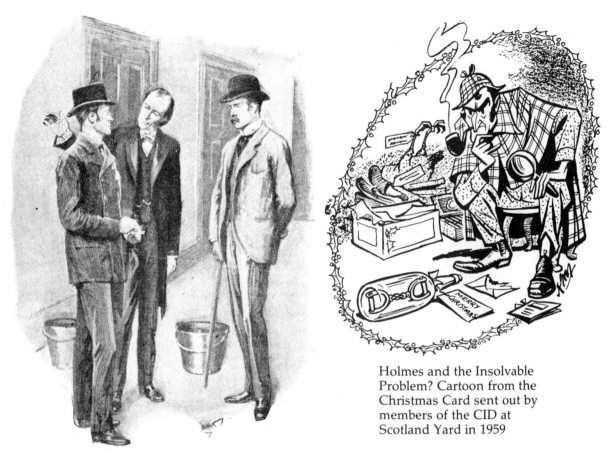

Holmes and the Insolvable Problem? Cartoon from the Christmas Card sent out by members of the CID at Scotland Yard in 1959

Sherlock Holmes with the Scotland Yard man he so often bemused, Inspector Lastrade, pictured by Sidney Paget

a dynasty. If there ever is a place to which old detectives as distinct from old soldiers go, he surely would there be regarded as a patriarch. The Wimseys, the Reginald Fortunes, the Campians and others would there be found acceptable. I find it difficult to imagine him admitting foreigners like Poirot and Van der Valk, and still less women like Miss Marple or Mrs Bradley. Though I suppose even they would have been preferable to a Barlow or a Gideon. For the professional policeman in the world of Sherlock Holmes played only a supporting rôle. Gregson and Lestrade, though the pick of a bad lot, were at their best never more than the assistants in the conjurer's troupe. It is, therefore, a cause for particular pleasure that I, a representative of that Force which Holmes always regarded with such tolerant derision, should a mere eighty-six years after his first detective feat—if that is not thought an unhappy choice of word—be entrusted with the task of honouring his memory. It is as if the Metropolitan policeman, like the leech and the apothecary of two centuries ago, has begun at last to emerge from the servants' quarters to take his place in the living room. Perhaps a further tentative exploration of the still recent and surprising discovery that players can actually be gentlemen just as gentlemen can occasionally play.

I doubt very much whether Holmes would have approved your choice of speaker. Still less would he have approved the reversal of the rôles of policeman and consultant detective which his retirement made possible. He was spared the early indications of that reversal when Wimsey's sister so forgot her station in life as to marry a Yard detective. Since then the policeman, if not actually achieving the status of the guest bedroom, is grudgingly regarded as the most competent, if not the most entertaining, counter to crime both fictional and real.

Holmes would find these sad days in other ways. The minions of Scotland Yard far from lurking in every corner are now so few in number as to be hard to find when they are wanted. Although he would, no doubt, say the same was true of his day. Perhaps unkindest of all is the increasingly vociferous clamour of the consultant detective or private detective of today to be licensed by the Home Office as a guarantee of respectability, the seal of approval to be given by Scotland Yard who would be unlikely these days to look with approval or tolerance on Holmes's occasional recourse to cocaine or for that matter to Watson's apparently unlicensed service revolver. I don't suppose the current medical warnings against tobacco would deter Holmes from his pipe but he would undoubtedly be disheartened by the disappearance of the Baker Street Irregulars either holidaying abroad or trend setting on television. But he has been spared worse. Throughout the whole of his distinguished career his findings were rarely doubted. It was sufficient for him to reveal his deduction to satisfy his following. Not for him the disillusionment of seeing truth dissipated by justice in the courts, or even worse, the tentative but happily unsuccessful attempts of the lawyers to usurp the position of consultant detective as folk hero.

Perhaps most merciful of all he was spared the realisation that his heirs and successors are not the Marshall Halls of one age or the Perry Masons of another but those who now fill the despised shoes or boots of Athelney Jones, of Lestrade, of Gregson and of Hopkins. This is not to imply any shortcomings, disillusionment or lessening of Holmes's stature. The change is compelled by the times in which we live. Holmes fulfilled the need for a folk hero against the believable background. Less than twenty murders yearly, four or five hundred burglaries and ninety or so robberies. A cosily domestic setting in which one brilliant individual could shine, especially in comparison with an illiterate police force with a musical tradition of relieving intoxicated gentlemen of their watches and chains. Now, alas, the 20,000 crimes of Holmes's day number 350,000, the twenty-nine murders ninety-three, the 500 burglaries 76,000, the ninety robberies 3,100, not to mention hi-jacking, bombing, race relations, trade disputes and the waves of fact, fiction and speculation generated by television, radio and the newspapers to a confused and bewildered public as anxious for reassurance as were the readers of Conan Doyle.

In such a setting it is not surprising that the police as a service are beginning, for the public, to add the rôle of protector to that of servant. A rôle too extensive for any one man, even Sherlock Holmes, to play. We pay in hardship and occasional danger for a status we never could have been accorded in Holmes's day. And in so doing we increasingly attract to our number men and women of a quality that even Holmes would have approved. But our reversal in rôles has not lessened the regard of the police for Holmes expressed long ago by Lestrade. He recalls an age, golden for us if for no one else, of a map of the world largely red, of gunboat diplomacy, of British infallibility, of a society in which everyone, particularly policemen, knew their place and in which foreigners were viewed with a very proper reserve. He was really the first person to make the investigation of crime respectable. And in the public mind to give that process the shape of the ancient morality play—right against wrong, good against evil. Time and changing social conditions have enabled us, the police, to assume that rôle and to inherit the public approval that he won for what had been regarded as a menial if not a worse activity. For this we shall always be in his debt though he would no doubt be horrified to know it.

Notwithstanding this inevitable change, his place in our history is secure. Not only in our own history but in that of the western world. For there is not an English-speaking country in which the words Scotland Yard and Sherlock Holmes require any explanation at all. They are two of the comparatively few symbols which bring to all minds the London which produced both. Though Holmes may not entirely welcome this posthumous union with the Yard it is nevertheless fitting, for never were two national symbols more closely associated. There could be no more happy continuance of that association than the presence in the Metropolitan force of two detectives rejoicing in the names of Holmes and Watson.

Holmes's immortality is assured and we at Scotland Yard are proud to share it.

The $64,000 Questions

In the summer of 1956 millions of American viewers were glued to their television sets as, week-by-week, Air Force Captain Thomas O'Rourke and his wife Bobbye, answered questions based on the Adventures of Sherlock Holmes in N.B.C.'s programme 'The $64,000 Question'. The couple eventually successfully completed the tests—though not without some heart-stopping moments of drama—and both won cheques of $32,000. Here are the questions they were asked so that you can test your own knowledge—though on this occasion no answers are given!

Mrs O'Rourke

Who was the medical man who was Holmes's closest friend?	64.00
Who was Holmes's arch enemy?	128.00
Who was the woman admired by Holmes?	256.00
Who was the boy who led the gang of street urchins known as the Baker Street Irregulars?	512.00
In what novel was Holmes first introduced?	1,000.00
In what country had Holmes spent the years before his return in 'The Adventure of the Empty House'?	2,000.00
In *A Study in Scarlet*, Holmes worked with two Scotland Yard inspectors. What were their names?	4,000.00
Give the name of the story in which Holmes assumed the following disguises: (a) a plumber with a rising business (b) an opium addict (c) a French workman in a blue blouse (d) an old woman	8,000.00
Give the stories associated with these numbers and tell who it was who brought the case to Holmes's notice: (a) 6 (b) 5 (c) 4 (d) 3	16,000.00
By what other names were the following known, and identify the story in which they appeared: (a) Arthur Pinner (b) Sutton (c) Mrs Norlett (d) Don Murillo (e) Hosmer Angel (f) Serge the Nihilist (g) Mr Cornelius	32,000.00

Capt O'Rourke

What was Holmes's street address?	64.00
Give the full name of Professor Moriarty's assistant	128.00

Who was the man used as the dupe in 'The Adventure of
the Red-Headed League'?   256.00
To what regiment was Watson attached?   512.00
In which case did Holmes recover the crown jewels?   1,000.00
What device was used to kill the Hon Ronald Adair?   2,000.00
What was the first case in which Holmes was engaged, and
what was the first case in which Holmes and Watson
were engaged?   4,000.000
Identify these manor houses, with the tales in which they
appear: (a) Riding Thorp Manor (b) Charlington Hall
(c) Deep Dene House (d) The Myrtles   8,000.00
Death came in what unusual ways to the following:
(a) Enoch Drebber (b) Bartholomew Sholto (c) Heidegger
(d) John Straker   16,000.00
By what other names were the following known, and
identify the story in which they appeared: (a) Waldron
(b) Signora Durando (c) Holy Peters (d) Jack McMurdo
(e) James Winter (f) Vandeleur (g) James Armitage   32,000.00

Sherlock Holmes's Horoscope

Walter Breen

With the tremendous interest in astrology, what more natural thing than to have an expert study Sherlock Holmes's birthdate—6 January 1854—and the stars and see what they reveal of the great man. And, not surprisingly, Walter Breen has come up with some remarkable facts in his report which is taken from Sybil Leek's Astrology Journal *of January 1971.*

FOR the illustrious Sherlock Holmes, as for few other characters whose exploits have been celebrated in fiction and legend the world over, we have unusually full biographical information. More or less as a matter of curiosity, following no doubt in the footsteps of many previous Baker Street Irregulars, I jotted down the birth data given by Dr. Watson for Holmes, then in a spare moment checked them against the 1854 ephemeris. I expected to find that either Conan Doyle had chosen some ludicrous impossibility of a day, or that possibly he might have made a lucky guess—in which one could speak of an amusing coincidence.

The one thing I was not prepared to find was that the birth data describes Holmes accurately, even to many progressions and transits for dated events of his later life. Probably any dyed-in-the-wool Irregular, committed (for the sake of the game) to the belief that there was a real Sherlock Holmes, will shrug and say 'Of course Holmes's horoscope would fit him.'

The chart shows Sagittarius rising, with Mercury (sextile MC); Sun conjunct Jupiter in Capricorn, square Moon in Aries—and trine Uranus in Taurus, which is loosely conjunct Pluto. Mars in Virgo widely opposes a conjunction of Venus-Neptune in Pisces, Venus being sextile Pluto and Ascendant, and at the midpoint between Sun and Moon. Saturn in Taurus is part of a Grand Trine in Earth, with Sun and Mars.

Mercury rising in Sagittarius, but without serious affliction, fits beautifully the picture of a gifted dilettante. Holmes, despite two brief periods at Christ Church College, Oxford, and Caius College, Cambridge, never stayed long enough to take a degree. As one might expect from Sagittarius rising, he had numerous hobbies and game-like pursuits, but at the same time—like every basically self-educated man—his education had serious gaps. Though he

Vernet and the Military Picture

FROM A CORRESPONDENT

The centenary of Horace Vernet, who died on January 17, 1863, recalls the long survival of the military tradition in French painting of the nineteenth century and Baudelaire's hatred of this artist as its most prolific and popular exponent. In his review of the Salon of 1846 and speaking as " the enemy of war and national folly ", Baudelaire declared with passion " I hate this art extemporized to the roll of drums, these canvases daubed at the gallop, this painting fabricated with pistol shots ".

His point of view is entirely comprehensible, though it has to be reconciled with the fact that many great Frenchmen had taken war as their theme, that it was indeed a major factor in French Romanticism. The campaigns of Napoleon had thawed the classical coldness of David, inspired the epic compositions of Baron Gros; could one then blame Vernet for responding to the same stimulus ? Born in the year of revolution, 1789, he was a young man still when the Napoleonic legend was taking pictorial shape. It was natural enough

Horace Vernet.

that he should follow his father, Carle Vernet, who, if best known for his caricatures of *Incroyables* and *Merveilleuses*, and of plethoric Englishmen suspiciously viewing the enemy capital in the time of truce, was capable also of painting a huge " Battle of Marengo ".

Was it any more reprehensible in Horace Vernet to paint battle scenes than in Géricault, his father's pupil, with whom for a while he was closely allied —alike in Bonapartist sympathies, a love of horseflesh, and a taste for a variety of sports ? It is necessary to distinguish between them on other grounds and in the important respect of what constitutes the difference between the great artist and the facile illustrator which was no doubt at the back of Baudelaire's mind. That superb energy of movement which Géricault was able to impart to horse and rider was beyond Vernet's power to achieve. Both the fury and the tragedy of war escaped him. What he did possess was an eye for circumstantial detail and a facility which had always been characteristic of his artist family. " No emotion at all and an encyclopaedic memory " was Baudelaire's way of estimating his talents.

It is interesting nowadays to see how the tendencies of the Romantic epoch in France appear in his work without anything of the Romantic spirit. He attempted the Byronic subject, and his picture of Mazeppa bound to his horse gained a European celebrity. He painted historical themes of the kind which answered to the Romantic desire to have done with ancient Greece and Rome and seek fresh colour elsewhere in the past, his " Edith of the Swan-Neck seeking the body of Harold after the Battle of Hastings " being an example. He shared in the search for the exotic which took him, like Delacroix, to North Africa, producing many a picture of Arab life. Yet in too few of these departures did he display the intensity of colour and feeling which was their best excuse.

The military picture remained his principal industry and the Napoleonic legend a theme demanded of him. Nicholas I of Russia paid 25,000 francs for a painting of the Emperor reviewing the Imperial Guard. Vernet covered acres of wall at Versailles with panoramas of battle. The military picture had become a commodity to be distinguished from the epics with which the century began or from such a record of the tramplings of conquest and of human suffering as Delacroix's " Massacres de Scio ". It is not a little curious that painters should still have been hypnotized by " le petit Caporal " and " la Grande Armée " for decades after Waterloo—not only Vernet but Charlet, Raffet, and finally Meissonier. An unabated thirst for " la gloire " required also a modern transposition ; from Adolphe Yvon who painted the Battle of Magenta. Isidor Pils who depicted the disembarkation of French troops in the Crimea, Meissonier with his picture of Napoleon III at Solferino. Vernet came up to date with his paintings of brisk skirmishes in North Africa such as the taking of the *Smala* of Abd-el-Kadir, near Algiers.

The decay of Romanticism and its absorption in the soft sands of bourgeois taste find a special instance in the military picture. The sentimentality of the new era is already foreshadowed in Vernet's "The Dead Trumpeter " (Wallace Collection) where horse and dog mourn in Landseerian fashion over the fallen youth. In other works the humorous anecdote crept in. The battle scenes became realistically unreal, with much circumstantial accuracy of uniform and a total absence of the actualities of warfare. Nevertheless, Vernet, like Meissonier, was treated as one of the demi-gods of art. Rulers doted on him, first King Jerome, then Louis-Philippe, the Tsar of Russia, Napoleon III. A little man, as frail-looking (so he was described) as a piece of glass, he travelled indefatigably in their service crossing frozen wastes of northern sea by sledge, and deserts on camel back, with an interval as director of the French Academy in Rome which incited him to paint a scene of brigandage and a meeting of Raphael and Michelangelo at the Vatican.

Military pictures, unless one includes Manet's " Execution of Maximilian ", have no place in the history of nineteenth-century French art as it has been fastidiously rewritten. Vernet has descended into the twilight of period. If one wishes to recapture the period feeling, an adventure, apart from aesthetic considerations, never without its attraction, it is possible to do so in those galleries of the Wallace Collection which enshrine a number of Lord Hertford's favourites, now fallen from grace. Here is Vernet, in company with other proscribed celebrities, his oil sketch of the siege of Constantine in 1837 with Meissonier's " Assassins " (and other " 5,000 francs per centimetre " pictures), with the replica of his son-in-law Paul Delaroche's " Princes in the Tower "; his Arabs, in grave discourse or cantering on their camels, partnering Decamps's souvenirs of the " Orient ". Vernet cannot be replaced on the pedestal from which Baudelaire roughly sought to dislodge him, but he still has a great deal to offer to the historian and student of Taste.

Sherlock's famous ancestor, Horace Vernet, the French painter could do the Bernard Berenson trick of identifying old masters from the style of brush strokes on paintings, or in spare time (1896) learn enough about medieval and Renaissance music to write a monograph on Orlando di Lasso's motets, he never became more than a gifted amateur in any of the arts. Artistic interest came naturally enough through his mother's connection with the Vernet family (French painters). Musical ability is indicated by his Venus-Neptune conjunction, but as this is obscurely placed and afflicted by Mars, we have ample reason for his not going further.

Holmes, despite his offhand disclaimers, had considerable athletic ability, which again he kept in the hobby class, not even bothering to try for a place in any of the teams when he was in college. Mars trine Uranus goes with strength; Moon in Aries confirms it—and athletic interest—but denied him staying power. Like many Sagittarius-rising people, he had a wiry rather than a brawny physique; the brawn which heavy Earth sign emphasis should have conferred was again denied by Moon in Aries. As it was, he developed considerable ability as an amateur lightweight boxer, swordsman and singlestick fighter—all these being dependent more on quick reflexes than on overwhelming strength. 'Amateur sport,' said he, 'is the best and soundest thing in England.'

At college, even as in later life, Holmes was a loner, making acquaintances but few friends, preferring to occupy himself with his diversity of intellectual interests. Already a few of these were being pursued strongly enough to become potential professions; others were to remain hobbies, still others were dropped. Holmes thus learned enough about ancient scripts to write a monograph on their use in dating documents (anticipating methods today in use); enough about organic chemistry to do later research in coal-tar derivatives (ancestor of today's multimillion-dollar dye, food-colour and plastics industries); enough about human morphology to anticipate the methods of modern criminology in his monographs on the form of the human ear (an identification technique only now beginning to be fully exploited); enough about certain byways in botany and geology to write of tobacco by analysis of the ashes, and to recognize at sight samples of soil as from particular locales. But he knew or cared little or nothing about religion, politics, economics, or even much of world literature, aside from certain favorite authors.

His most deeply pursued interests did share one feature: minute attention to detail and what could be deduced therefrom. 'Concentrate yourself on details. You know my method. It is founded on the observance of trifles,' he told Watson. This automatically points to an unusual Virgo emphasis. His chart shows an elevated slow-moving Mars in Virgo in High Focus—making it by far the strongest planet, and, throwing its sign into unusual relief; the more so since Mars (near the 10th cusp) is also the focus of a Grand Trine and a major opposition, and in aspect to everything else in the chart except Mercury and Venus. Now in more ordinary charts Mars in Virgo goes with craftsmanship of one or another kind; but here the craftsmanship is primarily

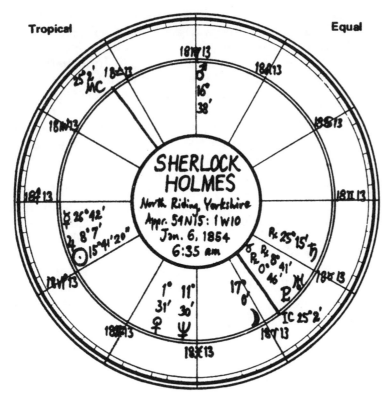

Tropical

Equal

SHERLOCK
HOLMES
North Riding, Yorkshire
Appr. 54N15: 1W10
Jan. 6, 1854
6:35 am

Sherlock Holmes's horoscope, as drawn by Walter Breen

mental (Moon in 3rd house, Sagittarius rising with Mercury), and we have already seen the evidence.

All this adds up to a cluster of interests and abilities which would have made detective work a natural choice. The Capricorn emphasis is obviously not only connected with a concern for law and order, but with patient assembling of materials, and an unusual reliance on logical methods, plus ambition to be the best of his kind. A Uranus-Pluto conjunction near the IC—4th house by Placidus, 5th by Equal House—guarantees extraordinary originality (Jupiter exactly trine Uranus) in situations or risk. (This and his Aries Moon near IC also account for his frequent shifts of residence in childhood.)

Since it is a 5th house conjunction, we may anticipate something very odd in his choice of love objects. (Venus is sextile Uranus, for confirmation.) A life-long bachelor, like many British Sagittarians of his generation, he distrusted women but manifested only the highest courtesy to them in practice; and they confided in him. He was, in a real sense, married to his profession.

And for him, there could be only one woman—the mysterious 'Irene Adler', sometime opera singer, sometime antagonist, his sole match among the women he met in the course of 26 years of professional life. (Baring-Gould suggests that he met her again in Montenegro in June 1891 and left her pregnant with a son who inherited his own extraordinary abilities, and who pursued a somewhat comparable though more sedentary life under the *nom de guerre* of Nero Wolfe.) For the kind of love and companionship most people see, in a wife—a 7th house matter, not a 5th—Holmes found Dr. Watson, early January 1881, when transiting Venus conjoined his natal Venus, transiting Mercury conjoined his Jupiter, and transiting Saturn sextiled his Ascendant.

In the 'Irene Adler' affair, Holmes used his remarkable gift for impersonation. This shows in his chart: Neptune is at $11\frac{1}{2}$ Pisces, at a degree-area commonly occupied in charts of actors; further, the Virgo-Pisces emphasis (Mars opposed Neptune) confers the actor's ability not only to take a variety of roles, but also to make many minutely crafted details contribute to the illusion. Nevertheless, acting was a blind alley for Holmes. During the summer of 1879, while his progressed Moon conjoined Neptune, Holmes—then impecunious—joined a troupe of actors, appearing as Horatio in Hamlet in London, to excellent notices (transiting Jupiter conjunct Neptune), departing for the USA five weeks later with the troupe. But clearly he realized, before the year was up, that his first love would never be acting, as it afforded him no outlet for his deductive abilities.

His Mars-Neptune opposition proved his weakness, despite all his Capricornian endurance. Holmes's tremendous exertions in spring 1887 left him a very sick, debilitated man (transiting Mars opposite natal Moon; Saturn opp. natal Sun), and he resorted to cocaine, later also to morphine, neither then being illegal. This must have seemed like just what the doctor ordered (progressed Moon trine Neptune, transiting Neptune conjunct natal Saturn), but naturally it left him addicted, and he is known to have remained so until the year 1896, when his 'kicking his habit' left him with little energy for anything else save for his monographs on cryptography (Secret Writings) and on Orlando di Lasso's motets.

It is possible to follow the Baring-Gould chronology of Holmes's exploits and vicissitudes, and find appropriate planetary transits or progressions or both for most of them. This holds true even for such things as his being beaten up in the summer of 1887 (transiting Mars over 7th cusp, then opposing natal Jupiter-Sun, square natal Moon; transiting Uranus sq. Jupiter), or Watson's return to Baker St. about 30 December, 1887 (progressed Jupiter conjunct natal Sun, transiting Sun over natal Jupiter!), and many more. But one of the strongest tests is that of the Reichenbach Falls episode, where Holmes and Moriarty were locked in a death struggle, 4 May, 1891. On that day there was a close conjunction of Mars, Neptune and Pluto, in early Gemini, squaring his Mars-Neptune opposition, closely sesquisquare his Midheaven; progressed Sun had reached the square of Saturn, but as his progressed Moon was without serious affliction, any astrology buff could have spotted that Holmes was not dead. And so it proved. Deceit and illusion were definitely at work (prog. Moon reaching opposition to Neptune), and nobody but his brother Mycroft and Col. Sebastian Moran knew he was still alive.

Holmes is said to have visited Tibet and other remote places in the ensuing three years. Two months after the Reichenbach Falls disappearance, Watson began placing short stories about Holmes's exploits in the *Strand Magazine*; this was an immediate source of funds for Watson, and potentially also for Holmes (Jupiter stationary sextile natal Sun, prog. Mercury trine MC, etc.). And on 5 April, 1894, Holmes returned to Baker St., when progressed Sun sextiled Mercury and prog. Moon trined Saturn—i.e. 'vacation's over now'.

For the rest, a month-to-month recital of events and planetary correlates would be dull reading—though doubtless Holmes would have approved of an investigation of such thoroughness. Suffice it that at Holmes's death (placed at his 103rd birthday in 1957 by Baring-Gould), progressed Saturn squared his Venus-Neptune, prog. Moon trined Saturn (happy release), prog. Sun was applying to conjunction with Pluto. The impression this leaves is that by now his connection with earth was tenuous indeed, his work done, death not feared but to be met with equanimity.

All of which raises a number of curious questions. The most important of these, perhaps, is that suggested by the curious event sworn to by Basil Rathbone, who long impersonated Holmes in the movies—a conversation with an aging British beekeeper, on a park bench, in which details of Rathbone's impersonations were gone over, odd scraps of Holmesian memories brought up, etc., leaving Rathbone (after his departure) with only one possible conclusion as to the man's identity.

Even if this be dismissed as illusion or practical joke (pointless like many British jokes), we are still left with the documented fact that the very birth data provided for Holmes fit the character incredibly closely. When Conan Doyle recorded Holmes's exploits, he was not as yet preoccupied with spiritualism, and he is not known to have been an astrologer. But even if he had asked an astrologer friend for a possible birth date for Holmes, how on earth could so perfect a choice have been made, were Holmes solely a figment of Conan Doyle's imagination? For in the 1890s, the rôles of Uranus and Neptune were not as yet well understood in astrology, and Pluto was not yet discovered. Nobody then would have had the insight to connect a strongly emphasized Mars-Neptune opposition, stimulated by transit, with a cocaine addiction. The Venus-Neptune conjunction was not yet known to be relevant to music. And so forth—many of the modern principles of interpretation herein used had not yet been devised.

It would be simple for a sceptic to claim that the interpretations are ambiguous enough to apply to almost anyone, or that they could have been easily applied after the fact. A ready way to test that comes at once to mind: show the chart, 'blind', without the name, to any astrologer and get his interpretations. You'll be surprised.

The remaining alternative, then, is that whoever Conan Doyle had in mind in writing about Holmes must have had not only these extraordinary characteristics (like the author himself and Dr. Joseph Bell of Edinburgh University Medical School) *but the same birth data*. Here we at once reach a situation like that of the Bacon-Shakespeare controversy, which was resolved by a wag who said that it wasn't Shakespeare who wrote the plays but 'somebody else of the same name.' So let it be with Sherlock Holmes.

Sherlock Holmes in Space

Evoe

There seems little doubt that Sherlock Holmes's popularity will continue to flourish far into the future, even though the world of Baker Street gets ever more distant from our modern space age. E. V. Knox, the contributor of this article, has been writing about Holmes under the pen-name 'Evoe' for some years, and here brings Holmes and Watson into contact with space technology in a story that might well be sub-titled 'The Great Detective meets Science Fiction'. It first appeared in PUNCH *on 23 November 1960.*

IT was not long after his return from Sussex that Holmes and I took a lease of the luxurious flat which had replaced our old lodgings in Baker Street. There installed we would not infrequently pay a visit to the new Planetarium, less than a hundred yards away, and spend the evening discussing the mysterious movements of the heavenly bodies.

My friend was in a particularly thoughtful mood on one of these occasions when, as we sat in our armchairs, he murmured 'Have you ever considered, Watson, how different from our own autumn must be the seasonal change in the Planet Pluto which takes two hundred and fifty of our years to complete a single revolution round the sun?'

I was meditating a suitable rejoinder to this observation when by a strange irony of circumstance we heard a thunderous banging at our door, as though a madman had assailed it. We opened it to reveal a figure in dishevelled attire, and in the last stages of exhaustion, with a look of horror in his eyes such as I have never seen on any human countenance. Staggering about the room he waved his two fists in the air and beat his head several times against the wall, dislodging one of my cherished Zulu assegais.

'Brandy!' commanded Holmes.

When we had plied him with the restorative and loosened his collar, what was our amazement to perceive writhing on the sofa the well-known and much photographed figure of the Minister for Hypersonic Affairs.

Between gasps and groans, he began to unfold the reasons for this unexpected visitation.

'You know, of course,' he said, 'that a certain Eastern Power that shall be nameless is attempting to launch an envoy, accompanied by a variety of domesticated fauna, into Space? The reasons are supposed to be scientific and the Americans are naturally competing with a similar enterprise. We now learn from our secret sources of information that this—'

'This nameless power,' suggested Holmes with a smile, 'has a further design up her sleeve. Her scientists have concocted a plan in connection with this ascent, so nefarious, so dastardly, that if realized it will enable them to plunge all the six continents of the earth into chaos and perpetual night.'

'The rascals!' I cried.

'It is a virus,' he continued, 'or perhaps I should say an opiate, which destroys all will-power, all desire for activity, thought, and progress. Disseminated, it will put an end to technical achievement, the nexus of trade, the very spirit of Democracy. Starvation will stalk the globe. The hand will fall from the plough, the fingers fail at the typewriter. Bulldozers will lie in the ditches. Savagery, nay, even cannibalism, will proliferate. Civilization as we know it will end.'

'Tut, tut, this is grave news,' said Sherlock. 'Would you kindly be rather more explicit about the functions of the machine?'

'It is a contrivance,' replied the Minister, 'which by means of a diffusory projectile shot from a space-car as it encircles the earth is enabled to pierce the non-gravitational zone and impregnate with its foul fumes the whole terrestrial atmosphere.'

'A squirt,' interjected my friend. His keen intelligence had pounced like a hawk on the very heart of the imbroglio.

'Precisely. And now let me apologize Mr. Holmes, for my somewhat abrupt and irregular arrival. I have run all the way from Downing Street, since the strike on the Underground and the congestion of vehicular traffic rendered any other means of approach impossible. But I do earnestly entreat you to help us if you can in this supreme emergency.'

I had myself in the meantime been pondering on the various implications of this diabolical strategem.

'Will not the weapon,' I suggested, 'rebound like a boomerang on those who utilize it? They will be hoist, or perhaps I should rather say depressed, by their own petard?'

'It was a point that I was about to propound myself,' said Holmes, 'but our good friend Watson anticipated me.'

'They are being immunized by the thousand every week with a cunning bacterial inoculation.'

'I will see what I can do,' said Holmes as he showed our unhappy guest to the door, and then turned to me.

'Run like a hare to the tobacconist, Watson,' he instructed me, 'we have no time to lose.'

For three days Holmes sat huddled in his chair without food or drink, while the smoke wreathed from his ancient briar in so thick a cloud that passers in the street took alarm, and on two occasions at least the fire-engine was summoned. On the morning of the fourth day the old gleam came into his eye, his figure stiffened, and 'Watson,' he cried, 'I think I have the solution.'

'I thought our opponents had that,' I said foolishly.

But he brushed my feeble witticism aside and sprang to the telephone.

I have mentioned more than once in my memoirs that there are occasions in the life of my friend when his supreme self-confidence suffered a setback as though ambition, in the words of the poet, had o'erleapt itself; and the world will not soon forget the dreadful accident, seemingly trivial at first, that befell the great detective only a few days later when he slipped and damaged his head while struggling to mount a No. 2 bus to Victoria. Unexpected complications followed and brain fever most unhappily supervened.

Messages of condolence naturally poured in from all the Crowned Heads, the Dictators and the Prime Ministers not only of Europe but the farthest isles of the outer seas, including even Galapagos and Waijiu, where the Episode of the Carnivorous Cabbages is still held in lively remembrance by the grateful aborigines.

Holmes and Watson in space. An illustration from *The Science Fictional Sherlock Holmes*, published in America in 1960

But my poor friend, alas, could not appreciate these tokens of sympathy. He was kept in seclusion and unable to see visitors; and even I myself, despite our years of friendship, despite my medical qualifications, was allowed only once to peep into his room. I saw nothing there but his pale bandaged face, and heard no more than a string of meaningless sentences from which only the words 'Moriarty—Silver Blaze—Swamp Adder,' clearly emerged.

The burden of my terrible knowledge at this time was almost too great to bear, and it became worse when the ascent of a new rocket launched by the distant Power of which we had spoken began to occupy the headlines of all the newspapers and set the minds of scientists agog with eager speculation.

I had no companion in whom I could confide except our great dog, Beowulf, a descendant of the well-known Baskerville strain whom we had bought from the breeder not long after our strange adventure on the Dartmoor bog. A grand specimen, he stood well over four feet high at the shoulder, even when the hackles were unraised. Now he would walk sadly to Holmes's chair, whine piteously, and return to his basket with a weary sigh.

As I sat there with him one evening, thinking over the many dramas in which Holmes and I had figured, the door opened quietly to admit, as I imagined, Evelina, the great-niece of Mrs Hudson, and now our daily help; but turning my head I perceived my mistake immediately. It was a stranger. Yet for all that, to my vast amazement Beowulf sprang upon him with barks of delight and began to lick him about the neck and chin, despite his singular, not to say astounding, choice of evening attire. He wore a mask and a helmet like the visor of a mediaeval knight, a metal cuirass and thick rubber overalls, the trousers of which ended in feet like those of a gigantic frog. Was it a madman who had entered the apartment? And if so, could it possibly be—? The thought had scarcely entered my mind when there came to my ears the best-loved voice in all the world uttering with complete calm and self-possession the simple words 'Good evening, Watson, the nights are drawing in.'

My head swam, my senses reeled. Question after question chased through my mind only to be rejected, until at last I managed to stammer out 'Holmes, my dear, dear fellow, so they've let you out!'

'Out of what?'

'Your loon—your mental home.'

'I never was in it.'

'But I saw you there!'

'A passable imitation, Watson. My simulacrum in wax from Madame Tussaud's.'

'But I heard you speak!'

'A tape-recorder under the bed.'

'Then where in heaven or earth have you been?'

'Recently in neither.'

And then, little by little, he began to recount the story of perhaps the most heroic and bewildering exploit that has ever adorned the annals of human history.

'I shall not weary you,' he said, 'with the methods I adopted of crossing the forbidden frontier, or worming my way into the good graces of the Alien Power that lies beyond. Suffice it to say that I secured false identity papers and represented myself as a descendant of an old Nihilist family, the local conservative stock from which so many of the most brilliant of our adversaries have sprung. It helped me not a little, too, that I was able to hurl the discus farther than their most redoubtable athletes, and to outpace them as easily as I once, on a famous occasion, outpaced you and the panting Lestrade. Finally, out of a hundred thousand applicants, I was chosen as Orbiter Number One, the first ambassador of that republic to engirdle the globe.

'I was entrusted with the awful Atomizer which would destroy the brains of mankind and reduce the inhabitants of the world to imbecile submission. I knew also the secret of its preventative. I was dressed as you see me now. I was encased in the mechanism of the Spatiometer. All was ready for a start, and then to my chagrin I saw that instead of the various animals—a yak, a couple of Chinese geese, and some white mice—with which I had hoped to make the journey, I was to be accompanied by a human fellow-passenger, one of their secret service men. I might have guessed it. They never permit an emissary to go abroad without a spy to report on his movements.

'So here we were, shut in together, only a foot apart, surrounded by complicated instruments, he the enemy, I the friend, of all that makes terrestrial life hopeful and endurable.'

'And what happened next?' I queried in an agony of suspense.

'A time had been given us at which to actuate the controls. I intended of course to disobey my injunctions, but I could see that my sinister companion was not so minded. At zero hour his hand went out to touch the button that would plunge threequarters of the dwellers on earth into the condition of stupified apes. I dealt him an upper-cut to the chin and almost at the same moment the whole of the space-car disintegrated into fragments and I became unconscious for a while.'

'And then?'

'I found myself floating in the sea, a contingency for which my present clothes had been designed. By an extraordinary stroke of luck I recognized my whereabouts. I was close to St Michael's Mount, which gave me some encouragement as a symbol that the Powers of Good were about to prevail. My fellow-traveller was floating by my side, but he was no swimmer and would have perished had I not dragged him ashore. He is now under lock and key in the hands of the sturdy Cornish Police.'

'And you, Holmes?'

'I chartered a helicopter at Penzance without troubling to change my clothes. It dropped me ten minutes ago in the middle of Queen Mary's Rose Garden.'

'Really, Holmes, this is well-nigh incredible!'

'It was a queer trip,' he admitted, 'and I shall have much to say tomorrow to the Prime Minister. I hold in my notebook all the details of their infernal chemistry, and am in a position to counter any further move they may make. In the meantime, when I have discarded this outfit, let us stroll to the Æolian Hall and listen to a little good music.'

Holmes Beyond
The Grave

This extraordinary item describes a séance at which it was claimed Sir Arthur Conan Doyle 'spoke' to a group of Sherlockians, the Six Napoleons of Baltimore, who attempted to make contact with him on the twenty-fifth anniversary of his death, on 7 July 1955. Doyle had, of course, been very interested in spiritualism during the later years of his life, and devoted much of his time and energy to investigating reincarnation, ghosts and even fairies. Understandably, the Sherlockians at the séance directed most of their questions to Sir Arthur about the Great Detective, and the following report from THE BALTIMORE SUN *gives a summary of the amazing events that occurred.*

SIR Arthur Conan Doyle, whose gifted pen created the legendary *Sherlock Holmes*, 'spoke' from the afterworld last night to a group of Baltimore devotees of the great sleuth.

At least, 'something' convincingly wrote the answers on a slate to a series of tough questions posed by members of the Six Napoleons.

The séance, an attempt to reach Sir Arthur on the twenty-fifth anniversary of his death, was the first ever held by the group. It was conducted in the office of Dr. Milton C. Lang, at 2117 Belair road.

Ray Hamby, director of the Hilltop Theaetr, who has studied spiritualism and made it a hobby, acted as the 'microphone, the broadcasting system', as his hand wrote out the messages.

He seemed to be in a deep trance, fully receptive and in harmony with the famed author who was communicating with the world of the living.

As one of the members noted, 'Mr. Hamby is not a member of the group. He knows virtually nothing of Holmesiana. It would take a scholar to answer some of the questions we asked—all of which were answered perfectly.'

Sir Arthur's 'messages from the dead' disclosed that his son, Adrian, is not in possession of missing Sherlock Holmes manuscripts, that these manuscripts are buried somewhere and that Sir Arthur is not happy since his body was removed recently to a new grave.

When asked 'Can we reach you, hereafter on this anniversary?' Sir Arthur plaintively replied: 'When do you come over?' He is not, it would seem, an unlonely spirit.

Attending the séance were Dr George Wells, James Bready, John Carter, Paul A. Clarkson, George R. Tullis, L. H. Denton and Dr Lang, all members of the Six Napoleons.

A 1920 newspaper story describing how Sir Arthur Conan Doyle
was tricked into believing photographs he saw of fairies were
genuine

How the fairy photographs were produced. A picture of a group of fairies is cut from an advertisement, photographed onto a glass plate and superimposed over a photograph of Conan Doyle

The group, named after the titles of one of the stories, meets monthly to read from their 'canon', the collected works of Conan Doyle, and to query each other on their reading about Sherlock Holmes, Doctor Watson and the other characters.

They are a part of the national organization, called the Baker Street Irregulars, with headquarters in New York, which was founded by Christopher Morley, Elmer Davis and Vincent Starratt. A quarterly journal, *The Baker Street Journal*, is published by the parent group.

The members believe that the stories were actually written by Dr Watson and marketed by Sir Arthur, whom they refer to as 'the literary agent'. They chose to meet in Dr Lang's office because Sir Arthur was also a general practitioner.

Mr Tullis opened the séance by asking the participants to 'establish a feeling of harmony in the room, to focus it in such a fashion as to make a circle between the terminals of the living and the dead.'

Then, as the members concentrated and Mr Hamby's hand began writing, these were some of the questions and answers:

'Are you happy in the afterworld, Sir Arthur?'—'Not entirely.'

'Are there other manuscripts you have written still undiscovered?'—'Yes' (very strong and large).

'Are they in the ground?'—'Yes.'

'Do you want us to look for them?'—'No.'

'Is Sherlock Holmes really dead?'—'I did not create for yesterday.'

'Is Professor Moriarty in heaven with you?'—'Yes. Heaven?'

'How many times was Dr Watson married?'—'Marriage is a state of mind.'

Or, more technical: 'Did Paddington Pollaky help you in publication of the Sherlock Holmes stories?' (Pollaky was a private detective. Certain persons are attempting to prove that Holmes was modelled on Pollaky)—'He was there.'

Sir Arthur also said 'I appreciate the work the Baker Street Irregulars do on behalf of Sherlock Holmes'. He promised to communicate again at a later date.

As the séance ended, the Six Napoleons declared they were extremely pleased by the accomplishments. They'll try again some time to learn more through spiritualism about their hero.

'Surely My Deductions Are Simplicity Itself...'

Solutions to the various competitions, crossword puzzles and quizzes contained in this book.

WORD SHIFT
(Page 18)
Spot slot slut glut glue CLUE.
Seek seed send fend FIND.

THE GAME OF THE NAME
(page 26)
Ace ado ale and any aye cad can cod con coo coy dan dey den (doc) doe don dye end lac lad lay led (loo) nan nay nod ode old one yen yon.

A SHERLOCK HOLMES COMPETITION
A. Conan Doyle
(page 27)

WHEN this competition was first mooted I went into it in a most light-hearted way, thinking that it would be the easiest thing in the world to pick out the twelve best of the Holmes stories. In practice I found that I had engaged myself in a serious task. In the first place I had to read the stories myself with some care. 'Steep, steep, weary work,' as the Scottish landlady remarked.

I began by eliminating altogether the last twelve stories, which are scattered through *The Strand* for the last five or six years. They are about to come out in volume form under the title *The Case-Book of Sherlock Holmes*, but the public could not easily get at them. Had they been available I should have put two of them in my team—namely, 'The Lion's Mane' and 'The Illustrious

Client', The first of these is hampered by being told by Holmes himself, a method which I employ only twice, as it certainly cramps the narrative. On the other hand, the actual plot is among the very best of the whole series, and for that it deserves its place. 'The Illustrious Client', on the other hand, is not remarkable for plot, but it has a certain dramatic quality and moves adequately in lofty circles, so I should also have found a place for it.

However, these being ruled out, I am now faced with some forty odd candidates to be weighed against each other. There are certainly some few an echo of which has come to me from all parts of the world, and I think this is the final proof of merit of some sort. There is a grim snake story, 'The Speckled Band'. That I am sure will be on every list. Next to that in popular favour and in my own esteem I would place 'The Red-Headed League' and 'The Dancing Men', on account in each case of the originality of the plot. Then we could hardly leave out the story which deals with the only foe who ever really extended Holmes, and which deceived the public (and Watson) into the erroneous inference of his death. Also, I think the first story of all should go in, as it opened the path for the other, and as it has more female interest than is usual. Finally, I think the story which essays the difficult task of explaining away the alleged death of Holmes, and which also introduces such a villain as Colonel Sebastian Moran, should have a place. This puts 'The Final Problem', 'A Scandal in Bohemia' and 'The Empty House' upon our list, and we have got our first half-dozen.

But now comes the crux. There are a number of stories which really are a little hard to separate. On the whole I think I should find a place for 'The Five Orange Pips', for though it is short it has a certain dramatic quality of its own. So now only five places are left. There are two stories which deal with high diplomacy and intrigue. They are both among the very best of the series. The one is 'The Naval Treaty', and the other 'The Second Stain', There is no room for both of them in the team, and on the whole I regard the latter as the better story. Therefore we will put it down for the eighth place.

And now which? 'The Devil's Foot' has points. It is grim and new. We will give it the ninth place. I think also that 'The Priory School' is worth a place if only for the dramatic moment when Holmes points his finger at the Duke. I have only two places left. I hesitate between 'Silver Blaze', 'The Bruce-Partington Plans', 'The Crooked Man', The Man With the Twisted Lip', 'The "Gloria Scott" ', 'The Greek Interpreter', 'The Reigate Squires', 'The Musgrave Ritual', and 'The Resident Patient'. On what principle am I to choose two out of those? The racing detail in 'Silver Blaze' is very faulty, so we must disqualify him. There is little to choose between the others. A small thing would turn the scale. 'The Musgrave Ritual' has a historical touch which gives it a little added distinction. It is also a memory from Holmes's early life. So now we come to the very last. I might as well draw the name out of a bag, for I see no reason to put one before the other. Whatever their merit—and I make no claim for that—they are all as good as I could make them. On the whole Holmes himself shows perhaps most ingenuity in 'The Reigate Squires', and therefore this shall be twelfth man in my team.

It is proverbially a mistake for a judge to give his reasons, but I have analysed mine if only to show any competitors that I really have taken some trouble in the matter.

The list is therefore as follows:

'The Speckled Band'
'The Red-Headed League'
'The Dancing Men'
'The Final Problem'
'A Scandal in Bohemia'
'The Empty House'

'The Five Orange Pips'
'The Second Stain'
'The Devil's Foot'
'The Priory School'
'The Musgrave Ritual'
'The Reigate Squires'

'I PLAY THE GAME FOR THE GAME'S OWN SAKE'
(*Page 46*)

1. Black Peter
2. Red Circle
3. Engineer's Thumb
4. Resident Patient
5. Boscombe Valley
6. Dancing Men
7. Six Napoleons
8. Last Bow
9. Thor Bridge
10. Copper Beeches
11. Noble Bachelor
12. Three Garridebs
13. Naval Treaty
14. Empty House
15. Speckled Band
16. Final Problem
17. Golden Pince-nez
18. Sign of Four
19. Gloria Scott
20. Three Gables
21. Study in Scarlet
22. Dying Detective
23. Abbey Grange
24. Card-Board Box
25. Red-Headed League
26. Five Orange Pips
27. Retired Colourman
28. Twisted Lip
29. Sussex Vampire
30. Crooked Man

A SHERLOCK HOLMES CROSSWORD PUZZLE
(*Page 66*)
Across
1. SH
2. Spurt
7. Scowrers
11. Joust
12. Cairo
14. EA
15. A Goose
17. Torn
18. Lestrade
21. Ninth
22. La
23. TE
24. Name
25. Bay
26. Nob
27. PT
29. Do
30. MS
31. Ass
32. Blue Carbuncle
36. DO
37. Three
40. Bone
41. Ski
43. An
44. Geo
45. Noose
46. Pip
47. Honey
48. Ear
49. Abe
50. Red
53. Recur

55. Dun	74. LV	102. Opium
57. DW	75. ND	103. Tea
58. To	76. Me	105. Three
59. ST	77. HA	106. Cocaine
60. Poe	81. PR	107. Oh
61. Miser	82. Nil	108. Two
63. Sob	84. Sir	110. HA
65. HP	85. York	111. Elman
66. Ettie	88. Holmes	113. NNE
67. Foot	91. SA	114. Pro
68. Up	92. Rent	115. Ir
69. Hat	93. Ring	116. Sneak
70. ACD	95. London	117. OR
73. SH	99. AM	118. EE
	100. Peerless	119. Mycroft

Down

1. Stan	33. Ebon	78. Brier
2. Sooty	34. Cooee	79. Hope
3. Push	35. Claret	80. CE
4. Use	37. TGP	83. Ian
5. Rt	38. Heir	84. SE
6. Wine	39. Rope	86. Orphan
7. Sol	42. Irene	87. Knee
8. Watson	45. Norwood	89. Mason
9. Evan	47. Hudson	90. Sloane
10. Seems	49. Alpha	94. Greek
11. Jonas	51. Edith	96. Opine
12. CO	52. Dust	97. Nine
13. Art	54. Copper	98. Due
16. Gibson	56. Neil	101. Scar
17. Table.	58. Thump	103. Thor
19. EC	61. Messy	104. AT
20. Dames	62. Rev	105. THS
22. Lobe	64. BT	107. ORC
27. Pansy	69. Hansom	109. Wit
28. Tree	71. China	112. MO
29. Dundee	72. Dartmoor	114. PY
31. Adair		

ON THE WALL
(*Page 75*)
(Remove some Ts): In the cupboard is a note
that says all you need to know.

Sherlock Holmes and American Presidents

(page 103)

1. Grant Munro (Monroe)
2. Cleveland
3. Hayes
4. Pierce
5. Baines (Baynes) (L.B.J.)
6. Stanford (Stamford
7. Prendergast (Prendergast) Truman
8. Nixon
9. Lincoln
10. Moffat (More fat)
11. Buchanan
12. Fillmore (Phillimore)
13. Teddy (Roosevelt)
14. Jefferson
15. Ford
16. Madison (Mad at son)
17. Lestrade (Let's trade)
18. Polk (poke, i.e. hit)
19. Taylor (tailor)
20. Arthur (author)

MYSTERY CODE

(page 119)

The map to the underground passage lies behind the fireplace.
(S=1, T=2, etc.)

ODDS AND ENDS

(Page 129)
MAIGRET

HOLMES SWEET HOLMES

(page 134)

'You know my methods, apply them!'
(*page 157*)

1. The Yellow Face
2. The Devil's Foot
3. A Case of Identity
4. The Dying Detective
5. His Last Bow
6. The Problem of Thor Bridge
7. The Blue Carbuncle
8. The Crooked Man
9. The Engineer's Thumb
10. The Creeping Man
11. The Man with the Twisted Lip
12. A Study in Scarlet
13. The Naval Treaty
14. The Golden Pince-nez
15. The Mazarin Stone

The Colonel Moran Quiz
(*page 173*)

The 7% Solution
The 6 Napoleons
The 5 Orange Pips
The Sign of (the) 4
The 3 Students
The 3 Garridebs
The 3 Gables
The 2 (nd) Stain
The Missing $\frac{3}{4}$
The Red O (Circle)
The Age of His Hans Sloan (And Others)
Irene Adler, 30
Cartwright, 14
Hayling, 26
Horner, 26
Patience Moran, 14
St Clair, 37

Significant Dates
1607—carved on Hurlestone Manor (Musg)
1742—original Baskerville Ms (Houn)
1858—Irene Adler born, New Jersey (Scan)
1860—John Ferrier died, 4 August (Stud)
1878—Watson graduates from University of London with M.D. (Stud)

CRYPTIC CROSSWORD
(*page 184*)

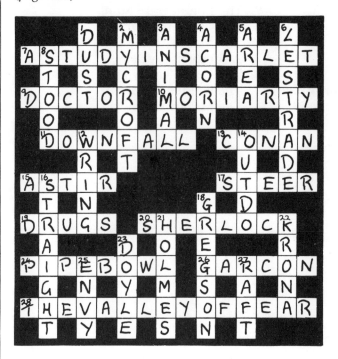

Sherlock Holmes, the Master Puzzle Solver, con-
founds Dr Watson once again. A Sidney Paget illustration for 'The Adventure of the Empty House', *Strand*,
1903

Acknowledgements

I should particularly like to thank Ken and Joan Chapman for their most generous help in the compiling of this book, and also for making available illustrations from Sherlockian publications from the presses of American publishers whom they represent: Luther Norris, The Pontine Press and The Aspen Press. (Copies of the books may be obtained from them at 2, Ross Road, London S.E.25.) My thanks also go to Bill Lofts for his help with research in England, and similarly John Bennet Shaw and his wife Dorothy for their help in America. I must also acknowledge the kindness of John Gardner, William E. Dunning, Sir Robert Mark and Walter Breen for their contributions, as well as the staffs of the British Museum and the London Library for their invaluable assistance. Thanks, too, to the following magazines, publishers and organisations: *Baker Street Journal*, *The Sherlock Holmes Journal*, The Sherlock Holmes Society of London, BBC, Methuen & Co Ltd, Messrs Sheed & Ward, *The Railway Magazine*, *The Bookman*, London Transport, British Tourist Board, *Reader's Digest*, St Bartholomew's Hospital, *The Cornhill Magazine*, Lisel Haas Photographs, *The Sphere*, *The Times*, *Daily Telegraph*, Marvel Comics, *John O'London's Weekly*, *Punch*, Hammer Films, BP Singer Features, *The Spectator*, Harry Price Library, *The Baltimore Sun*, *Evening Standard* and Abbey National Building Society. The illustrations are all from my own collection, except where acknowledged to another source, and I would like to thank Dr Julian Wolff, Christopher Lee and Peter Cushing for their help in this connection.

P.H.